*D*OUBTING JESUS' RESURRECTION

What Happened in the Black Box?

SECOND EDITION

Endorsements and Praise for this Book

"As Kris Komarnitsky notes in his book, I am on record with an explanation of the belief in Jesus' resurrection that is essentially identical with his own. The difference is that I merely proffered this explanation, while he provides a full, vigorous, and nuanced argument for it. Not surprisingly, I am persuaded."
— **David Berger, Ruth and I. Lewis Gordon Professor of Jewish History and Dean, Bernard Revel Graduate School of Jewish Studies, Yeshiva University**

"If you liked my book *Beyond Born Again*, you're going to love this one by Kris Komarnitsky! He shows great acuity of judgment and clear-eyed perception of the issues. He does not claim to have proof of what happened at Christian origins, but he does present a powerfully plausible hypothesis for what might have happened, which is all you need to refute the fundamentalist claim that things can only have gone down their way. By now it is a mantra – it is also nonsense, and Kris shows that for a fact."
— **Robert M. Price, Ph.D. Theology, Ph.D. New Testament**

"Komarnitsky is addressing an important topic in a considered and rational way. This book offers the open-minded reader an opportunity to work through some of the key questions surrounding the Easter mystery that lies at the heart of Christian faith."
— **Gregory C. Jenks, Ph.D., author of *The Once and Future Bible* (2011) and *Jesus Then and Now* (2014)**

"Komarnitsky offers a nice overview of cognitive dissonance concepts followed by a series of jaw dropping stories from history – each showing the extreme contradictions believers can accommodate."
— **Valerie Tarico, Ph.D. Psychology (first edition)**

"*Extremely* well researched and presented." (Emphasis is original.)
— **Why Won't God Heal Amputees Discussion Forum (first edition)**

"Komarnitsky has taken a theory from social psychology, Festinger's explanation of cognitive dissonance, and effectively and plausibly applied it to the greatest 'black box' mystery of history, namely the stories of the resurrection of Jesus and the related beliefs. Whether or not you agree with Komarnitsky's conclusions, in the first five chapters your thinker will become a better thinker, in the final chapter your heart will become a bigger heart, and putting them together you will see life with more perceptive eyes."
— **E. H. Stecher, M.Div., M.A. Psychologist (first edition)**

"Even with an MA in NT studies and seven years of Greek under my belt, I am extremely impressed by the author's command of the material (he is a confessed layman). His advocacy of Festinger's theory of cognitive dissonance…and his explication of Ps. 16:10 as the most likely source of the 'on the third day,

according to the scriptures' tradition, to name just two of his arguments, make this book well worth your while if you are even remotely concerned with the fact/legend of the resurrection of Jesus."
— **Shelfari Review (first edition)**

"An even-handed treatment of all major perspectives on the resurrection – traditional and modern, conservative and liberal – and an irenic style and tone that match the balanced discussion. This is more remarkable since Komarnitsky is examining one of the most emotionally charged questions in Christianity. Komarnitsky's answers are well-documented and carefully considered, and his central thesis is intriguing. Highly recommended."
— **Rev. Chuck Jones, Atlanta, Georgia (first edition)**

"Getting into this sort of thing is kind-of like a championship boxing match. The title doesn't change hands on a draw. The challenger has to actually win. Komarnitsky never delivers the knockout punch in *Doubting Jesus' Resurrection* – nor could he. It was not his intention to do so....What ought to give the believer pause is that the author managed to exhibit a perfectly credible scenario that doesn't appeal to unseen and unprovable entities....In short, [his book] shows that doubting the Resurrection is a reasonable and honest – an honorable – posture."
— **Amazon Review (first edition)**

$\mathcal{D}$OUBTING JESUS' RESURRECTION

What Happened in the Black Box?

SECOND EDITION

Kris D. Komarnitsky

STONE ARROW BOOKS
Draper, Utah

Published 2014 by Stone Arrow Books.

Komarnitsky, Kris D., KrisKomars1@gmail.com, 1964-
Doubting Jesus' Resurrection: What Happened in the Black Box?
Second Edition (paperback and e-book)
Includes bibliographical references and index
ISBN: 978-0-9825528-9-6
Library of Congress Control Number: 2013951554

10 9 8 7 6 5

To those whose honest doubts

lead them to inquire into other possibilities.

About the Second Edition

Although improvements to clarity have been made throughout this second edition, the basic explanation offered for Christian origins remains unchanged from the first edition. The main addition is a chapter that compares the hypothesis in this book to the resurrection hypothesis using the historian's method of inference to the best explanation.

Contents

Introduction

Doubt is an understandable human reaction to the claim that Jesus resurrected from the dead. This is true not only for atheists who logically rule out Jesus' resurrection on the basis that there is no God, but also for those of us who accept the possibility of God. The problem is firsthand personal experience. Many of us have never experienced God intervene within human history in the way suggested by the resurrection, that is, in a *physically direct* way. We now and then hear of an incredible event from someone else, a miracle, but it is never anything we can personally verify. We sometimes experience a confluence of events, but closer examination often reveals those events to be more connected than we thought or indistinguishable from random chance. There are times when we think God *should* intervene within human history in a physically direct way, but it does not happen. When there is a big gap between firsthand personal experience and a given claim, there is doubt. From a logic perspective it is simple – when we weigh the evidence for any claim, our personal experience affects the result; it is the first piece of evidence to go on the scale and its weight is equal to the confidence that we have so far learned to place in our own experiences.

We see the effect of experience-based doubt toward Jesus' resurrection in two of our nation's founding fathers, both of whom believed in God. Thomas Paine declared:

> [Jesus' disciple] Thomas did not believe the resurrection; and, as they say [in the Gospels], would not believe, without having occular and manual demonstration himself. *So neither will I*; and the reason is equally as good for me and for every other person, as for Thomas.[1]

Thomas Jefferson took scissors and paste to the Bible creating his own *Jefferson Bible*...without the resurrection in it. Although many people are not as skeptical as Paine and Jefferson, experience-based doubt has at the very least caused many people to honestly ask, could there be something other than Jesus' resurrection that plausibly explains the evidence before us?

Many defenders of Jesus' resurrection insist there is not. For example, two of the world's leading scholars on Jesus' resurrection assert, "Jesus' resurrection from the dead is the only plausible explanation for the known facts."[2] This sentiment has filtered down to and been expressed very successfully by laymen as well, one notable example being Lee Strobel in his best-selling book *The Case for Christ*. Strobel, an award winning legal editor for a major newspaper who documented his conversion to Christianity, proclaims, "I was ambushed by the amount and quality of the evidence that Jesus is the unique [resurrected] Son of God....I had seen defendants carted off to the death chamber on much less convincing proof!"[3] Certainty that the historical evidence overwhelmingly leads to only one conclusion is also prevalent in the blogosphere: "The evidence is simply overwhelming. If you believe in gravity, you have to believe that Christianity is also true."[4]

When trying to assess the historical reality of Jesus' resurrection, many people turn to the Gospels. However, there is significant controversy over their historical reliability. In general terms, traditional scholarship argues that the four canonical Gospels are each historically reliable and that as a group they form a powerful combination of independent attestation of events. In contrast, non-traditional scholarship argues that none of the Gospels can be considered historically reliable, and none are truly independent from the others because they all draw from a common pool of circulating oral traditions and/or from each other. The most controversial example of the non-traditional view is probably in the works of the Jesus Seminar, a group of over one hundred scholars who have concluded that the majority of the words and deeds of Jesus in the Gospels are later legendizations about him.[5] *

---

* This book will use the terms "traditional" and "non-traditional" to refer to the two sides of the resurrection issue – the traditional side believing that Jesus did resurrect from the dead, and the non-traditional side believing that he did not. This designation is an attempt to avoid the baggage that usually comes with terms like critical/uncritical, liberal/conservative, and skeptic/believer.

With the exception of an essay in the appendix that looks at how fast legends can grow and how fast the historical core of events can be lost, this book will not attempt to tackle the voluminous topic of Gospel reliability or the degree of their interdependence, so this book is not, nor does it pretend to be, a complete assessment of Jesus' resurrection. Instead, this book will take what I think is a unique approach.

This book will begin by looking at just one Gospel tradition in isolation, the discovered empty tomb tradition. Considering scholarship from both sides of the aisle, it will be argued that there is good reason to conclude that this tradition is a legend. Following up on this possibility, this book will then move on to its main topic, which is to address a much more basic and interesting question that automatically follows from the conclusion that there never was a discovered empty tomb. This question springs from what the apostle Paul wrote to one of his Christian congregations about twenty years after Jesus' death:

> For I handed on to you as of first importance what I in turn had received: that Christ died for our sins in accordance with the scriptures, and that he was buried, and that he was raised on the third day in accordance with the scriptures, and that he appeared to Cephas [Peter], then to the twelve. Then he appeared to more than five hundred brothers and sisters at one time, most of whom are still alive, though some have died. Then he appeared to James, then to all the apostles. (1 Corinthians 15:3-7)

Based on other evidence that it is not necessary to discuss here, and with some caveats that will be mentioned later, the beliefs and traditions stated above by Paul are thought by virtually all scholars to have been passed on to him within six years after Jesus' death, well before Paul wrote the above passage and well before any of the Gospels were written.[6] Because of this, this passage is by far the earliest and most valuable piece of evidence we have of early Christian beliefs and traditions, and it leads to an interesting historical question: If the discovered empty tomb tradition is a legend and Jesus did not resurrect from the dead, what then caused the rise of these beliefs and traditions? This book is the result of an inquiry into this specific question.

The type of problem we are tackling here is similar to that described by a researcher in an entirely different field of study. Jim Collins, a highly respected management researcher, was trying to determine the elusive root causes of corporate success, and he likened his investigation to trying to determine what is in a black box when given the input and output of the box but limited direct evidence of what is actually in it. He described the process of his investigation this way:

> [It was] an iterative process of looping back and forth, developing ideas and testing them against the data, revising the ideas, building a framework, seeing it break under the weight of evidence, and rebuilding it yet again. That process was repeated over and over, until everything hung together in a coherent framework of concepts.[7]

That same process was used here except that in our case Jesus' crucifixion is the input that went into the black box and the output is the beliefs and traditions we see in 1 Corinthians 15:3-7.

Jesus Crucified ⟹ ? ⟹ Beliefs and Traditions in 1 Cor 15:3-7

What Happened in the Black Box?

In order to make this book much thinner than it would otherwise be, I will not present the iterative process that was used when trying to figure out what happened in the black box; I will only present the final conclusion arrived at. I will also not present the many different ways that the various pieces of Christian origins evidence can be interpreted; I will only present *one* plausible way to interpret each piece of evidence and only *one* plausible way to

4

connect them together into an overall explanation. My intent is not to claim that the explanation in this book is the *only* plausible explanation for the rise of the beliefs and traditions in 1 Corinthians 15:3-7, only that it is *one* plausible explanation. The goal is to present the reader with a single, clearly laid out hypothesis for the birth of Christianity that they can assess for themselves and compare to the traditional explanation or any other explanation in order to decide which one makes the most sense to them.

At this point I should define what I mean by the term "plausible". No matter what happened at Christian origins – a resurrection or something else – we are dealing with a very rare or, from our perspective as humans not knowing the intentions of God, an *improbable* event. In other words, whatever happened, the *odds* of it happening are very low based on how often we see the same or similar events happen in human history. However, rare events are a fact of history. As New Testament scholar N.T. Wright points out, "[History] is mostly the study of the unusual and unrepeatable."[8] So if we know ahead of time that the answer to Christian origins is going to be *improbable*, how do we judge whether or not it is *plausible*? To help with this I will use a very down to earth and practical definition of plausible that comes from evangelical New Testament scholar Michael Licona: "Many times in historical research, the data is so fragmented that historians are only warranted in judging that their hypotheses are 'plausible'; in other words, one can imagine without too much of a stretch that it could have happened this way."[9] That is what this book is aiming for – an explanation of Christian origins that can be *imagined* without too much of a stretch that it could have happened that way.[*]

---

[*] A "possible" explanation is an explanation that does not contradict itself or a piece of the known evidence. A "plausible" explanation is a possible explanation that can be imaged without too much of a stretch that it could have happened that way. A "probable" explanation is a plausible explanation that has a greater than 50% chance of being true. In this way an "improbable" explanation (an explanation which has a less than 50% chance of being true) can still be "plausible".

If this book is successful in presenting a plausible non-traditional explanation for the rise of the beliefs and traditions in 1 Corinthians 15:3-7, it comes full circle and impacts on the historical reliability of the Gospels. Why? Because 1 Corinthians 15:3-7 is used by many traditional scholars as "external evidence" for the historical reliability of the Gospels. As Craig Blomberg, a leading defender of Gospel reliability says about Paul's 1 Corinthians 15:3-7 passage:

> Paul in fact displays a fairly detailed knowledge of the Gospel traditions if one reads him carefully....[The] awareness of these details is a significant confirmation of the early existence of the traditions that went into the formation of the Gospels....Perhaps the most spectacular example of Paul's early familiarity with the historical Jesus appears in 1 Corinthians 15:3-7, with his knowledge of Jesus' death and resurrection....[This] external evidence for the Gospel traditions reinforces the confidence in their historical reliability...[10]

There is an implicit assumption in Blomberg's use of 1 Corinthians 15:3-7 to support Gospel reliability. He is assuming that the events reported in the Gospels – Jesus' rock-hewn tomb burial, the discovery of that tomb empty on the third day after his death, and Jesus' corporeal post-mortem appearances – are the *only* events that could cause the rise of the much more generally expressed beliefs and traditions in 1 Corinthians 15:3-7 (Jesus was "buried", was "raised on the third day", and "appeared" to many people). But if something else gave rise to these beliefs and traditions in 1 Corinthians 15:3-7, the Gospel events that Blomberg is assuming lies behind them could just as easily be legends springing from the beliefs and traditions themselves. As Blomberg's colleague N.T. Wright points out:

> A good deal of study has been devoted to the task of proposing alternative explanations for the rise of early Christian belief. Any of these, if sustainable, could challenge the argument of the previous section [that *only* a discovered empty tomb and post-mortem "meetings" with Jesus could lead to early Christian belief], leaving the Easter stories to be explained as aetiological

or apologetic attempts to flesh out a faith arrived at on other grounds.[11]

When investigating the birth of Christianity like we are doing here, a traditional cultural commentator cautions:

> If we cherish the distinctive ideals of Western civilization, and believe as I do that they have enormously benefited our civilization and the world, then whatever our religious convictions, and even if we have none, we will not rashly try to hack at the religious roots from which they spring. On the contrary, we will not hesitate to acknowledge, not only privately but also publicly, the central role that Christianity has played and still plays in the things that matter most to us.[12]

I agree that efforts like this should not be taken on rashly. In the conclusion of this book I will affirm those things about Christianity that I believe have benefited our world. I will also explain why I think inquiries like this are still legitimate and important. By the end of this book, my hope is that the reader will find it to be what it is intended to be – a look at another possibility for Christian origins driven by honesty and experience-based doubt, not a rash or angry attack on Christianity.

Because I am a layman with no formal credentials in religious studies, nothing in this book can, or should be, given the weight it might be if it were written by a credentialed expert. However, almost everything in this book is backed by a credentialed expert somewhere, and in every case I cite the expert or experts referred to so the reader can follow up on an idea if desired. Because of this, this book is best viewed as a synthesis of ideas that are already out there. It is in this sense that others might find this book useful even though it is written by a layman.

Two things have already been presupposed in this introduction: Jesus existed and 1 Corinthians 15:3-7 is not a later editorial insertion into Paul's letter to the Corinthians. Both of these presuppositions are vigorously contested by some scholars. Needless to say, if either of these two presuppositions is wrong, then this book is completely on the wrong track. In addition to these two presuppositions, the following three are added, the first two being widely accepted by scholars on both sides of the aisle, the last one being contested by some in non-traditional scholarship: 1) around 50-60 C.E. (twenty to thirty years after Jesus' death) Paul wrote at least the following seven epistles: Romans, 1 and 2 Corinthians, Galatians, 1 Thessalonians, Philippians, and Philemon, 2) the Gospel of Mark was written before the Gospels of Matthew, Luke, and John, and 3) the earliest Christians did not just believe that Jesus was *spiritually* raised from the dead; they believed he was *bodily* raised from the dead, that his corpse was gone from its final human resting spot (I am only presupposing a *belief* here; I am not presupposing that Jesus' corpse was in fact gone from its final human resting spot).[*]

Since Christian origins can be a difficult topic of study, five things are worth mentioning that might make reading this book a little easier. First, the endnotes in the back of the book contain *only* bibliographical source information or, very occasionally, something that would only interest someone who is interested in the bibliographical source information, so there is no need to keep flipping to the back of the book to see if the endnotes have further elaboration on the main text. Second, various scholars are referred to throughout this book whose names I do not imagine many readers will recognize. This is not important; the names are used only because they are the easiest way to introduce ideas that have already been formed. Third, there will be times when it may be helpful (though it is not necessary) to have a Bible handy so you can confirm for yourself that I have not misrepresented or abused the text or context of a passage referred to. Fourth, for those who would like to see a basic outline of the hypothesis that will be presented in this book before reading the actual arguments, read the two page summary presented in Chapter Six first. The fifth and final thing that will make reading this book easier is being clear

---

[*] My conclusion that the earliest Christians believed Jesus' body was gone from its final human resting spot is primarily based on Paul's seed/plant analogy in 1 Corinthians 15:35-54 – seed transforms into plant, corpse transforms into spiritual body. There is no seed remaining behind after the seed becomes a plant, so there would be no corpse remaining behind after the corpse becomes a spiritual body.

ahead of time on the structure of the presentation. After arguing that the discovered empty tomb tradition is plausibly a legend, the rest of this book will simply step through all of the questions that *must* be answered in order to produce the beliefs and traditions in 1 Corinthians 15:3-7 without a discovered empty tomb. It will be argued in every case that each one of these questions has a plausible answer and that together they form an overall plausible answer to what happened in the black box.

Chapter 1

The Discovery of an Empty Tomb, Fact or Fiction?

Whether we are a historian with a PhD, or a layperson trying to make sense of Christian origins, we have a decision to make when we come to the tradition of the discovered empty tomb – it is either history or it is legend. There are two things in the written record which suggest it is the latter.

Paul's Silence on the Discovered Empty Tomb

A discovered empty tomb days after Jesus' death should have been a key part of any argument for Jesus' resurrection from the very beginning. Yet the apostle Paul does not seem to know anything about it when arguing for Jesus' resurrection.

According to John Dominic Crossan, Paul was no amateur at defending ideas:

> Paul [received] a first-class education in the synagogue at Tarsus with a strong emphasis on apologetics for Judaism and polemics against paganism. He was educated…for debates within Judaism…for debates with paganism…[and] for debates within Judaism about paganism.[1]

Since Paul usually wrote to Christian communities that did not doubt Jesus' resurrection, there was usually no reason to defend Jesus' resurrection in his letters to them. However, in his first letter to the Corinthians, Paul was writing to one of his more troublesome congregations. The Corinthian congregation was one of his more troublesome groups because of the competing Greek religions there and its over eight hundred mile separation from Christian beginnings in Palestine. Immersed in Greco-Roman philosophies that emphasized the soul, the Corinthians would have had great difficulty with a raised corpse. That this was precisely the part of the resurrection message that some of them were having difficulty with is evident in the doubts that some of them expressed, which are quoted by Paul in his letter back to them: "There is no resurrection of the dead....How are the dead raised? With what kind of body do they come?" (1 Cor 15:12, 35).

Given the Corinthian's Greco-Roman beliefs, and the difficulty they would have had with a raised corpse, it makes sense that they were doubting both Jesus' bodily resurrection and the future bodily resurrection of believers at the end of time. Even if the Corinthians somehow saw Jesus as an exception and they were only doubting the future general resurrection (as some scholars propose), they would soon have their doubts about Jesus' resurrection because Paul points out the obvious in his letter back to them: "If there is no resurrection of the dead, then Christ has not been raised" (1 Cor 15:13). After pointing this out, Paul had to know that he needed to defend Jesus' resurrection in the same letter. The highly respected evangelical *Expositor's Bible Commentary* agrees that Paul is trying to defend Jesus' resurrection in his letter to the Corinthians:

> In one of the reports Paul received concerning what was going on in Corinth, he heard that some were claiming "that there is no resurrection of the dead" (1 Cor 15:12)....Paul was so deeply concerned about this theological position that he gave an extended discourse in ch. 15 *to prove the resurrection of Christ* and to set a timetable for the final return of Jesus and the resurrection of the dead [emphasis added].[2]

We see Paul's defense of Jesus' resurrection in 1 Corinthians 15:1-19. There, Paul starts out by cautiously reminding the Corinthians that they had previously accepted Jesus' resurrection:

> Now I should remind you, brothers and sisters of the good news that I proclaimed to you, which you in turn received, in which also you stand, through which also you are being saved, if you

hold firmly to the message that I proclaimed to you – unless you have come to believe in vain. (1 Cor 15:1-2)

Paul then repeats a core Christian creed which includes the assertion that Jesus was "buried" and then "raised" and that this has been confirmed in the scriptures (1 Cor 15:3-4). Paul goes on to remind the Corinthians that Jesus appeared to many people, including over five hundred "at one time", most of whom "are still alive", implying that some of them were still available to be asked about their experience (1 Cor 15:5-7). Paul then draws on the influence of authority and group appeal by asking the Corinthians, "Now if Christ is proclaimed [by Paul, the Twelve, the apostles, and the five hundred] as raised from the dead, how can some of you say there is no resurrection of the dead?" (1 Cor 15:12). Paul finishes off by going into detail on the dire consequences if Jesus did not resurrect from the dead: "our proclamation has been in vain", "your faith has been in vain", we are guilty of "misrepresenting God", our "faith is futile", "you are still in your sins", those Christians who have died have "perished", and "we are of all people most to be pitied" (1 Cor 15:14-19).

Given Paul's ability to defend ideas, and given his effort above to defend Jesus' resurrection, it is hard to understand why Paul did not mention a *discovered* empty tomb if he knew about it. It would have been a great bolstering point for Jesus' resurrection and in turn for the general resurrection, which Paul argues for right after arguing for Jesus' resurrection (1 Cor 15:20-57), including giving a seed/plant analogy that attempts to describe how a dead body is raised (1 Cor 15:35-54). The discovered empty tomb is the only piece of major evidence missing from Paul's argument for Jesus' resurrection.

Although the evangelical *Expositor's Bible Commentary* acknowledges that Paul is defending Jesus' resurrection in 1 Corinthian 15, they give no explanation for Paul's silence on the discovered empty tomb. Of the traditional commentators that do try to address this issue, the typical response seems less than adequate. For example, one traditional scholar says, "[Paul] focuses on resurrection witnesses rather than the empty tomb."[3] But why wouldn't Paul focus on both?

Some say that the buried-raised sequence mentioned by Paul – "and that he was buried, and that he was raised" (1 Cor 15:4) – implies a discovered empty tomb. Actually, it only implies the *belief* in an empty tomb or empty burial location. It does not imply that Jesus' tomb or burial location was actually *discovered* empty.[*]

Some say that the third-day reference in Paul's letter – "he was raised on the third day" (1 Cor 15:4) – is referring to the discovered empty tomb on the third day after Jesus' death. But this is just using the Gospels to fill in what is not said. While it is a great question to ask what the origin of the third-day belief is, and this will be covered in detail later (Chapter Five), it is unbelievable that "on the third day" served as Paul's reference to a discovered empty tomb. No defender of Jesus' resurrection would say just that without mentioning the discovered empty tomb itself.

Some have suggested that the discovered empty tomb was so well known that in context it was unnecessary for Paul to explicitly mention it. But if this were true, there would be no need for Paul to mention any of the basic creed (1 Cor 15:3-4), nor the list of appearances (1 Cor 15:5-7), nor Paul's own appearance (1 Cor 15:8), nor the consequences if Jesus did not resurrect (1 Cor 15:14-19), since all of these too must have been well known to the Corinthians.

Paul's silence on the discovered empty tomb suggests that the discovered empty tomb tradition did not yet exist when Paul was writing his letter about twenty years after Jesus' death or that Paul knew it was an emerging legend. As Geoffrey Lampe says:

> If Paul and the tradition which he cites lay no emphasis on the [discovered] empty tomb the question arises whether Paul nevertheless may have known of it. Many New Testament scholars hold that he did. Certainly it would be quite unsafe in the ordinary way, to infer that he did not from the fact that he does not actually allude to it. But in this case I think that the argument from silence has unusual force. For the situation in which Paul wrote I Corinthians 15 was that some of the

---

[*] The circumstances surrounding Jesus' burial and how the belief that Jesus was bodily raised could have come about without a *discovered* empty tomb will be discussed in the next two chapters.

Corinthians were denying that there is a resurrection of the dead (I Cor 15:12). In answer to them Paul marshals every possible argument, and in particular, he adduces the known fact that Jesus was raised from the dead as the foundation for belief in the future resurrection of Christian people. If Jesus' resurrection is denied, he says, the bottom drops out of the Christian gospel. And the evidence that he was raised consists in the appearances to himself and to others. Had he known that the tomb was found empty it seems inconceivable that he should not have adduced this here as a telling piece of objective evidence.[4]

The Ending to the Gospel of Mark

A second aspect of the Christian origins record also leads to the conclusion that the discovered empty tomb tradition could be a legend. Of interest here is the last sentence in the earliest written account of the discovered empty tomb, which is also the last sentence in the entire Gospel of Mark.

In almost all Bibles today, there is a clearly annotated short and long ending to the Gospel of Mark (Mk 16:9 and Mk 16:9-20). Everyone agrees that these endings were not written by Mark. A few scholars think these endings were an honest attempt by later writers to reconstruct an ending that Mark had written. However, it is much more widely accepted, even among traditional scholars, that the last sentence in the original Gospel of Mark was chapter 16 verse 8. There are primarily two things which point to this conclusion. One, the earliest surviving manuscripts end at verse 16:8. Two, it goes against the odds of chance that Mark's Gospel would get chopped off in a way that would produce a complete sentence. As Bruce Metzger says, "...on the basis of good external evidence and strong internal considerations it appears that the earliest ascertainable form of the Gospel of Mark ended with 16.8."[5] Verse 16:8 reads: "[The women] fled from the tomb, for terror and amazement had seized them; and they said nothing to anyone, for they were afraid."

It has long puzzled scholars why Mark would end his *entire* Gospel with fear-induced silence if the women had experienced only a few moments of numbness and then went and told others about their incredible discovery of an empty tomb, as it is reported they did in the later Gospels. A representative explanation from the traditional side of scholarship for this strange ending to Mark's Gospel comes from Craig Blomberg:

> Mark is writing to Christians who would not likely have come to faith in the first place had they not heard the story of the resurrection. So he can assume knowledge of it and deliberately cut it [his Gospel] short to call attention with riveting abruptness to the women's initial fear and failure, knowing full well, and knowing that his audience knew well, the story of how they later overcame their fear and spread the word. Most probably, Mark wants to encourage beleaguered Christians in Rome shortly before or during the Neronic persecution in the 60s that they, too, can overcome any failure they may have experienced or that they may fear and that it remains their task to spread the gospel too.[6]

Blomberg is basically saying that Mark ended his Gospel with fear-induced silence in order to encourage those Christians who already knew that the women at the tomb had overcome their fears, to overcome their own fears and failures and to spread the good news. Although not an impossible proposal, why would Mark cut off the very end of an otherwise complete story in order to convey a practical message of encouragement that he could have conveyed in a half page letter to the same audience? Additionally, wouldn't Mark have been at least a little concerned that cutting his story short might confuse potential new recruits to the church who were not yet completely familiar with or convinced how the story ended, as well as future members of the church who might read his Gospel when his message of encouragement was no longer relevant or of such high priority? Mark could also have had it both ways. He could have completed the story and gotten the same message across to beleaguered Christians simply by emphasizing the women's fear and then, while continuing the story, emphasizing their success at overcoming that fear.

Another explanation for the ending to Mark's Gospel comes from non-traditional scholarship. Some have long pointed out that the ending to Mark's discovered empty tomb account makes perfect sense if, in this first version of the discovered empty tomb legend (appearing decades after Jesus' death), the women's fear-induced silence "[gave] an answer to the question why the women's story of the empty tomb remained unknown for so long."[7] Looking at Mark's ending this way, the shock and awe in Mark's last sentence brings Mark's entire Gospel to a climax in support of Jesus' resurrection – Jesus' tomb was actually *discovered* empty, but nobody has ever told about it…until now. In this explanation, the shock and awe in Mark's last sentence of his discovered empty tomb story matches the shock and awe of Mark's Gospel as a whole. The matching effect seems to make this explanation plausible. Gerd Ludemann even concludes, "…Other attempts to trace the riddle of the tradition behind Mark 16:1-8 have failed."[8]

Some think that in a patriarchal society where men were considered the most reliable witnesses, the use of female witnesses in Mark's discovered empty tomb account counts against the conclusion that it is a legend. But the use of women in a legend which is trying to explain why the discovered empty tomb story remained unknown for so long actually makes perfect sense. As Earl Doherty says, "Mark is portraying them [the women] exactly as…women were regarded in first-century Palestine….All they can do is react in fear and terror."[9] Michael Goulder agrees: "You know what women are like. They were so scared that they never passed the message on."[10] Although Mark's tradition does not include how the discovered empty tomb became known if the women did not tell anybody, such means are not usually the focus in a growing legend. For someone listening to the story, it is easily assumed that the information was leaked out years later from one of the women or some confidant of one of the women.

Some think that a decades long silence by the women would have sounded implausible to Mark's audience – implausible that nobody asked the women what they saw and what followed when they stayed back and watched Jesus' crucifixion (Mk 15:40), and implausible that the women continued to remain silent even after people proclaimed that Jesus appeared to them. However, this objection assumes a critically thinking audience, which is often not the case when legends are growing, especially in a largely uneducated population. Additionally, given the low reputation of women in the first century, even someone listening to the story critically might simply assume that the women remained silent out of stupidity, fear of public attention, or some other unexplained reason. The low reputation of women would also explain why nobody would have bothered to ask the women what they saw and what followed when they stayed back and watched Jesus' crucifixion.

Some think Mark intended the women's silence to be only temporary because Mark foreshadowed the appearances of Jesus to the disciples in Galilee by having an angel at the tomb command the women to go tell the disciples that they would see Jesus in Galilee (Mk 16:7). However, anyone thinking critically about the story would realize that it does not matter if the women followed through on the angel's command or not, Jesus still would have appeared to the disciples in Galilee.

Some think Mark intended the women's silence to be only temporary because that is how Mark's earliest literary interpreters, Matthew and Luke, understood Mark (Mt 28:8; Lk 24:9). However, we do not know if this is how Matthew and Luke (or their sources) really understood Mark or if this is further legendary development. As the highly respected Catholic scholar Raymond Brown says:

> True, we have in the Matthean and Lucan accounts...an early interpretation of Mark; but...there is a very high possibility that these two evangelists have changed and developed the Marcan outlook. Consequently, I shall not use Matthew and Luke as a primary guide to Mark's intention.[11]

Although some may say the explanation for Mark's ending offered by non-traditional scholarship above is simply a mirage seen only by those intent on finding legends, it is worth noting that had the discovered empty tomb account with the fear-induced silence ending occurred in any Gospel other than the first one written, the above legendary explanation would not be possible. It is the fact that this strange ending occurs in the *earliest* account of the discovered empty tomb that is significant. Non-traditional scholarship may be guilty of looking too hard for legends, but if they are wrong in this case, it is a cruel coincidence of history that Mark's innocent message to beleaguered Christians was put in the earliest written account of the discovered empty tomb giving the impression of an emerging legend that had not been heard of before.

Together, Paul's omission of the discovered empty tomb in his letter to the Corinthians and the awkward ending to the Gospel of Mark plausibly suggests that the discovered empty tomb tradition is a legend.

The Jewish Charge of a Stolen Body

According to the Gospel of Matthew, Jesus was buried in a tomb that his followers knew the location of and that the authorities posted guards at (Mt 27:62-66). Then, according to the Gospel of Matthew, the guards passed out from fear when an angel came to open the tomb (Mt 28:1-4). After that (according to Matthew) the guards were paid off by the authorities to keep quiet about the angel and to say instead that Jesus' disciples stole his body while they slept (Mt 28:11-15). Writing decades after Jesus' death, Matthew then states that this lie – that Jesus' disciples stole the body while the guards slept – "is still told among the Jews to this day" (Mt 28:15).

This last statement by Matthew strongly suggests that there was an actual charge of a stolen body from some Jews at the time Matthew was writing. Since this charge is from Christianity's opponents, and because this charge presupposes that Jesus' tomb was discovered empty, it is sometimes used as evidence that Jesus' tomb really was discovered empty.

However, since this charge is recorded in a Gospel written *after* the Gospel of Mark, this charge could just as easily be the result of apologetics and legendary growth *after* the discovered empty tomb tradition came into circulation. It would have been natural two thousand years ago, just as it would be today, that some people would have accepted the Christian claim of a discovered empty tomb at face value and responded simplistically. The result could have been a sequence of charges and countercharges between unsophisticated Jews and Christians that developed something like this:

- Christian legend arises that Jesus' tomb was found empty.

- Some Jews counter that his followers probably stole the body.

- Christian legend arises that the tomb was guarded.

- Jewish legend arises that the guards fell asleep.

- Christian legend arises (reflected in Matthew's Gospel) that the Jewish claim of sleeping guards comes from the guards being paid off (decades earlier) by the authorities to *say* they fell asleep instead of reporting the supernatural angel they saw.

The entire sequence could be a series of legends and counter-legends driven by apologetics from both sides over a period of years or decades. That there never were any guards at Jesus' burial spot is supported by three things. First, the Gospels of Mark, Luke, and John say nothing about guards at the tomb. Second, Matthew's comment that this "is still told *among the Jews* to this day" (Mt 28:15) suggests that the source of the stolen body/sleeping guards charge was not from any official Jewish source, or even the guards themselves, but from the general populace. The third thing that supports the conclusion that there never were any guards at Jesus' burial spot is an interesting coincidence in the Gospel of Matthew.

Matthew is both the only Gospel to post guards at the tomb and the only Gospel to have Jesus *publicly* predict his future resurrection.* In Matthew, Jesus' public prediction of his future resurrection cites Jonah 1:17 and goes like this: "For just as Jonah was three days and three nights in the belly of the sea monster, so for three days and three nights the Son of Man will be in the heart of the earth" (Mt 12:40). Later on, when Matthew narrates the posting of the guards, it is done like this:

---

* I am excluding the non-canonical Gospel of Peter (which does have a guarded tomb) because we're missing much of that gospel and therefore we do not know if it also has a public prediction of Jesus' future resurrection. I predict that it will if the rest of that gospel is ever found.

...the chief priests and the Pharisees gathered before Pilate and said, "Sir, we remember *what that impostor said* while he was still alive, 'After three days I will rise again.' Therefore command that the tomb be made secure until the third day; otherwise his disciples may go and steal him away, and tell the people, 'He has been raised from the dead', and the last deception would be worse than the first." (Mt 27:62-64)

Regarding the connection between the Jonah 1:17 announcement and the posting of the guards, C.H. Giblin says:

In [Matthew] 27.63 [the passage above], when the Pharisees recall what Jesus said while he was still living, they must be referring principally to what was told them in [Matthew] 12.40 [the Jonah 1:17 announcement]. For [Matthew] 12.40 is the only place where a burial-prediction, able to be construed as a resurrection-prediction was made to them or even stated publicly.[12]

Further confirming the connection that Giblin is referring to, the Gospel of Matthew has Jesus direct his Jonah 1:17 resurrection prediction specifically at the "scribes and Pharisees" (Mt 12:38), the same general authorities who ask Pilate to have the tomb guarded – "the chief priests and the Pharisees" (Mt 27:62). These things give the impression that Matthew (or the tradition he drew from) has a public announcement about Jesus' future resurrection for the sole purpose of posting guards at the tomb, for in order to post guards at the tomb, one must first show that the chief priests and Pharisees have a *reason* for posting guards at the tomb (in this case to prevent Jesus' disciples from stealing his body in order to fulfill his resurrection prediction). Adding further to the impression of fabrication or legend, the public prediction of Jesus' future resurrection in Matthew creates a difficulty in the larger Christian storyline – the Jewish authorities understood Jesus' Jonah 1:17 resurrection prediction but his own disciples did not, even after Jesus told them in plain language (see Mk 9:9-10, 31-32).

According to Raymond Brown: "[Regarding the] existence of a guard...there is neither internal nor external evidence to cause us to affirm historicity."[13] Even evangelical scholar William Craig, after a valiant attempt to defend the guard at the tomb, concludes, "Although there are reasons to doubt the existence of the guard at the tomb, there are also weighty considerations in its favor. It seems best to leave it an open question."[14] But Craig also points out, "The vast, vast majority of New Testament scholars would regard Matthew's guard story as unhistorical....I can hardly think of anybody who would defend the historicity of the guard at the tomb....Most scholars regard the guard at the tomb story as a legend or a Matthean invention."[15]

If everyone agrees that the guards at the tomb are, or at least *could* be, a fiction, then it is easy to explain the existence of the Jewish charge of a stolen body – it was just a simplistic response by some unsophisticated Jews to the Christian claim of a discovered empty tomb. If the Jewish charge of a stolen body is so easily explained this way, then the Jewish charge of a stolen body is not good evidence in support of the discovered empty tomb.

The Jesus Seminar sums it up nicely:

> [The Gospel of] Matthew reflects the view that in some quarters the empty tomb story backfired as an attempt to demonstrate the historicity of Jesus' resurrection. Unbelievers countered the story of the empty tomb with the charge that the body had simply been removed from the tomb by the disciples. Matthew creates a story to counteract that charge and to buttress the account of the empty tomb. The posting of the guard is reported only by Matthew among the canonical gospels....The Fellows of the Seminar concluded that the original story of the empty tomb was a Markan fiction and that the subsequent fiction of the guards at the tomb and the charge and countercharges were equally fictive.[16]

Conclusion

In conclusion, it is plausible that the discovered empty tomb tradition is a legend. If so, then a great deal of other questions automatically follow that must be answered in order to explain the rise of the beliefs and traditions expressed in 1 Corinthians 15:3-7. The rest of this book will simply step through each of these questions and attempt to show that each has a plausible answer.

Chapter 2

An Obscure Burial

If there never was a discovered empty tomb, how could a belief that Jesus was bodily raised have emerged and survived if his followers could have simply checked the location where Jesus' body was buried and seen that his corpse was still there? There seems to be only one possibility, and it has been suggested before – Jesus was removed from the cross and buried in a location unknown to his followers. In this case, his followers would not have been able to check the location of his body to see if his corpse was there or not. But is such a scenario plausible?

According to the Gospels, Jesus was arrested by the Jewish authorities, given a trial, convicted of blasphemy or some other unidentified infraction, handed over to the Romans who put him on trial again, and then crucified. Although disagreeing that formal trials ever took place or that Jesus was convicted of blasphemy, the arrest by Jewish authorities and the handing over of Jesus to the Romans for crucifixion is accepted even by the Jesus Seminar:

> [We] approved on three different occasions over a ten-year period the statement that Jesus performed some anti-temple act and spoke some word against the temple. More than a hundred scholars participated in these affirmations....[It is suggested that] Jesus precipitated some kind of temple incident by his aggressive criticism of the commercialization of the temple cult....[The arresting party] probably consisted of temple police and perhaps those attached to the service of the high priest....[Those] messengers of the temple bureaucracy would have brought him under arrest to the high priest....The Fellows were dubious that the ranking priests consulted widely with the elders and scholars

and they seriously doubted that the whole Council or Sanhedrin was involved....[Some] Jewish officials, probably the high priest and his associates, urged Pilate to execute Jesus as a threat to public order. For his part, Pilate needed little convincing...it is quite possible that he had issued a standing order for dealing with troublemakers, in which case the "trial" may have been a very brief discussion with the handiest local centurion.[1]

Whether the Gospel accounts leading up to Jesus' crucifixion are correct or the Jesus Seminar's version is correct, the handing over of Jesus by the Jewish authorities to the Roman authorities is what is important here.

Out of the thousands of people crucified by the Romans in the decades surrounding Jesus' death, it is universally accepted that almost all were simply left on the cross to decay, eventually eaten by birds and other wild animals. This practice served as a deterrent to others and as a symbol of Roman power, especially during times of rebellion such as those that occurred in 4 B.C.E., 66 C.E., and 70 C.E.

However, there appears to have been exceptions during peacetime, where crucified bodies were sometimes allowed to be removed from the cross and buried. Many have pointed out the reasons why Jesus' body could plausibly have been removed from the cross for burial.[2] The main reasons are given below.

The following Jewish traditions show that the *Jewish* authorities would have had a strong *desire* to see Jesus buried:

1) Deuteronomy 21:22-23: "If a man has committed a crime punishable by death and he is put to death, and you hang him on a tree [a cross], his body shall not remain all night upon the tree, but you shall bury him the same day, for a hanged man is accursed by God; you shall not defile your land which the Lord your God gives you for an inheritance." This tradition shows up across a very large body of Jewish literature, including Ezekiel 39:11-16; Joshua 8:28-29; 10:25-27; War of the Jews 4.5.2; Antiquities of the Jews 4.8.24; John 19:31; Gospel of Peter 2:3; 5:1; and Mishnah Sanhedrin 6:4-5.

2) Even the wicked, divinely judged, and enemies slain in battle are to be buried (Num 11:33-34; 1 Kgs 11:15; Ezek 39:11-16; Against Apion 2.29; cf. 2.26).

3) Of all of Tobit's virtues, it is his burying the dead that is his greatest (Tobit 1:18-20; 2:3-8; 4:3-4; 6:15; 14:10-13).

4) Burial of a corpse takes precedence over study of the Law, circumcision, or offering the Passover lamb (b. Meg. 3b).

5) A high priest is obligated to bury a neglected corpse if there is no one else to do it (Sipre Num. §26 (on Num 6:6-8)).

6) The importance of care for the dead and their proper burial is well attested in scripture: Genesis 23:4-19; 50:4-14; 50:22-26; Joshua 24:32; 1 Samuel 31:12-13; 2 Samuel 2:4-5; 21:12-14; Numbers 11:33-34; 1 Kings 11:15; Ezekiel 39:11-16.

The following evidence and arguments indicate that peacetime Roman administrations sometimes respected local burial sensitivities, and that they may have done so in the case of Jesus:

1) The archaeological discovery of the skeletal remains of a first-century crucifixion victim in a family tomb just outside of Jerusalem (Giv'at ha-Mivtar) suggests that a Roman governor in Jerusalem had at least once released the body of a crucifixion victim for burial. Since it was only by accident that the victim's remains were preserved in a way that identified him as a crucifixion victim, there were probably others.[*]

2) Philo writes in the early first century that on the eve of Roman holidays in Egypt, crucified bodies were sometimes taken down and given to their families (Flaccum 10.83-84).

---

[*] There was a knot in the wood of the victim's cross that caused one of the nails to bend 180 degrees back on itself and become unremovable. The nail and the piece of wood were buried with the victim with the nail still imbedded in the skeletal remains.

3) Cicero mentions in 70 B.C.E. a governor in Sicily who released bodies to family members in return for a fee (Verrem 2.5.45).

4) The Digest of Justinian (48.24) has Augustus in the early first century giving crucified bodies back to their families and Paulus in the third century saying that crucified bodies should be given to any who seek their burial.

5) On the eve of Passover, a holiday that celebrates Israel's liberation from foreign domination, Pilate may not have wanted to risk provoking the Jewish population and so may have allowed Jesus to be buried.

6) The assertion in the Gospel of Mark that Pilate "used to release for them one prisoner for whom they asked" (Mk 15:6) suggests that during the first century C.E. one could at least plausibly tell stories of Roman judicial clemency, especially around religious holidays.

7) Five Gospels (including the non-canonical Gospel of Peter), Paul's epistles (Rom 6:4-6), and the earliest Christian creed (1 Cor 15:4), texts and traditions designed to sustain Christian belief in the first century, all tell of a crucifixion victim being buried. That these texts proved successful in sustaining Christian belief shows that the removal of a crucifixion victim from the cross during a major Jewish festival was considered at that time a plausible event.

If the Roman authorities allowed Jesus to be removed from the cross in deference to Jewish burial sensitivities, what would have become of Jesus' body and what would Jesus' family, friends, and followers have done? To answer these questions, we have to look at how first-century Jews buried their poor and the difference between an honorable and a dishonorable Jewish burial.

First-Century Jewish Burial of the Poor

It is widely acknowledged among archaeologists and biblical scholars that first-century Jews who were poor were not normally buried in rock-hewn tombs. Instead, they were buried in the ground:

> The eight hundred tombs thus far discovered in the vicinity of Jerusalem do not reflect the totality of the burials. Kloner estimates at 50 the highest average number of burials in a single tomb. The corresponding number of deaths in Jerusalem from the third century B.C.E to the first century C.E. (period of the finds) would then be only 40,000. Kloner's estimate of the number of deaths is about 750,000 for this period; such a figure would mean that, at best, only about 5 percent of the tombs have been found. Presumably these tombs belonged to the middle and upper classes, with *the rest of the population buried in simple shallow pits that have long since disappeared.*[3]

> Because of the expense associated with hewing a burial cave out of bedrock...only upper class and upper-middle class Jerusalemites could afford rock-hewn tombs. The poorer members of Jerusalem's population apparently disposed of their dead in a manner that has left few traces in the archaeological record, for example in simple individual trench graves dug into the ground....The majority of victims crucified by the Romans belonged to the lower classes – precisely those who could not afford rock-hewn tombs....Because trench graves are poor in finds and are much less conspicuous and more susceptible to destruction than rock-hewn tombs, relatively few examples are recorded....Jesus' family did not own a rock-hewn tomb.[4]

In Jeremiah 26:23 King Jehoiakim is said to have slain the prophet Uriah "and cast his dead body into the burial place of the common people". That these "graves" designate a communal burial ground is suggested not only by the language of throwing or casting of the corpse, but also by 2 Kings 23:6, for Josiah is there said to have taken the ashes of the Asherah he had burned and "threw its dust on the graves of the common people", a description which does not pass well with tombs [see too Jer 31:40]. It may well have been the case that these burial plots were reserved for persons too poor to afford a tomb for burial.

Similarly, in Matthew 27:7 the high priests are said to have taken Judas' blood money and "bought the Potter's Field as a burial place for strangers". Tombs are not located in a field, and foreigners who die far from home will not have tombs in Jerusalem awaiting use.[5]

Some think poor criminals were the exception, that they received a rock-hewn tomb burial in a specially designated criminal's graveyard. This conclusion is based on a passage from the Mishnah which says:

> They did not bury the condemned in the burial grounds of his ancestors, but there were two graveyards made ready for the use of the court, one for those who were beheaded or strangled, and one for those who were stoned or burned. When the flesh [of the criminal] had wasted away they gathered together the bones and buried them in their own place [the family burial place]. (Mishnah Sanhedrin 6:5-6)

The reference in this passage to gathering the bones and burying them with the family is called "secondary burial" and usually occurred about a year after the "primary" (or initial) burial. The passage above strongly suggests that rock-hewn tombs were used for criminals so that their bones could be easily collected at a later date for burial with the family.

However, going against this conclusion in the case of poor criminals is that virtually all archaeological discoveries of Jewish ground burials (those of poor people) have only *individuals* in them. As archaeologist Boaz Zissu says, "In most cases, the Beit Safafa graves [two miles southwest of Jerusalem] contained only one body each."[6] Zissu goes on to say that none of the graves had more than two bodies. Hershel Shanks finds the same thing at Qazone (43 miles southeast of Jerusalem) and Qumran (14 miles east of Jerusalem): "...each grave [at Qazone] contained a single body, as did almost all...at Qumran."[7] Shanks also goes on to say that no grave ever contained more than two bodies. Similar graves of individuals have been found at Ein el-Ghuweir (16 miles southeast of Jerusalem).[8] These finds suggest that poor people did not have a place where they consolidated the bones of family and therefore did not practice the secondary burial suggested in the Mishnah passage above.

If poor people did not practice secondary burial, then the Mishnah passage above, with its implied rock-hewn tomb, most likely applied only to criminals wealthy enough to expect a secondary burial in a family tomb or, for those only moderately wealthy, in an ossuary. This would leave the poorest criminals to be buried in the ground, and only once. This conclusion is supported by archaeologist Jodi Magness:

> There is no evidence that the Sanhedrin or the Roman authorities paid for and maintained rock-hewn tombs for executed criminals from impoverished families. Instead, these unfortunates would have been buried in individual trench graves or pits.[9]

A final thing to look at regarding first-century Jewish burial of the poor is how their graves were marked. According to Jodi Magness:

> After the trench was filled in, a rough headstone was often erected at one end. [Today,] the headstones are uninscribed, although some may once have had painted decorations or inscriptions that have not survived.[10]

In contrast to what Magness found, Boaz Zissu found at the Qumran graves mentioned earlier fewer graves marked by headstones and more marked with just a pile of loose rocks: "each...is marked by a cairn or, less often, a large standing stone."[11] According to Jon Davies, some graves may not have been marked even by a cairn, but only the mark described in the Mishnah to give warning of uncleanness: "whiting [chalk] mingled with water and poured over the grave."[12]

All of the above suggests that Jesus, whether buried in a criminal's graveyard or not, would have under normal circumstances been buried in the ground. If there were no family or friends present at the burial, and especially if Jesus was buried dishonorably, both of which will be suggested next, it is plausible that those who buried Jesus did not make any special effort to gather a headstone and inscribe Jesus' name on it, but simply marked the grave with whiting or with a pile of loose rocks to show that someone was buried there and therefore that spot was unclean.

Dishonorable Versus Honorable Burial

Regardless of whether the charge brought against Jesus was legitimate or not, if Jewish officials urged Pilate to execute him, they most likely would have followed through and treated him as a criminal in his burial too. This would have entailed the Jewish authorities taking possession of Jesus' body to make sure he received a dishonorable burial.

Virtually all scholars agree that rites of mourning were not allowed at a dishonorable burial. In the Old Testament it is said of a criminal's burial, "They shall not lament for him..." (Jeremiah 22:18). A continuation of the earlier Mishnah passage suggests that no mourning was allowed for those criminals who received a secondary burial, which would imply the same restriction existed at their primary burial:

> The kinsmen came and greeted the judges and the witnesses as if to say, "We have nothing against you in our hearts, for you have judged the judgment of truth." And they used to *not make open lamentation*, but they went mourning, for mourning has its place in the heart. (Mishnah Sanhedrin 6:6, emphasis added)

The Talmud also restricts mourning: "For those executed by the court, no rites whatsoever should be observed..." (Semahot 2:6). Although the Jewish court did not themselves execute Jesus, they nevertheless handed over Jesus to the Romans with the intent that he be crucified and so this passage would seem to apply.

The texture of a dishonorable burial is further filled out by the Jewish historian Josephus, who suggests that few would attend: "He that blasphemeth God, let him be stoned; and let him hang upon a tree all that day, and then let him be buried in an ignominious and *obscure* manner" (Antiquities of the Jews 4.8.6, emphasis added). Although Jesus may not have been charged with blasphemy as the Gospels claim, Josephus' remarks nevertheless reflect the obscure nature of a criminal's burial in general. Josephus also makes reference to a "night" burial, which may have been another way of giving someone an obscure burial: "...and there let him be stoned; and when he has continued there for one whole day, that all the people may see him, let him be buried *in the night*" (Antiquities of the Jews 4.8.24, emphasis added). Referring to a thief Josephus says, "...he was immediately put to death; and attained no more than to be buried *in the night* in a disgraceful manner, and such as was suitable to a condemned malefactor" (Antiquities of the Jews 5.1.14, emphasis added).

It is unclear if a dishonorable burial entailed the banning of all attendance or only the attendance of those who might mourn. However, even if the latter, it is unlikely that any of Jesus' followers who thought they could keep from mourning would have attended Jesus' burial. Without a family burial place to later move Jesus' bones to, and with his burial spot in Jerusalem days away from where most of his followers lived in Galilee, knowing the exact spot where Jesus was buried would not have been very important. More significantly, because Jesus at the moment must have looked like a failure, those who were associated with him may all have avoided the burial to avoid public humiliation. There would also have been an incentive for Jesus' followers to avoid his burial due to fear of being identified by Roman or Jewish authorities who could make reprisals against them or use them to get to other followers of Jesus whom the authorities might still have seen as potential troublemakers. Such behavior by the authorities is noted by first-century historian Tacitus. He noted that as people lingered around the corpses of those executed by the Romans in 32 C.E. (within a year or two of Jesus' crucifixion), "Spies were set round them, who noted the sorrow of each mourner..." (Annals 6.19). All of the above suggests that if Jesus was buried dishonorably, it is doubtful that any of his family, friends, or followers would have attended the burial.

But what if Jesus was for some reason buried honorably? It turns out that nothing substantial changes, for in this case mourners still would not have been allowed to attend the burial. This conclusion is based on a Mishnah passage which reads, "A mourner must not observe mourning on festivals, for it is written:

'And thou shalt rejoice on thy feast' [Deut 16:14]" (Moed Katan 3:7-9). As William Craig says about this passage:

> According to the Mishnah, lamentation for the deceased is actually *forbidden* during a Jewish feast to all but the next of kin (Moed Katan 3.7-9)....Executed by crucifixion during the juxtaposed feasts of Passover and Unleavened Bread, he [Jesus] could not be publicly lamented by his followers.[13] *

Although the context of the above passage allows mourning by next of kin, even the Gospels do not place a next of kin at Jesus' burial. Regarding the woman named Mary with different sons referred to in the burial accounts – "Mary the mother of Joses" (Mk 15:47), "Mary the mother of James" (Lk 24:10), and "the other Mary" (Mt 27:61) – R.E. Brown says:

> The possibility that this Mary is the same person known to John as Mary of Clopas [Jn 19:25] is good....In John alone the mother of Jesus is at Golgotha [observing Jesus' crucifixion]; but she and the disciple whom Jesus loved seem to depart before Jesus' death (19:27), and they are absent from the burial account.[14]

In conclusion, whether Jesus was buried honorably or dishonorably, mourning would have been prohibited. In this case, attendance at the burial, if not altogether banned, would have been restricted to those who could keep from mourning. However, it is likely that even those followers of Jesus who thought they could keep from mourning stayed away from the burial to avoid public humiliation and out of fear of reprisal or monitoring by the Roman and Jewish authorities. In this case, none of Jesus' followers would have been present at Jesus' burial and so none would have known the spot where he was buried.

---

* This Jewish restriction on mourning would apply even if the Passover Seder was on the night *after* Jesus' crucifixion (as is suggested in Jn 18:28; 19:14; and GPeter 2:5). In this case, the afternoon of Jesus' death would still be a festival – Passover instead of the Festival of Unleavened Bread.

The Rock-Hewn Tomb Burial
Legend in the Gospel of Mark

The Gospels say that Jesus was buried in a rock-hewn tomb and that his followers knew the location of the tomb. But the above analysis suggests that the most likely outcome for a person in Jesus' situation was an obscure ground burial. If an obscure ground burial occurred, it is worth asking why the burial accounts emerged as they did in the Gospels.[*]

Mark's burial account is of paramount interest because that is the earliest burial account that we have. As Raymond Brown, again, a highly respected Catholic scholar says:

> True, we have in the Matthean and Lucan accounts of the burial an early interpretation of Mark; but...there is a very high possibility that these two evangelists have changed and developed the Marcan outlook. Consequently, I shall not use Matthew and Luke as a primary guide to Mark's intention.[15]

Because of the primacy of the Gospel of Mark, Mark's burial account will be looked at in detail below. It is worth noting that the historicity of Joseph of Arimathea does not matter for this analysis. Even if he was a member of the Sanhedrin and buried Jesus, the use of his name in burial legends years later that relate allegiances and actions that he never had or did would not be surprising if he was by that time dead or not in the locale where the story was growing.

The following is the entire burial account, including the lead into it, from chapter 15 of the Gospel of Mark. The items most germane to the burial are underlined.

> Then Jesus [on the cross] gave a loud cry and breathed his last. [38]And the curtain of the temple was torn in two, from top to bottom. [39]Now when the centurion, who stood facing him, saw that in this way he breathed his last, he said, "Truly this man was

---

[*] Those who consider such a question a moot point because legends often go in all kinds of unexplainable directions can skip this whole section. Skip ahead to the section at the end of this chapter entitled "A Few Other Considerations Related to Jesus' Burial".

God's Son!" [40]There were also <u>women looking on from a distance</u>; among them were Mary Magdalene, and Mary the mother of James the younger and of Joses, and Salome. [41]These used to follow him and provided for him when he was in Galilee; and there were many other women who had come up with him to Jerusalem. [42]<u>When evening had come, and since it was the day of Preparation, that is, the day before the sabbath,</u> [43]<u>Joseph of Arimathea, a respected member of the council, who was also himself waiting expectantly for the kingdom of God, went boldly to Pilate and asked for the body of Jesus.</u> [44]Then Pilate wondered if he were already dead; and summoning the centurion, he asked him whether he had been dead for some time. [45]When he learned from the centurion that he was dead, <u>he granted the body to Joseph.</u> [46]<u>Then Joseph bought a linen cloth, and taking down the body, wrapped it in the linen cloth, and laid it in a tomb that had been hewn out of the rock.</u> He then rolled a stone against the door of the tomb. [47]<u>Mary Magdalene and Mary the mother of Joses saw where the body was laid.</u> (Mk 15:37-47)

The intentions behind Mark's burial account that will be suggested below operate under the assumption that the *primary* goal of Mark's burial account, as part of a growing legend, was to explain *how* Jesus followers were able to see *where* he was buried, for one must know where a body is buried in order to later discover that burial location empty.

In Mark's Gospel, Jesus is a convicted criminal in the eyes of the Jewish authorities (even though a false conviction of blasphemy, Mk 14:55-64; 15:9-10). If behind Mark's burial account lies the common knowledge by the author and the author's audience that Jesus would normally under the circumstances have been buried in the ground with none of his followers present (for the reasons outlined previously), then a certain logic becomes apparent that explains why the women were able to see *where* Jesus was buried. But before focusing on that aspect of Mark's burial account that explains why some of Jesus' followers were able to see *where* he was buried, every other detail of Mark's burial account needs to be thoroughly addressed in order to solidify the rest of the picture because that picture often shifts around as people try to reconcile Mark's burial account with the burial accounts in the later Gospels. As I go through each of these details, I rely heavily on the highly esteemed opinion of Catholic scholar Raymond Brown.

Before his burial account, Mark twice makes it clear that "the whole council" was complicit in the death of Jesus (Mk 14:55; 15:1). He then refers to Joseph of Arimathea in his burial account as "a respected member of the council" (Mk 15:43). Regarding this characterization of Joseph in light of the fact that the whole council was complicit in the death of Jesus, William Lyons says:

> ...the use of βουλευτής ["member of the council" (Mk 15:43)] here clearly serves to indicate to the readers that Joseph was one of those responsible for his death....Being esteemed as a member of the council responsible for the death of Jesus is unlikely to suggest to Mark's readers that they should themselves respect Joseph. In this context it [the word "respected"] is more probably intended to explain Pilate's decision to grant Joseph's request [for Jesus' body].[16]

Lyons' conclusion is consistent with the "boldness" it took for Joseph to ask Pilate for Jesus' body (Mk 15:43), this qualifier suggesting that Pilate did not always grant or appreciate such requests. R.E. Brown agrees with Lyons: "Mark wanted his readers to know that Joseph was a distinguished member of the Sanhedrin....[There] is nothing in Mark's first item of information about Joseph to make readers think of him as a follower or supporter of Jesus."[17]

Regarding Mark's characterization of Joseph as someone "who was also himself waiting expectantly for the kingdom of God" (Mk 15:43), Donald Senior says:

> This suggests that he [Joseph] was not yet a disciple, but is someone open and responsive to the message Jesus proclaimed (cf. Mk 1:14-15). In similar language Jesus had blessed the Scribe who instinctively understood and accepted Jesus' teaching on the primacy of the love command [Mk 12:28-34]....In both instances, a person from the ranks of those who seem to be Jesus' unyielding foes – the scribes and the council –

is stirred by Jesus and in so doing moves closer to the Kingdom they seek.[18]

R. E. Brown agrees:

> If Mark had wished to describe the burial of Jesus by a disciple, that could easily have been made unambiguous, as in the instance of the burial of John's body by "his disciples" (Mk 6:29)....[Mark's Joseph] might be described as a pious Jew who awaited the kingdom of God in the sense that he sought only to obey the commandments, much as the scribe of Mk 12:28...."A respected council member who was also himself awaiting the kingdom of God" meant that Joseph was a religiously pious Sanhedrist who, despite the condemnation of Jesus by the Sanhedrin, felt an obligation under the Law to bury this crucified criminal before sunset...the inability of Jews to carry a corpse on the Sabbath [being] a practice surely forbidden in NT times (cf. John 5:10) and specifically [forbidden] in *m. Sabb.* 10:5 [the Jews counted days from sunset to sunset, so the Sabbath began at sunset on Friday].[19]

Regarding Joseph's request for only Jesus' body (among the three that were crucified, see Mk 15:27), Mark's account may intend that the other two crucifixion victims were not yet dead since sometimes it took more than a day for crucifixion victims to die. Supporting this conclusion is Pilate's response to Joseph's request for Jesus' body: "[Pilate] wondered if he were already dead" (Mk 15:44). Only after summoning the centurion and confirming Jesus' death did Pilate grant the body to Joseph. R.E. Brown suggests another possibility that explains why Joseph requested only Jesus' body in Mark's burial account: "We have to assume that the story in the Synoptics has been narrowed down in its focus to Jesus, ignoring the two others who were no longer theologically or dramatically important."[20]

Regarding Mark's "linen cloth" used to wrap Jesus' body (Mk 15:46), R.E. Brown notes:

> It is not justified to claim that *sindōn* ["linen cloth"] was of such quality that readers would have to recognize the burial as

honorable. *Byssos* is the really fine linen. To specify that the *sindōn* he took over from Mark would befit a burial rendered to Jesus by a disciple, Matthew (27:59) adds "clean white" (*katharos*). The argument of Shea that if Joseph were not a disciple of Jesus and were just burying a criminal, he would have wrapped the body in ragged, torn, dirty winding sheets makes little sense....This is a hasty, impromptu gesture by Joseph. Are we to suppose that he would go home (to Arimathea?) or go into the city to friend's homes asking them for some dirty cloths? Rather he went and purchased what was readily available, and stores certainly did not sell torn cloths for interring criminals....Some have puzzled whether Joseph had sufficient time to go and buy such a cloth....[However, one could] take the verbs that describe his action causatively: "having had a linen cloth bought" – a cooperation that would have sped up the process. Similarly, although Mark seems to have Joseph himself "take down" Jesus, Joseph would have had him taken down by others. Sometimes confirmation for this is found in the words spoken at the empty tomb in Mark 16:6: "See the place where *they* placed him."[21]

Mark describes the tomb as having a "very large" stone (Mk 16:4) to block the entrance, and the women visiting the tomb ask, "Who will *roll* away the stone for us?" (Mk 16:3). With the help of the later Gospels, most notably Matthew's burial in a "rich man's" tomb (Mt 27:57), many have concluded that Mark intends a *disc-shaped* stone for the tomb's entrance and therefore a very extravagant tomb. However, it is more likely that a square/rectangular stone is intended not only in Mark, but Matthew as well. Archaeologist Amos Kloner explains:

> More than 98 percent of the Jewish tombs from this period, called the Second Temple period (c. first century B.C.E. to 70 C.E.), were closed with square blocking stones...only four are known to have used round (disk shaped) blocking stones...[and] they occur only in the more elaborate cave tombs, which had at least two rooms or, as in one case, a spacious hall....Matthew, Mark and Luke all describe the stone being "rolled" (in John it is "taken away") [see Mt 27:60; 28:2; Mk 15:46; 16:3-4; Lk 24:2; Jn 20:1], and thus it is only natural to assume that the stone was

round. But we must remember that "rolled" is a translation of the Greek word *kulio*, which can also mean "dislodge," "move back" or simply "move". This ambiguity in the text, combined with the archaeological evidence, leads me to agree with the scholar Gustave Dalman, who, as early as 1935, suggested that Matthew 27 does not refer to a round blocking stone....In Matthew 28 an angel sits on the stone after "rolling" it back [Mt 28:2]. If the stone had been rolled back between two walls, as was the case with Second Temple period round stones, it would have been impossible to sit on it [the top of the disk would normally be enclosed within the two walls]. Indeed, it would be difficult to sit on the edge of a disk-shaped stone even if it had been pulled back from the tomb entrance. A square blocking stone would make a much better perch. Of course, with angels anything can happen, but it seems likely that the human author of the Gospel would have described the angel sitting on a square stone....Most likely Jesus' tomb [that is being described in the Gospels] was a standard small burial room, with a standing pit and burial benches along three sides...[22]

R.E. Brown agrees:

Apparently Matthew 28:2 supposes a boulder, since the angel who rolls away the stone sits on it – a wheel-shaped stone would most likely have been rolled back into a rock recess or flat along the outside of the tomb and thus not available for sitting....The reason for mentioning the size of the stone [Mk 16:4] is to increase the miraculous element in the stone's being rolled back when the women visit the tomb on Sunday.[23]

A final detail to address in Mark's burial account is that it may intend the women closed the distance between them and the burial enough to see inside the tomb: "[they] saw *where* the body was laid" (Mk 15:47). However, this verse may instead intend that the women only saw *which tomb* Jesus was laid in, never moving from the spot in the "distance" (Mk 15:40) that they watched the crucifixion from. It is noteworthy that Mark never narrates the women moving from their spot in the distance. Either possibility is compatible with the later statement by the angel: "look, there is the *place* they laid him" (Mk 16:6) – the angel may be pointing out the bench/niche that the women saw Jesus laid on, or the angel may be pointing out the bench/niche that *he* knew Jesus was laid on. Whichever Mark intends, either is compatible with the analysis presented here.

So in summary up to this point, we have in Mark's Gospel a Joseph of Arimathea who is a pious Sanhedrist who only desires to carry out the Jewish law and bury this crucified criminal before sunset. With this established, we can now look at that aspect of Mark's burial account that answers what I am proposing here was the most important thing that his burial account needed to answer – how it was that Jesus' followers knew *where* Jesus was buried.

Richard Carrier points out the urgency of sundown in Mark's burial account:

> ...before even asking for the body, "evening had already come" (Mark 15:42 [NASB translation])....Since Mark specifically says it was still the day *before* the Sabbath, the word for "evening" (*opsia*, "late" sc. "hour") must refer to the hour or minutes just before sunset....and there was yet further delay awaiting the centurion to confirm the death of Jesus (Mark 15:44), and then all the walking involved (both to and from Pilate, then from the cross to the grave)....[The] phrases used for the time of burial imply that the sun was virtually in the process of going down once Joseph arrived and had the permission to get the body....Likewise, we are told that the women assumed the burial was not completed (they went to complete the anointing on Sunday [Mk 16:1-2]), so we even have some positive evidence that there wasn't enough time [to complete all the desired burial actions].[24]

R.E. Brown agrees: "Mark describes the sparsest type of burial, marked by haste and lacking in amenities."[25]

If behind Mark's burial account lies the common expectation that Jesus would normally under the circumstances have been buried in the ground with none of his followers present, Mark's burial account appears to be conveying the idea that Jesus' followers were able to see *where* Jesus was buried because the trip to the place of burial (the criminal's graveyard or perhaps the Kidron or Hinnom valley), and the time required to dig and/or fill in a ground burial, was cut short by sunset, causing Joseph of Arimathea to put Jesus temporarily in an available rock-hewn tomb very close to or at the site of the crucifixion. In other words, Mark's rushed burial into the closest available rock-hewn tomb conveys to a first-century audience *why* the women were able to see *where* Jesus was buried, knowing where Jesus was buried being a necessary condition for what follows – the discovery of that burial location empty. Archeologist Amos Kloner agrees that a temporary burial is intended in Mark's Gospel:

> Jesus' burial took place on the eve of the Sabbath. His would have been a hurried funeral, in observance of the Jewish law that forbade leaving the corpse unburied overnight....The body was simply and hastily covered with a shroud and placed on a burial bench in a small burial cave....I would go one step further and suggest that Jesus' tomb was what the sages refer to as a "borrowed or temporary tomb." During the Second Temple period and later, Jews often practiced temporary burial. This is reflected, for example, in two quotations from rabbinic sources involving burial customs and mourning:
>
>> Whoever finds a corpse in a tomb should not move it from its place, unless he knows that this is a *temporary* grave. (Semahot 13:5, emphasis added)
>>
>> Rabbi Simeon ben Eleazar says: "Rabban Gamaliel had a *temporary* tomb in Yabneh into which they bring the corpse and lock the door upon it..." (Semahot 10:8, emphasis added)[26]
>>
>> [See too Talmud Baba Bathra 102b: "People do not plant [vines] with the object of pulling them out, [but a burial] may sometimes take place at twilight and it is put down *temporarily*."]

It is worth asking, if Mark intends a temporary burial, when in such a situation would Joseph of Arimathea most likely return to the tomb to rebury Jesus where he was supposed to be buried in the ground? The most obvious answer might seem to be as soon as the Sabbath ended at sunset on Saturday. However, if a Saturday night return by Joseph was a likely option, it seems Mark's audience would have naturally concluded from Mark's Gospel that the women found an empty tomb on Sunday morning simply because Joseph had moved the body the previous night, in which case Mark's discovered empty tomb account would have failed as an argument for Jesus' resurrection. That Mark's Gospel did not fail as an argument for Jesus' resurrection suggests that there was something about Jewish burial practices, or some other practical matter, that would have made it unlikely that Joseph returned to the tomb Saturday night. Perhaps the fact that it was dark when the Sabbath ended was reason enough to wait until Sunday for such a mundane transfer of a corpse (as opposed to the intentional night burials mentioned earlier by Josephus to inflict dishonor on the buried person at their initial burial). Further suggesting that a Saturday night return to the tomb would not have occurred for some practical reason is that in Mark's account the women do not return to the tomb on Saturday night even though they buy spices that same night for anointing Jesus' body the next morning (Mk 16:1). If behind Mark's burial account was the common knowledge that Joseph would not normally have returned to the tomb before Sunday, Mark's Gospel further reveals its intent to convey a temporary burial by eliminating the possibility that the women missed a first light Sunday morning transfer of Jesus' body. Mark's Gospel does this by placing the women at the tomb just as the sun was rising: "they came unto the sepulchre *at the rising of the sun*" (Mk 16:2 KJV, Young, Webster, and NLT translations).

In conclusion, it makes sense that a hurried rock-hewn tomb burial legend would emerge out of an obscure ground burial in order to explain *how* some of Jesus' followers were able to see *where* he was buried, seeing where Jesus was buried being a necessary precursor to the discovered empty burial location legend. It also makes sense that all burial accounts after Mark's would continue to have Jesus buried in a rock-hewn tomb, not only because that was the tradition passed down to them, but because the much more important tradition – the discovered empty burial location legend – was by then based on a rock-hewn tomb.

A Few Other Considerations Related to Jesus' Burial

If Jesus received an obscure ground burial, it is not surprising that this does not show up in either the Jewish or Christian literature. Before the Christian claim of a discovered empty tomb showed up a decade or more after Jesus' death, the details of Jesus' burial would have been unimportant and not part of any historical core that anyone should expect to be preserved in Jewish or Christian records. When some Christians finally claimed a discovered empty tomb, with its associated rock-hewn tomb burial, most Jews probably just ignored the claim, for unless one actually *saw* the burial, how is one supposed to argue that a ground burial instead of a rock-hewn tomb burial occurred for a poor person buried over a decade earlier? But even if some Jews responded that Jesus should have been, or was, buried obscurely in the ground, it would not be surprising if this response was not preserved in the Jewish literature given how little the Jews wrote about Jesus. We can say this with confidence because the Jewish charge of a stolen body does not show up in the Jewish literature anywhere even though we know it existed because it appears in the Christian literature (as discussed in the previous chapter). Furthermore, it is likely that the only reason Christians recorded the Jewish charge of a stolen body was because they had an apologetic response to it (the tomb was guarded). In contrast, there would be no reason for Christians to record the Jewish charge of an obscure ground burial if they had no apologetic response to it, and especially if they had already answered that charge as best they could with the Gospel accounts of a rock-hewn tomb burial and the story of that rock-hewn tomb being discovered empty.

Although the above explains why Jesus' obscure ground burial would not show up in Jewish or Christian records, as an interesting aside, there may actually be one literary attestation of Jesus being buried in obscurity in the ground. In the non-canonical Secret Gospel of James, written around 100-150 C.E., there is a scene where Jesus appears to his disciples after his death and says:

> You have not yet been abused and have not yet been accused unjustly, nor have you yet been locked up in prison, nor have you yet been condemned unlawfully, nor have you yet been

crucified without reason, nor have you yet been buried *in the sand*, as I myself was.[27]

If this passage is referring to a ground burial, which it appears that it is, it is significant because it is unlikely that a rock-hewn tomb burial would be legendized into a ground burial. More likely the legend would develop in the opposite direction. Therefore, this piece of literature may preserve a distant memory of Jesus' burial in the ground, and the much more spectacular story of a rock-hewn tomb burial and discovered empty tomb is simply what won the day among the populace.

Another question that often pops up in discussions about Jesus' burial is why didn't the Jewish authorities simply exhume Jesus' body from the ground and parade it around to debunk the belief that Jesus was raised? This assumes the Jewish authorities paid any serious attention to the earliest Christians, which they probably did not. But even if they did, Gerald Bostock points out why such action would have been counterproductive:

[The] production of the body would have involved the priestly party in taking seriously the resurrection claims of the disciples, and with it the admission that they might have crucified God's Messiah....[It would also make them guilty of the] heinous offense of despoiling a grave....What is more there was no reason at all for them to produce the body until the time of Pentecost, when the disciples made the first public statement about the resurrection. By then, however, seven weeks had passed, and at that stage the corpse would not have been easily demonstrated to be the body of Jesus. The time-lag would have made the production of the body a futile exercise, even if its production could have proved anything of significance.[28] *

A final consideration related to Jesus' burial involves tomb veneration. That Jesus' burial location was unknown to his followers is consistent with the absence of evidence that Jesus' burial location was ever venerated in the first decades after his

---

* As will be shown in Chapter Five, most corpses in the Palestinian climate started to become unrecognizable after only three days.

death. The absolute earliest evidence of people venerating a tomb associated with Jesus is 135 C.E., but most think there was no tomb veneration until the fourth century. Both are well after the discovered empty tomb tradition came into circulation and therefore it would not be surprising if some tomb was by that time thought to be the one Jesus had been in even if the real place of Jesus' burial was never known.

I do not understand how some use the absence of early tomb veneration as evidence that Jesus' tomb was actually found empty, the logic being that because it was found empty, the earliest Christians did not care to venerate it. Even if Jesus' tomb was found empty, no one could have stopped early Christians from flocking to visit and venerate the site where the miracle of Jesus' resurrection took place, just as thousands of Christians today flock to the two competing sites for Jesus' burial in Jerusalem. As Peter Carnley says, "The pious interest in the alleged site of the Holy Sepulchre in our own day seems to render such an argument [that lack of tomb veneration points to a discovered empty tomb] completely impotent."[29]

Conclusion

In conclusion, it is plausible that Jesus was buried in the ground in a location unknown to his followers and that the Gospel burial accounts are legends. In this case, the only thing historical on this topic that is preserved in the literary record is that Jesus was buried, and that is exactly how it appears in the early passage that this book is trying to explain: "he was buried" (1 Corinthians 15:4).

Chapter 3

The Belief That Jesus Died for Our Sins and Was Raised

1 Corinthians 15:3-4: "...Christ died for our sins in accordance with the scriptures, and...he was raised...in accordance with the scriptures..."

If there never was a discovered empty tomb, and if Jesus was buried in a location unknown to his followers, what plausibly could have caused the nearly instantaneous rise of the radical beliefs that Jesus died for our sins and was raised from the dead? Some have proposed that post-mortem hallucinations of Jesus kick-started these beliefs. However, this seems implausible to me primarily for one of the reasons that others have found it implausible:

> Precisely because such encounters [visions of a recently dead person] were reasonably well known, they *could not possibly*, by themselves, have given rise to the belief that Jesus had been raised from the dead....[Jesus' followers] said what nobody had ever said about such a dead person before, that they had been *raised from* the dead.[1]

In other words, if a regular post-mortem hallucination of a recently deceased loved one gave birth to the belief that Jesus had been raised from the dead, then we should see beliefs in resurrected loved ones scattered throughout Jewish history. But we do not see that. The only explanation that seems to me to be capable of explaining the nearly instantaneous rise of such radical beliefs is the just as radical human phenomenon of cognitive dissonance reduction.

What is Cognitive Dissonance Reduction?

Most non-traditional scholars doubt that Jesus ever claimed he was the Messiah. However, Jesus obviously made a big impression on some people. Because of this, it is plausible that some thought or hoped he was the Messiah, perhaps a sentiment like that expressed in the Gospel of Luke: "...we had hoped that he was the one to redeem Israel" (Lk 24:21). How might people like this, Jesus' most ardent followers who thought or hoped he might be the Messiah, have reacted to the harsh reality of his death? For most people most of the time, the reaction in such a situation would be the depressing realization that expectations were wrong. But sometimes people do not follow that route. We human beings have a tendency, when we deeply believe or want to believe in something, to look for and arrive at conclusions that confirm what we already believe or want to believe. This sometimes leads to extraordinary displays of rationalization when strongly held beliefs are inescapably disconfirmed by reality. The internal tension caused by a disconfirming event is called "cognitive dissonance" by psychologists, and the release of this tension due to a rationalization (or any other action that releases the tension) is called "cognitive dissonance reduction". The 1999 *Baker Encyclopedia of Psychology and Counseling* (the most recent edition available) defines cognitive dissonance and cognitive dissonance reduction this way:

> An individual holds beliefs or cognitions that do not fit with each other (e.g., I believe the world will end, and the world did not end as predicted). Nonfitting beliefs give rise to dissonance, a hypothetical aversive state the individual is motivated to reduce....Dissonance may be reduced by changing behavior, altering a belief, or adding a new one.[2]

Using this psychological phenomenon to explain the rise of early Christian belief has been critiqued by two traditional scholars,

N.T. Wright in 2003 and William Craig in 2011.[3] The controversy surrounding this theory can be seen in Wright's strong disagreement with it and the response of a non-traditional scholar to Wright's critique. According to Wright, "The flaws in this argument [that cognitive dissonance caused early Christian belief] are so enormous that it is puzzling to find serious scholars still referring to it in deferential terms."[4] Non-traditional scholar Robert M. Price responds to Wright's critique this way:

> ...there are many viable explanations [for the rise of the belief that Jesus resurrected], not least Festinger's theory of cognitive dissonance reduction, whereby more than one disappointed sect has turned defeat into zeal by means of face-saving denial. Wright suicidally mentions this theory, only to dismiss it...with no serious attempt at refutation.[5]

I agree with Price. Wright does not adequately rebut this idea, and in my opinion neither did Craig when he critiqued it in 2011. Below is further explanation of this psychological phenomenon and an application of it to the early Christian beliefs that we are interested in. At the same time, the explanation below addresses all of Wright's and Craig's objections for anyone who might read or listen to their critiques.

The study of cognitive dissonance was pioneered in the 1950s by the late social psychologist Dr. Leon Festinger. After his death in 1989, Festinger's peers put together a collection of his best works, including his study of cognitive dissonance, and referred to him as "the dominant figure in social psychology since Kurt Lewin" and "a towering figure in contemporary social science and one of the foremost adventurers of the mind."[6] A decade later, the American Psychological Association's Scientific Conference Program dedicated one of its volumes to Festinger's theory of cognitive dissonance where they said, "Festinger's theory of cognitive dissonance has been one of the most influential theories in social psychology."[7]

Although the Scientific Conference Program report fans out into a diverse array of studies related to cognitive dissonance, included in it is one of Festinger's initial experiments from the

1950s.[8] In this experiment, Festinger infiltrated a small cult group and observed firsthand their behavior when their religious beliefs were disconfirmed by the harsh reality of events. This experiment is fully documented in Festinger's original 1956 book *When Prophecy Fails*.[9] This experiment will be summarized below and it serves as both an initial explanation and the first of four examples of the extraordinary effects of cognitive dissonance and cognitive dissonance reduction.

It is important to point out that the actual beliefs of the cult group below, which are quite bizarre and no doubt related to the UFO craze of the 1950s, are not being compared to Christianity in any way. The only thing that is being illustrated below is that people can sometimes come up with ingenious and complex explanations in order to make sense of a disconnect between deeply held beliefs and the harsh reality of events. It is this concept that will be later applied to the formation of the early Christian beliefs that Jesus "died for our sins" and was "raised".

The cult group consisted of eleven hardcore members and numerous transitory participants. It was led by a woman who believed she was receiving mental messages from spacemen on another planet. The cult received a message in August 1954 that great cataclysm would ensue around the world on December 21st of that same year. The cult publicly declared this belief and attracted much media and public attention. Additional messages from the spacemen led the cult to believe that at midnight on the eve before the cataclysm they would be removed from the planet and spared from the destruction. In order for this to happen, they were instructed to wait inside certain identified parked cars and the spacemen would then transfer them from the parked cars to a flying saucer. Imposter cult members (three social psychologists) infiltrated the group and were able to observe firsthand over a period of weeks the buildup to these expectations and the reaction of the hardcore believers to the shock of disconfirmation on December 21st when none of the events occurred as they expected.

When none of the events occurred as they expected, two of the hardcore cult members rejected their beliefs and left the group. But the other nine did not. Instead, they went through a period of intense rationalization over a period of hours. Many explanations were floated as the group wrestled with their catastrophic disappointment.[10] For example, they reasoned that the spacemen must have given them the wrong date. Another explanation was that the events had been postponed, possibly for years, so that more people could prepare to "meet their maker". Yet another was increasingly more complex: The message from the spacemen, which had them waiting in parked cars from which they would be moved to the flying saucer, must be symbolic because parked cars do not move and hence could not take anyone anywhere; therefore, the parked cars must symbolically refer to their physical bodies, and the flying saucer must symbolically refer to the importance of their own inner "strength, knowing, and light" for their rescue. The small group even considered leaving the disconfirmation unexplained while insisting that the plan had never gone astray, accepting that they did not have to understand everything for it all to still be essentially true.

During this rationalization period, one of the social psychologists feigned frustration and walked outside. One of the hardcore members, a medical doctor (Dr. Armstrong), followed and offered verbal support. Here are the words of a normal human being who has staked everything on a belief, only to have that belief cruelly disconfirmed by reality:

> I've had to go a long way. I've given up just about everything. I've cut every tie. I've burned every bridge. I've turned my back on the world. I can't afford to doubt. I have to believe. And there isn't any other truth....I won't doubt even if we have to make an announcement to the press tomorrow and admit we were wrong. You're having your period of doubt now, but hang on boy, hang on. This is a tough time but we know that the boys upstairs are taking care of us....These are tough times and the way is not easy. We all have to take a beating. I've taken a terrific one, but I have no doubt.[11]

In the end, the group settled on a rationalization provided by the group's leader, which was based on a timely message she received from the spacemen. She said that the steadfast belief and waiting by their small group had brought so much "good and light" into the world, that God called off the pickup and the cataclysm.[12] This rationalization was jubilantly received by the group. Dr. Festinger explains:

> The group was able to accept and believe this explanation because they could support one another and convince each other that this was, in fact, a valid explanation. Although their belief was momentarily shaken by the disconfirmation, the members were able to maintain their membership in the movement because of the mutual social support which they received. Furthermore, the conviction of the members who had waited together did not show any signs of faltering several weeks after the disconfirmation (when the study was concluded). In fact, so powerful was the increased social support that two of the members who had occasionally expressed mild skepticism about a few tenets of the movement, now firmly believed all of them.[13]

Although the mental health of all the cult members was not open for examination, there was an opportunity for professional psychiatrists to evaluate one of the hardcore cult members. The only reason this psychiatric examination was conducted was because relatives questioned the person's sanity and sought to gain custody of his children. The cult member, the medical doctor (Dr. Armstrong), and a believer in the cult all the way through the disconfirmation and beyond, was cleared by two court-appointed psychiatrists. The psychiatrists concluded that although Dr. Armstrong had some unusual ideas, he was "entirely normal".[14]

There have been two objections to Festinger's experiment. First, since the cult group studied was very small, there is no way to rule out the possibility that the three imposter cult members influenced the cult in a way that actually caused the results. To avoid this possibility would require infiltrating a much larger cult group and being present during a disconfirmation of beliefs. While I am sure there are many social psychologists who would love to do just that, I assume such opportunities are rare. This limitation of Festinger's experiment will be addressed shortly when we turn to three examples of cognitive dissonance in much larger religious movements. The second problem sometimes cited with Festinger's cult group study is that it did not follow the cult members for longer than one month after the disconfirmation event. For all we know, belief in their rationalization only lasted a month and then faded away. Because of this, Festinger's cult group study is only useful for showing that a disconfirmation can produce new beliefs; it is not useful for showing that such new beliefs can be *sustained*. This limitation of Festinger's experiment will also be addressed in the next examples involving larger religious movements where the new beliefs were sustained. The basic theory of cognitive dissonance and cognitive dissonance reduction is summarized by Festinger:

> Suppose an individual believes something with his whole heart; suppose further that he has a commitment to this belief, that he has taken irrevocable actions because of it; finally, suppose that he is presented with evidence, unequivocal and undeniable evidence, that his belief is wrong: what will happen? The individual will frequently emerge, not only unshaken, but even more convinced of the truth of his beliefs than ever before....The dissonance [conflict between belief and reality] would be largely eliminated if they discarded the belief that had been disconfirmed....Indeed this pattern sometimes occurs....But frequently the behavioral commitment to the belief system is so strong that almost any other course of action is preferable....Believers may try to find reasonable explanations and very often they find ingenious ones....For rationalization to be fully effective, support from others is needed to make the explanation or the revision seem correct. Fortunately, the disappointed believer can usually turn to others in the same movement, who have the same dissonance and the same pressures to reduce it. Support for the new explanation is, hence, forthcoming.[15]

The second example of cognitive dissonance reduction involves a large religious movement called the Millerites. The Millerite movement began in 1818 with a man named William Miller and by the 1840s had membership in the thousands across many cities. Miller believed that the Bible predicted Jesus' second coming would be sometime between March 21st 1843 and March 21st 1844. When the later date came and went without incident, the movement did not crumble. Instead, despite heavy ridicule, the group's founder and his apostles rationalized that there must have been some minor error in calculating the exact time, but the end was nevertheless still near. A corrected date came from a follower within the movement by the name of Reverend Samuel Snow. Despite the objections of the group's leaders that the exact date could not be known, Snow declared October 22nd 1844 as the new date for Jesus' second coming. Belief in this date by the Millerites took on a life of its own as described by a Millerite newspaper editor:

> At first the definite time was generally opposed; but there seemed to be an irresistible power attending its proclamation, which prostrated all before it. It swept over the land with the velocity of a tornado, and it reached hearts in different and distant places almost simultaneously, and in a manner which can be accounted for only on the supposition that God was [in] it....The lecturers among the Adventists were the last to embrace the views of the time....It was not until within about two weeks of the commencement of the seventh month [about the first of October, the editor is using the Jewish year], that we were particularly impressed with the progress of the movement, when we had such a view of it, that to oppose it, or even to remain silent longer, seemed to us to be opposing the work of the Holy Spirit; and in entering upon the work with all our souls, we could but exclaim, "What were we, that we should resist God?" It seemed to us to have been so independent of human agency, that we could but regard it as a fulfillment of the "midnight cry".[16]

Based on this new date, things reached an incredible pitch of fervor, zeal, and conviction. One of the elders in the Millerite movement described it this way:

> The "Advent Herald", "the Midnight Cry", and other Advent papers, periodicals, pamphlets, tracts, leaflets, voicing the coming glory, were scattered, broadcast and everywhere like autumn leaves in the forest. Every house was visited by them....A mighty effort through the Spirit and the word preached was made to bring sinners to repentance, and to have the wandering ones return.[17]

But October 22nd 1844 came and went with no second coming of Jesus. This second disconfirmation almost killed the movement, but still, yet another and this time much more complex rationalization emerged – the date had been correct, but Jesus' second coming had occurred in heaven not on earth, Jesus had begun an investigative judgment of the world, and when he is done he will return to earth, but no one knows exactly when.[18] This rationalization was sustained and continues to this day with membership in the millions. It is known as the Church of Seventh-day Adventists.[*]

The third example of cognitive dissonance reduction is documented in a one thousand page tome by the late Gershom Scholem, President of the Israel Academy of Sciences and Humanities. This example of cognitive dissonance reduction occurred in the seventeenth-century Jewish messianic movement of Sabbatai Sevi (sometimes spelled "Zevi"), a Jew who publicly proclaimed himself to be the Messiah in 1665. Sevi, an adherent to a popular Jewish theology called Lurianic Kabbalism, was a charismatic manic-depressive who would deliberately and spectacularly break the law of Moses, eat forbidden foods and utter the sacred name of God, and then claim he had been inspired to do so by special revelation. Sabbatai gained a huge following spanning Italy, Holland, Germany, and Poland. His followers thought he was to usher in a new age of redemption for Israel. When Sabbatai traveled to Istanbul in 1666, he was arrested and imprisoned by Muslim authorities. The Sultan gave him a choice: conversion to Islam or death. Sabbatai chose Islam. Gershom Scholem explains the effect of Sabbatai's shocking choice on his followers:

> Sabbatai's apostasy burst like a bombshell, taking by surprise the messiah's closest associates as well as the most vehement unbelievers. Neither literary tradition nor the psychology of the

---

[*] Three other date specific second-coming-of-Jesus examples of cognitive dissonance reduction rationalizations which enabled the movements to continue after a disconfirmation include the second-century Montanists, the sixteenth-century Anabaptists, and the nineteenth-century Joanna Southcott movement (the latter concerned a messiah-like figure, not necessarily Jesus).

ordinary Jew had envisaged the possibility of an apostate messiah....In order to survive, the movement had to develop an ideology that would enable its followers to live amid the tensions between inner and outer realities....The peculiar Sabbatian doctrines developed and crystallized with extraordinary rapidity in the years following the apostasy. Two factors were responsible for this, as for many similar developments in the history of religions: on the one hand, a deeply rooted faith, nourished by a profound and immediate experience...and, on the other hand, the ideological need to explain and rationalize the painful contradiction between historical reality and faith. The interaction of these two factors gave birth to Sabbatian theology, whose doctrine of the messiah was defined by the prophet Nathan in the years after the apostasy.[19]

The theology defined by the prophet Nathan after Sevi's apostasy was that Sevi's apostasy was part of an intentional strategy to assume evil's form and then kill it from within. Scholem explains:

The resultant doctrine was necessarily novel and even heretical in terms of traditional Judaism. The doctrine of the messiah as expounded by Nathan of Gaza and his disciples during the ten years following the apostasy emphasized three novel points....[1] Redemption had begun, but had yet to be fully realized and consummated amid pain and suffering – including the anguishing shame of the messiah's apostasy....[2] All other saints [before Sevi] had "raised" the holy sparks from the depths of the *qelippah* while keeping themselves aloof from the danger zone. Only the messiah performed the terrible *descensus ad inferos*....[3] Lurianic kabbalah had taught [that]...evil existed by virtue of the vitality which it drew from the sparks of good that it had snatched and held imprisoned. Once these sparks were released and "raised," evil, impotent and lifeless as it is by itself, would automatically collapse. At this point, Sabbatian doctrine introduces a dialectical twist into the Lurianic idea. According to the new, Sabbatian version, it is not enough to extract the sparks of holiness from the realm of impurity. In order to accomplish its mission, the power of holiness – as incarnate in the messiah – has to descend into impurity, and good has to assume the form of evil. This mission is fraught with danger, as it appears to strengthen the power of evil before its final defeat. During

53

Sabbatai's lifetime the doctrinal position was that by entering the realm of the *qelippah*, good had become evil *in appearance* only. But there were more radical possibilities waiting to be explored: only the complete transformation of good into evil would exhaust the full potential of the latter and thereby explode it, as it were, from within....It was along such lines that the subsequent theology of the Sabbatian radical developed.[20]

Summarizing the process of rationalization in the Sevi movement Scholem says, "When discussing the Sabbatian paradox by means of which cruel disappointment was turned into a positive affirmation of faith, the analogy with early Christianity almost obtrudes itself."[21]

The fourth and final example of cognitive dissonance reduction involves another Jewish Messiah movement, this one from the 1990s. A group of Hasidic Jews called Lubavitch (or Chabad, a subgroup of Orthodox Jews), were headquartered in New York City and had approximately two hundred thousand followers worldwide. Beginning in 1991, there grew an increasing fervor among the Lubavitch that their spiritual leader – the Rebbe Menachem Mendel Schneerson ("Rebbe" is the formal title for the Lubavitch spiritual leader) – might be the long-awaited Jewish Messiah, the one who would usher in the end times redemption. Rebbe Schneerson never explicitly claimed that he was the Messiah, but he made such a big impression on so many of his followers that many thought he might be.

In March 1992, the eighty-nine year old Rebbe Schneerson had a stroke that rendered him paralyzed on the right side of his body and unable to talk. Dr. Simon Dein, a psychiatrist, social anthropologist, and Senior Lecturer in Anthropology and Medicine at University College London, was living in a Lubavitch community in Stamford Hill, England at the time, studying another aspect of the Lubavitch. Dein explains how Rebbe Schneerson's followers made sense of the Rebbe's new disabilities in light of their belief that he might be the Messiah:

> Despite his profound incapacity, messianic fervor in the Lubavitch community intensified, culminating in plans to crown

him as Mosiach [the Messiah]. Lubavitchers referred to Isaiah 53, "a man of sorrows, and familiar with suffering", and argued that his illness was a prerequisite to the messianic arrival....that the Rebbe himself had chosen to become ill and had taken on the suffering of the Jewish people.[22]

Two years later, on March 10, 1994, Rebbe Schneerson had another stroke, this one rendering him comatose. His followers were unshaken, again holding fast to their belief that he could be the Messiah. One Lubavitch Rabbi gave the following rationalization:

> The Rebbe is now in a state of concealment. The Jews could not see Moses on Mount Sinai and thought he was dead. They built the golden calf and had a vision of him lying dead on a bier, whereas he was in fact alive and in a state of concealment. The Rebbe is in a state of Chinoplet, a trancelike state where the soul leaves the body. The soul of the Rebbe has to go down to lower realms to drag up the souls of the sinners. He must do this before he declares himself as Moshiach [the Messiah]. The spiritual energy required to bring Moshiach is very great and his body is depleted of energy. It is only now that we have the medical technology to keep him alive. We should not be sad. The attitude to adopt is one of *Simha* (joy). We are of course sad that the Rebbe is suffering but must be joyful that he is undergoing the process of transformation to reveal himself as Moshiach.[23]

According to Dein:

> [Rebbe Schneerson's] faithful followers saw this [the second stroke] as a prelude to his messianic revelation and the arrival of the redemption. As he lay dying in intensive care, several hundred followers assembled outside Beth Israel Medical Centre singing and dancing – anticipating the imminent arrival of the redemption....Supporters and believers signed petitions to God, demanding that he allow their Rebbe to reveal himself as the long-awaited Messiah and rise from his sickbed to lead all humanity to their redemption.[24]

Three months after this second stroke, on June 12, 1994, Rebbe Schneerson died. Incredibly, this still failed to extinguish the belief among his followers that he could be the Messiah. Dein, who was still with the Lubavitch community in Stamford Hill when Rebbe Schneerson died, observed yet another and this time even more startling rationalization: "Many Lubavitchers expressed the idea that he would be resurrected." [25] Dein watched the funeral procession in New York City via satellite on the same day that Schneerson died and saw Lubavitchers "dancing and singing in anticipation of his resurrection and imminent redemption."[26] One observer on the street said of these people celebrating, "They were certain that any second, the hoax would end and the Rebbe would get up and lead us to the redemption right then."[27]

Although exact numbers are unknown, the idea that Rebbe Schneerson would resurrect from the dead soon swept through the Lubavitch community worldwide and gained a significant following. In Stamford Hill Dein reported, "Very soon, the overwhelming feeling in the community was that the Rebbe would resurrect and that the redemption would arrive."[28] Five days after the Rebbe's death, a full-page advertisement in a widely circulated Jewish Orthodox weekly in New York City (the *Jewish Press*) declared that Rebbe Schneerson would be resurrected as the Messiah. [29] Two years after Rebbe Schneerson's death, the *International Campaign to Bring Moshiach* set up a huge billboard beside New York's George Washington Bridge proclaiming Rebbe Schneerson was the Messiah.[30] Seven years after the Rebbe's death, David Berger, professor of Jewish History, past president of the Association for Jewish Studies, and outspoken critic of the Rebbe Schneerson movement gave this assessment of the movement:

> [A] large majority of Lubavitch hasidim believe with perfect faith in the return of the Rebbe as Messiah son of David....The dominant elements among hasidim in the major Lubavitch population centres of Crown Heights in Brooklyn and Kfar Chabad in Israel – perfectly normal people representing a highly successful, very important Jewish movement – believe that Rabbi Menachem Mendel Schneerson will return from the dead...and lead the world to redemption.[31]

Berger goes on to say, "With the exception of Sabbatianism, Lubavitch messianists have already generated the largest and most long-lived messianic movement in Jewish history since antiquity."[32]

In trying to make sense of and explain the rationalization process that led to this religious movement, Dein says:

> [The] Lubavitch are not a group of fanatics....They are sane people trying to reason their way through facts and in the pursuit of understanding....Like many groups whose messianic expectations fail to materialize, resort is made to eschatological hermeneutics to explain and reinforce the messianic ideology....The Rebbe's illness and subsequent death posed cognitive challenges for his followers. They made two predictions that were empirically disconfirmed: that he would recover from his illness and that he would usher in the Redemption. In accordance with cognitive dissonance theory...they appealed to a number of post hoc rationalizations to allay the dissonance.[33]

Dein goes on to say, "Not surprisingly, these new beliefs have attracted a lot of derision from the wider Jewish community and, on account of their proclamations of the imminent resurrection of Schneerson, some have labeled [them]...'Christians'." [34] Berger adds:

> The stunning speed with which this belief has spread in the absence of a scintilla of evidence should capture the attention of all historians who have struggled to explain and reconstruct the development of the early Christian belief in the resurrection and the empty tomb....Though largely ignored thus far, this is a development of striking importance for the history of world religions...[35] *

---

* It is also worth noting that some Lubavitch rationalized that the Rebbe never died. In this view, the Rebbe's death was in appearance only, he is concealed at this time, and he will become visible again at the time of the redemption. Simon Dein and Lorne Dawson also report, "A few Lubavitchers go as far as to hold the Rebbe to be God incarnate and worship him as such" ("The

Although Dein says there is "no empirical evidence" that Christian beliefs influenced Rebbe Schneerson's followers, it is impossible to rule this out.[36] But even if the Rebbe Schneerson movement beliefs were influenced by Christianity and are not "pure", all it would mean is that they needed a little nudge from others who went first in rationalizing a dead Messiah who would resurrect from the dead. This nudge would not take away from the conclusion that the Rebbe Schneerson movement is a powerful example of a cognitive dissonance reduction rationalization.

The Rebbe Schneerson example above may by itself be enough to convince many people that early Christian belief could have come about in the same way. If some twentieth-century Jews who knew where their dead Messiah was buried could rationalize that he had taken on the suffering of the Jewish people and would resurrect from the dead, it is not much of a stretch to imagine that some first-century Jews, not knowing where their dead Messiah was buried, could rationalize that he died for their sins and had already resurrected from the dead. However, it is worth taking a close look at the specifics of Christian origins to see if a cognitive dissonance reduction rationalization for early Christian belief holds water.

Before doing so, there are two other points to make. First, all four of the examples above show that when cognitive dissonance reduction results in a new belief, unless someone is there to observe and document the initial rationalization process, the historical record will leave little or no trace of the cause of the new belief. The new belief will seem as if it just appeared out of thin air. If the Gospels are not a reliable record of early Christian events, that is how the beliefs in 1 Corinthians 15:3-7 look. The second point concerns the veracity of beliefs formed by a cognitive dissonance reduction rationalization. There is no reason to think that the most ardent believers in all of the examples above would not have been willing to die for their beliefs if faced with a choice

---

'Scandal' of the Lubavitch Rebbe: Messianism as a Response to Failed Prophecy," *Journal of Contemporary Religion* 23.2 (May 2008), 169; see too Berger, who says this belief is not that uncommon and discusses it extensively in *The Rebbe, the Messiah, and the Scandal of Orthodox Indifference* (2008)).

of recanting or death. Therefore, if some of the first Christians went to their deaths as martyrs insisting that Jesus was the Messiah and that he was raised from the dead, this too would be consistent with a cognitive dissonance reduction rationalization.

Cognitive Dissonance Reduction Applied To Christian Origins

In 1956, Festinger made only passing comment on how his theory might be applied to Christian origins. He noted that the applicability of cognitive dissonance reduction to Jesus' followers rested on the question of whether or not Jesus' followers were surprised by his death. If Jesus predicted his death was a necessary thing to his followers, then his death would not have been a disconfirmation of beliefs and therefore could not have caused cognitive dissonance. However, Festinger notes that if Jesus' followers had no expectation of a dead Messiah, "[then] the crucifixion and the cry Jesus uttered on the cross were indeed an unequivocal disconfirmation."[37]

Today, many New Testament scholars doubt the historicity of the Gospel accounts of Jesus predicting his own death (Mk 8:31; 9:31; 10:34; Mt 17:23; 20:19; Lk 9:22; 18:33; 24:7; Jn 2:19).[38] The Jesus Seminar for example concludes that all of these predictions were put on Jesus' lips after his death as a form of legendary embellishment that Jesus knew all along exactly what was going to happen.[39] Although Jesus' followers must have been aware that Jesus was putting himself in a precarious situation by going to Jerusalem and instigating an incident at the temple, if they had already begun to hope or think that he might be the Messiah, they probably never imagined that God would let events get so out of hand that the Messiah would be put to death. Jesus' most ardent followers may even have imagined that the Jerusalem authorities, or at least some of them, might see the same greatness they saw in Jesus. If Jesus' followers had no expectation of his death, then like any human beings, they would have been subject to the powerful influence of cognitive dissonance and the desire to reduce that dissonance through rationalization when faced with Jesus' crucifixion.

Paul M. van Buren considers there to be three possible origins to the earliest belief that Jesus died for our sins and was raised: a

59

discovered empty tomb, a visual experience of Jesus after his death, or "the discovery of a new and positive way in which to speak of Jesus' death and of Jesus after his death, that is, a new way of perceiving Jesus, was itself the event of Easter."[40] Van Buren's last possibility is exactly what is being proposed here.

Like the earlier examples of cognitive dissonance reduction, a sustaining rationalization for Jesus' death would most likely have emerged very quickly and in the presence of others who could offer mutual encouragement. Therefore, if after Jesus' death his inner circle fled Jerusalem as a group back to their homes in Galilee seventy miles to the north, it seems most likely that it was on that several day trek, or very shortly after arriving in Galilee, that the ideas contained in 1 Corinthians 15:3-4 were born. That the resurrection belief started in Galilee, not Jerusalem, is supported not only by the fact that Galilee is logically where Jesus' followers would have gone, but also by the earliest recorded written reference to a post-mortem appearance of Jesus with a location mentioned in it: "But go, tell his disciples and Peter that he is going ahead of you to *Galilee*; there you will see him, just as he told you" (Mk 16:7). The rationalization did not need to be perfect, but it did need to adequately answer what would to them have been the two most natural and pressing questions: Why did the Messiah have to die, and how can a dead person be the Messiah?

I suggest that these two pressing questions resulted in the following initial two-part rationalization among some of Jesus' followers: 1) Jesus died for our sins and 2) Jesus will be back soon to reign as the Messiah should. The second part of this rationalization, that Jesus will be back soon, is not expressed in the 1 Corinthians 15:3-7 passage. However, we know that the imminent return of Jesus and the ushering in of a new kingdom was widely believed throughout the early Christian community (1 Thess 4:13-18; 1 Cor 1:6-8; 7:25-31; Rom 13:11-12; Phil 1:6-10; Mk 8:38-9:1; 13:24-31); therefore, this belief could have existed much earlier and been part of the initial rationalization.

If Jesus was going to come back soon to reign as the Messiah should, a third component of the rationalization automatically follows – Jesus' resurrection from the dead. Although Jesus' followers could have reasoned that he would resurrect later, at the time he was to begin his reign and perhaps at the same time ushering in the general resurrection (just like some Lubavitchers rationalized for Rebbe Schneerson after his death), I hope to show below that the Jewish and surrounding Greek beliefs of the first century would have favored the conclusion that Jesus was bodily raised up to heaven *now* and would return later from there.

However, before trying to show this, there are two side issues that need to be addressed. The first can be posed as a question – why did Rebbe Schneerson's followers rationalize that he would resurrect later instead of rationalizing that he was already raised to heaven and would return later from there as it is proposed Jesus' followers did? There are three possibilities. One, in the back of the Lubavitchers' minds when they were rationalizing they may have realized that a resurrection *now* conclusion could potentially have been dashed with a relatively quick grave check. Two, the modern-day realization that heaven is not a physical place located just beyond the clouds that a body could go to would have made a bodily raised to heaven rationalization difficult for those Lubavitchers with a scientific/rationalist bent. Three, which is probably the most influential, it was part of Lubavitcher theology that a "prince", in this case Rebbe Schneerson, *must* be present in this world in some capacity in order to mediate the world's divine force or the world would cease to exist.[41] Since the world existed, it would have been extremely difficult for Rebbe Schneerson's followers to rationalize that he had already been raised to heaven. For these reasons, a resurrection *later* rationalization would have been much easier for Rebbe Schneerson's followers to arrive at than a bodily raised to heaven *now* rationalization.

The second side issue that needs to be addressed is the suggestion by some that a dead person being bodily raised up to heaven instead of on earth is not really "resurrection"; it is "translation" or "assumption".[42] Adding confusion to this issue, the exact definition of translation/assumption is not clear from the Jewish literature. We *know* that it is used to refer to persons being bodily raised up to heaven *before* death (clear examples of this will be given later), but it is possible that it is only the transportation up to heaven that is of interest in these instances, not the timing of when it occurs (before or after death). However, no matter which way the term translation/assumption is understood, a dead person who has been brought back to life in their body has clearly been resurrected from the dead. If the formerly dead person's final location is heaven, it simply means that in addition to being resurrected from the dead, they have also been transported up to heaven (or translated/assumed up to heaven if one adopts the second understanding of this term mentioned above). In short, if Jesus' followers believed he was bodily raised up to heaven, they would have said he was resurrected from the dead.

With these two side issues addressed, the main question in defending the three part rationalization proposed earlier is whether or not there was sufficient raw material in the Jewish and surrounding Greek culture to feed such a rationalization. The answer is that there was plenty. Below is a summary of the religious and cultural influences which would have served as raw material for the rationalization that Jesus "died for our sins" and "was raised" (and would return very soon).

Jesus Died for Our Sins

John Dominic Crossan notes that first-century Judaism and its surrounding Greek culture was rich with the theme of atoning sacrifice by blood:

> The world of Paul's time took it for granted that sacrifice was how you established and maintained peaceful unity with a god, a goddess, the gods, or God. You offered something that belonged to you to the divine. It could be as small as a libation, the first sip of wine poured out before a private banquet, or as large as a hecatomb, one hundred oxen slain before a public temple....Everyone in Paul's world, Jews and pagan alike, understood that "reconciliation" could involve "a sacrifice of atonement by blood".[43]

In Judaism, the theme of sacrifice also had a sense of "measure for measure" when dealing with God, that is, the sacrifice was proportional to the need or reward.[44] One Jewish tradition that reflects this idea of measure for measure sacrifice in return for God's blessing is the account of Abraham's near-sacrifice of his son Isaac (Gen 22:1-19). In this account, Abraham is ordered by God to sacrifice his son Isaac. Abraham ties his son up, and with knife in hand ready for the killing, an angel from God tells him to stop. But Abraham's *willingness* to sacrifice his son is rewarded:

> ...because you have done this and have not withheld your son, your only son, I will indeed bless you, and I will make your offspring as numerous as the stars of heaven and as the sand that is on the seashore. And your offspring shall possess the gate of their enemies. (Gen 22:16-17)

This tradition of the near-sacrifice of Isaac reflects the idea that when dealing with God, everything is measure for measure; you get back in equal measure that which you give. Abraham was *required* to be willing to sacrifice Isaac in order to get the blessings for Israel in return. In effect, the willingness of Abraham to sacrifice Isaac, even though unaccomplished, was a vicarious sacrifice on behalf of Israel.

By the first century, the Abraham/Isaac story had undergone modification to further accentuate its vicarious sacrifice theme. Now, Abraham's son Isaac is depicted as a *willing* sacrifice, an idea that is not present in the original Genesis story. This idea is captured in a retelling of the Abraham/Isaac story by the Jewish historian Josephus: "Now Isaac was twenty-five years old....Isaac was of such a generous disposition as became the son of such a father, and was pleased with this discourse....So he went immediately to the altar to be sacrificed" (Antiquities of the Jews 1.13.2-4).

The use of the Abraham/Isaac vicarious sacrifice theme was not just confined to what transpired in the past between Abraham and Isaac. It was also used by first-century Jews to help them make sense of present difficult situations. This is reflected in a first-century Jewish passage where it was said to Jewish martyrs before they went into battle: "Remember whence you came and at the hand of what father Isaac gave himself to be sacrificed for piety's sake" (4 Maccabees 13:12). Here, the soon to be martyrs are told that their sacrifice is "for piety's sake", that is, theirs is a vicarious sacrifice for the sake of Israel as a whole. First-century Jews were comparing Isaac's unaccomplished sacrifice to the present real deaths of Jewish martyrs.

Although the theme of willing, measure for measure, vicarious sacrifice had strong attachments to the Abraham/Isaac tradition, it also became a standalone theme that by the first century could be expressed without specific reference to Abraham or Isaac. The language of "atonement for sins" also materialized by the first century. Both concepts are captured in this first-century Jewish text which is speaking of already martyred comrades:

> These, then, who have been consecrated for the sake of God, are honored, not only with this honor, but also by the fact that because of them our enemies did not rule over our nation, the tyrant was punished, and the homeland purified – they having become, as it were, *a ransom for the sin of our nation*. And through the blood of those devout ones and *their death as an atoning sacrifice*, divine Providence preserved Israel... (4 Maccabees 17:20-22, emphasis added)

Even if the above phrase "ransom for the sin of our nation" is a form of metaphor, as is suggested by the phrase preceding it "as it were", a metaphor is still a way of expressing ideas that you either cannot yet come right out and say, or as a way of saying what you want to say but qualifying it so that you can claim you are not really saying it. Addressing the use of this phrase in later Judaism, Gershom Scholem notes, "[The Jews] neutralize[d] their daring utterances by a qualifying 'as it were' or 'so to speak.' With the aid of this formal reservation they attenuated their symbols in appearance but saved them in reality."[45]

Paul M. van Buren makes the connection between the 4 Maccabees passage above and the early Christian belief that Jesus died for our sins:

> The principle of measure for measure, coupled with the association of the Maccabean martyrs with Isaac, also accounts for [a]...phrase in 4 Maccabees (17:21), which calls their deaths "a ransom for the sin of our nation, as it were." The affirmation of the next verse is even more striking (17:22): "Through the blood of these righteous ones and through the propitiation of

their death the divine providence rescued Israel..." In Romans 3:25 Paul used the same word – *hilasterion*, "propitiation" – with reference to Christ's death....[The] language of the primitive gospel seems very much at home in the interpretive world of the Jewish literature in which the *aqedah* [the Abraham/Isaac tradition] was developing.[46]

But if Jesus' followers concluded that God offered up his own Messiah as a sacrifice, to whom did Jesus' followers think the offering was being made to? Van Buren answers, "The question has no answer, perhaps because it is irrelevant. What matters is that the principle of 'measure for measure' has been radicalized – one might say extended to the breaking point..."[47] Gershom Scholem agrees, "Both Christianity and the Sabbatian movement took as their point of departure the ancient Jewish paradox of the Suffering Servant which, however, they stressed with such radicalism that they practically stood it on its head."[48]

In conclusion, there was enough raw material available in the Jewish tradition and surrounding Greek culture for Jesus' followers to rationalize that Jesus "died for our sins".

Jesus was Raised

According to Bruce Chilton and Jacob Neusner, first-century Jewish beliefs were very diverse:

In the case of Judaism in the first centuries BC and AD, for example, we find a variety of documents that scarcely intersect. If we invoke any criterion we think likely to characterize a variety of writings – a single doctrine concerning the Torah, the Messiah, the definition of who and what is "Israel," for example – we find no one answer present in all writings, and no point of agreement which unites them. Not only so, but both archaeological and text analysis insist that the various writings were produced by diverse groups and do not speak for one and the same community at all....[In] antiquity as today, many Judaisms competed....[The] dogma of a single, valid Judaism contradicts the facts of history at every point in the history of Judaism.[49]

This diversity in first-century Jewish beliefs can be seen in their beliefs about the general resurrection – the Pharisees and Sadducees could not even agree that there would be such a thing (the Pharisees said yes, the Sadducees said no). Within this mix of Jewish beliefs about the general resurrection, there was the belief that great prophets were sometimes bodily translated or assumed up to heaven *before* death. For example, the Old Testament has this occur to both Enoch and Elijah (Gen 5:24; 2 Kings 2:11; see too Heb 11:5 in the New Testament). Moses too may have been thought by some Jews to have received the privilege of live bodily translation/assumption. Speaking of Moses, the Old Testament says, "He was buried in a valley in the land of Moab, opposite Beth-peor, but no one knows his burial place to this day" (Deut 34:6). Belief by some Jews in Moses' bodily translation is more clearly expressed in the first-century writing of Philo Judaeus:

> ...the end of virtuous and holy men is not death but a translation and migration, and an approach to some other place of abode....[In] this instance something marvelous did take place; for he [Enoch] was supposed to be carried off in such a way as to be invisible, for then he was not found....This mercy also was bestowed on the great prophet [Moses], for his sepulcher also was known to no one. And besides these two there was another, Elijah, who ascended from the things of earth into heaven... (Philo Judaeus, Questions and Answers on Genesis, Book I, #86)

The Jewish historian Josephus also alludes to belief in Moses' bodily translation/assumption:

> Now as he went thence to the place where he was to vanish out of their sight, they all followed after him weeping...and as he was going to embrace Eleazar and Joshua, and was still discoursing with them, a cloud stood over him on the sudden, and he disappeared in a certain valley, although he wrote in the holy books that he died, which was done out of fear, lest they should venture to say that, because of his extraordinary virtue, he went to God. (Antiquities of the Jews 4.8.48)

The possibility of bodily translation/assumption up to heaven may also have applied to other Jews. Based on a comparison of Ugaritic texts to clarify the meaning of Hebrew texts, Mitchell Dahood of the Pontifical Biblical Institute says of the authors of Psalms 16:10, 49:15, and 73:24 (below), "The psalmist firmly believes that he will be granted the same privilege accorded Enoch and Elijah; he is convinced that God will assume him to himself, without suffering the pains of death."[50]

Psalm 16:10: "For you do not give me up to Sheol, or let your faithful one see the Pit."

Psalm 49:15: "But God will ransom my soul from the power of Sheol, for he will receive me."

Psalm 73:24: "You guide me with your counsel, and afterwards you will receive me to glory."

There is also one example of Jews experimenting with belief in persons being bodily raised to heaven *after* death, i.e. resurrection followed by transportation up to heaven (or followed by translation/assumption up to heaven if one understands this term can be used after death). In the Testament of Job, written sometime in the first century B.C.E. or the first century C.E., the bodies of some children killed in the collapse of a house are portrayed as having been raised up to heaven alive:

She asked him [the commanders of some soldiers] saying: "I ask as favor of you, my Lords, that you order your soldiers that they should dig among the ruins of our house which fell upon my children, so that their bones could be brought in a perfect state to the tombs..." [As the narrator of the story, the woman's husband then says,] And the kings gave order that the ruins of my house should be dug up. But I prohibited it, saying "Do not go to the trouble in vain; for my children will not he found, for they are in the keeping of their Maker and Ruler". And the kings answered and said: "Who will gainsay that he is out of his mind and raves? For while we desire to bring the bones of his children back, he forbids us to do so saying: 'They have been taken and placed in

the keeping of their Maker'. Therefore prove unto us the truth".
But I said to them: "Raise me that I may stand up", and they
lifted me, holding up my arms from both sides. And I stood
upright, and pronounced first the praise of God and after the
prayer I said to them: "Look with your eyes to the East". And
they looked and saw my children with crowns near the glory of
the King, the Ruler of heaven. And when my wife Sitis saw this,
she fell to the ground and prostrated [herself] before God, saying:
"Now I know that my memory remains with the Lord".
(Testament of Job 39-40)

The Jewish beliefs in the general resurrection, the bodily
assumption of individuals before death, and the resurrection of
children after death were probably rooted in feelings of the just
reign of God. Since this world is far from fair, God would make
things right in a future mass resurrection, vindicating the righteous
and punishing the wicked, a measure for measure recompense by
God according to what each person was due but did not receive in
this life. The bodily assumption of great prophets up to heaven was
a reward for one's supreme moral virtue, and the raising of dead
children up to heaven was an answer to the meaningless loss of
innocence.

The surrounding Greek culture also had raised heroes.
Although such beliefs were usually centered on a person's raised
"soul", such as the belief by most people in Jesus' time that the
emperor Augustus had been raised from the dead, there were also
beliefs that the bodies of special people were sometimes assumed
or translated to the place of the gods before or right at the moment
of death. Here are four such examples:

Herakles, having abandoned hope for himself [he was ill],
ascended the pyre and asked each one who came up to him to
light it....[Philoctetes] lit the pyre. Immediately lightning fell
from the heavens and the pyre was wholly consumed. After this,
when the companions of Iolaus came to gather up the bones of
Herakles and found not a single bone anywhere, they assumed
that, in accordance with the words of the oracle, he had passed
among men into the company of the gods. (Diodorus of Sicily,
Library of History 4:38:3-5, written in the first century B.C.E.)[51]

A severe battle took place not far from Lavinium and many were slain on both sides, but when night came the armies separated; and when the body of Aeneas was nowhere to be seen, some concluded that it had been translated to the gods... (Dionysus of Halicarnassus, Roman Antiquities 1.64.4-5, written in the first century B.C.E. or the first decade or two of the first century C.E.)[52]

Romulus, when he vanished [after a battle], left neither the least part of his body, nor any remnant of his cloths to be seen....[The] senators suffered them not to search, or busy themselves about the matter, but commanded them to honor and worship Romulus as one taken up to the gods. (Plutarch, Lives of the Noble Greeks and Romans, Romulus 2:27, written in the first or early second century C.E. with Romulus living in the eighth century B.C.E.)[53]

Xisouthros got out [of a boat], with his wife and daughter and with the helmsman, and he kissed the ground and dedicated an alter and sacrificed to the gods. Then he and those who had disembarked with him disappeared. Those who had remained on the boat and did not get out with Xisouthros then got out and looked for him, calling for him by name; but Xisouthros himself was no more to be seen by them. Then a voice came from up in the air, commanding that they should honor the gods. For Xisouthros had gone to dwell with the gods because of his piety; and his wife and daughter and the helmsman had shared in the same honor. (Berossos, Babyloniaca, third century B.C.E., preserved in Syncellus, Ecloga Chronographica 55, ninth century C.E.)[54]

According to Stephen Patterson:

In the broader Hellenistic world, it was commonplace to speak of great heroic individuals who had been taken up to dwell among the gods as a reward for and the vindication of a life well lived. This tradition, too, would have been influential in the Hellenized Jewish environment of the first century, and it no doubt influenced the formulation of early Christian claims about Jesus.[55]

That the surrounding Greek culture had ideas that were similar to and therefore could have been influential in the formation of the Christian belief that Jesus was raised from the dead, is also evident in this statement by second-century Christian apologist Justin Martyr when speaking to pagans:

> When we say...that He, Jesus Christ, our Teacher, was crucified and died, and rose again, and ascended into heaven, we propound nothing different from what you believe regarding those whom you esteem sons of Jupiter. (Justin Martyr, First Apology, Chapter 21)

As an aside, Justin Martyr then goes on to explain this similarity between Christian and pagan belief as a case of the devil knowing ahead of time that Jesus' resurrection and ascension were prophesied in the Jewish scriptures and, with the intent to deceive the human race, creating *imitations* of resurrecting and ascending people in Greek mythology *before* the time of Jesus:

> But those who hand down the myths which the poets have made...have been uttered by the influence of the wicked demons, to deceive and lead astray the human race. For having heard it proclaimed through the prophets that the Christ was to come...the devil...said that Bacchus...having been torn in pieces, he ascended into heaven. And he [the devil]...gave out that Bellerophon...ascended to heaven on his horse Pegasus. And when they heard it said...[that Jesus would] by His own means ascend into heaven, they pretended that Perseus was spoken of. (Justin Martyr, First Apology, Chapter 54. This concept is also expressed by Justin Martyr in his Dialogue with Trypho, Chapters 69-70)

Given the diverse mixing pot of ideas – belief in bodily resurrection of the masses at the end of time, belief in bodily assumption of great prophets before death and the resurrection of children after death, belief in raised souls and bodies of Hellenistic heroes, belief in the vindication of and reward for the righteous, a sense of justice about what ought to be – and given the inescapable reality of Jesus' death, there was plenty of raw material and creative potential for the belief to emerge that Jesus was bodily raised to heaven after death. As Stephen Patterson says:

> Peter...and John...had known Jesus and had been in his company. Long before his death, they had committed themselves fully to Jesus' vision of the Empire of God. They believed in his cause as God's cause. It was people like these who would have been the first to say, "God raised Jesus from the dead"....Just as they had given themselves over to this cause during Jesus' lifetime, so now they would give themselves over to the belief that God would not allow the cross to remain as the final word on Jesus' life....It was not necessary for Christians to have had experiences of the risen Jesus, or to have discovered an empty tomb, in order to say this. They could have said it, and would have, even if Jesus' body had been [buried]...and never seen again.[56]

Belief in the vindication of and reward for the righteous, as evident in Jewish traditions like the bodily assumption of great prophets up to heaven to be with God, and as evident in Greek traditions like the immediate raising of the souls and bodies of Hellenistic heroes to become gods at the time of their deaths, would have favored this rationalization over one in which Jesus stayed dead until the time his reign was to begin.

A Spiritually Raised Messiah Rationalization?

Many first-century Jews believed that a person's body was required for any kind of consciousness or presence anywhere. The soul could not "live" in any meaningful sense separate from the body, and if the body was dead, the soul was for all practical purposes dead too, or at the very least deeply "asleep" (see for example Isa 26:19, Dan 12:2, Hos 6:2, and LXX Hos 13:14). The rationalization proposed in the previous section is consistent with this view that the body and soul were for all practical purposes inseparable. If Jesus' followers believed he was raised, they would have believed that both his body and soul were raised.

However, other first-century Jews believed that the body and soul were separate, that the soul of a dead person was still alive in some sense and was capable of more than just a sleep state. N.T. Wright, known for his exhaustive study of ancient Jewish beliefs about the afterlife, summarizes the beliefs that such Jews had about the souls of dead people: "They are, at present, souls, spirits or angel-like beings...Where are they? They are in the hand of the creator god; or in paradise; or in some kind of Sheol, understood now not as a final but as a temporary resting-place".[57] If Jesus' followers were among those Jews who believed that consciousness and presence was possible for a soul without a physical body, it opens up the door to a rationalization that some think would have been much easier for Jesus' followers to arrive at and just as effective at reducing their cognitive dissonance.

Some propose that had Jesus' followers rationalized his death, they would have rationalized that Jesus' *spirit* (instead of his body) had been assumed up to heaven and that his messiahship would be vindicated when his spirit was reunited with his body later at the general resurrection. The appeal of this rationalization is that it would have been in much less tension with the Jewish belief that bodily resurrection of the dead was only supposed to occur at the end of time.

Determining which rationalization is more likely – a spiritually-raised Messiah or a bodily-raised Messiah – is difficult because we do not know what Jesus' followers believed about the body-soul connection. If all we can do is guess, then the bodily-raised rationalization remains just as plausible an option as the spiritually-raised option.

However, let's do a thought exercise and assume that Jesus' followers were among those Jews who believed that consciousness and presence were possible for a soul without a physical body. Where does this lead us? First of all, it should be admitted up front in this case that a spiritually-raised rationalization *would* have been viable in the eyes of Jesus' followers. However, even if this rationalization was viable in the eyes of Jesus' followers, I think a bodily-raised rationalization would have been more attractive, or at least just as attractive, for the following reason.

According to Wright, no matter where and under what kind of conditions, or in what kind of state, different Jews thought a dead person's soul waited for their future resurrection, Jews who believed in bodily resurrection saw bodily resurrection as (in Wright's words) the "ultimate prize", the "reward", the "final state of blessedness".[58] This suggests that first-century Jews who believed the soul could exist separately from the body saw that existence as being in some sense less than would be enjoyed when the soul was later reunited with its final immortal body. Given the belief by some Jews that the soul died with the body (or remained deeply asleep), it makes sense that there would have been a range of beliefs about this lesser existence of the soul – from those who believed the soul was barely awake, to those who believed the soul enjoyed an active existence just short of what would be enjoyed when reunited with the physical body. Wright confirms this in a general sense: "The idea of a soul separable from the body, with different theories as to what might happen to it thereafter, was widespread in the varied Judaisms of the turn of the eras."[59]

If Jesus' followers did not think a very inspiring existence awaited the soul after death before being reunited with its body at the general resurrection, then a bodily-raised rationalization for Jesus would have been more attractive to them than a spiritually-raised rationalization. A bodily-raised rationalization would have been further favored by Jesus' followers if the Hellenistic belief in bodily raised heroes at the time of death was an influence on them.

But the question also arises, where and to what sort of existence did Jews think Enoch, Elijah, and Moses went to after their live bodily assumptions into heaven? According to Wright, "No account is available of what sort of existence they had gone to or, in particular, of the kind of heavenly world in which Elijah could still possess his body."[60] Wright goes on to say that how Jews made sense of the bodies of Enoch, Elijah, and Moses being in heaven is "a question of particular relevance, one might think, to later developments about the resurrection".[61] How Jews made sense of the bodies of Enoch, Elijah, and Moses being in heaven would also seem to be of particular relevance to how Jesus' followers would have rationalized Jesus' raising – as one that was spiritual or one that involved the body.

There seems only two ways that Jews could have made sense of the bodies of Enoch, Elijah, and Moses being in heaven – either their bodies eventually died and decayed in heaven, or their bodies had attained the "final state of blessedness". The latter is suggested by the Jewish tradition that Elijah, after his live bodily assumption, was going to return to earth before the general resurrection (2

Kings 2:11; Malachi 4:5; Mark 6:14-15). The only way it seems he could do that after a thousand years is if his body was already in its final immortal state.

If Jesus' followers believed that Enoch, Elijah, and Moses had already attained the final immortal state, the "final state of blessedness", the "reward", the "ultimate prize", and they also believed that Jesus was the long awaited Messiah, the *greatest* of all the prophets, it seems doubtful that they would have chosen a rationalization that entailed Jesus going to an existence that was less than what Enoch, Elijah, and Moses had already attained. Therefore, a *bodily*-raised rationalization would have been more attractive to Jesus' followers than a spiritually-raised rationalization even if they thought a fairly favorable existence awaited the soul in heaven before the general resurrection.

Make James the Messiah?

Some propose that Jesus' followers, instead of rationalizing his resurrection, would more likely have accepted Jesus' death and rationalized that Jesus' brother James, being of the same blood line, was the new Messiah. Rationalizing that a brother was the new Messiah is what sometimes happened in other messianic movements when the leader died. However, it is hard to see how Jesus' followers could have rationalized this if James did not show any interest in and was not even a part of the Jesus movement when Jesus was alive, which it is widely agreed was the case. James may also simply not have had the charisma or inspired others enough to think he could be the Messiah.

A Dead Messiah Could Never Be Rationalized?

Some propose that Jesus' death would have prevented *any* rationalization that entailed Jesus still being the Messiah. After all, Jews had no concept of a Messiah who, instead of establishing David's throne in Jerusalem, would be humiliatingly executed by his enemies and defeated. While true, Jesus' followers did not have to view Jesus as defeated if their initial rationalization included the belief that Jesus would *return* very soon in *victory*. The three part rationalization proposed in this book – Jesus died for our sins, was raised from the dead, and will be back very soon – has this

74

component, and it reflects all of the logic one would expect of a human rationalization trying to maintain the view that Jesus was still the Messiah despite his death.

Some point to the dozen or so other Jewish Messiah movements in the first and second centuries that died out when their Messiah died as supporting evidence that a first-century dead Messiah could never be rationalized. However, there is actually a good reason why none of these other Jewish Messiah movements were able to rationalize their Messiah's death. All of them were *military* messiah movements that were crushed *militarily*. The followers of these movements would have had a much harder time rationalizing their man was still the Messiah after he had just been killed by the same enemies he promised his followers that he was going to kill. His followers would have had to rationalize not only their Messiah's death, but their Messiah's massive miscalculation of his own military prowess or his intentional lie. As James Crossley points out about two of the larger of these movements, "Simon bar Giora [70 C.E.] and bar Kochbah [135 C.E.] were military figures expecting military victories. Of course their deaths would be deemed as a failure."[62]

But the best evidence that Jews could rationalize a dead non-military Messiah is the previously mentioned modern-day Rebbe Schneerson movement that did just that. Even if Christianity in some sense paved the way for their rationalization, Jewish messianic expectations have not changed in two thousand years and it still would have been extremely difficult for Rebbe Schneerson's followers to deal with a dead Messiah. As Simon Dein points out:

> In Chabad [Lubavitch] eschatology the arrival of *Moshiach* [the Messiah] is integrally tied to the notion of the Redemption and all that it entails: utopia, the rebirth of the dead, the end of persecution...and the joyful gathering of all Jews in Israel.... Maimonides in his *Mishneh Torah* [an authoritative text used by the Lubavitch] states: "If a king arises from the house of David...defeats all the nations surrounding him, builds the Temple in its place, and gathers the dispersed of Israel, then he is surely the Messiah."[63]

Given these expectations for the Messiah, David Berger, a Jew and a historian, explains the difficulty Rebbe Schneerson's followers would have had rationalizing a dead Messiah: "[Lubavitch is] a major movement located well within the parameters of Orthodox Judaism....There is no more fundamental messianic belief in Judaism than the conviction that the Davidic Messiah who appears at the end of days will not die before completing his mission....[A person] is invalidated as a potential Messiah the moment that he dies in an unredeemed world."[64]

This statement by Berger explains his reaction when he saw his fellow Jews rationalize after Rebbe Schneerson's death that Rebbe Schneerson was still the Messiah and would resurrect from the dead:

> ...My sense of puzzlement, bewilderment, disorientation began to grow. The world appeared surreal, as if I had been transported into Alice's Wonderland or a Jewish Twilight Zone. The rules of Judaism seemed suspended....Here was a movement of posthumous false messianism self-evidently alien to Judaism that no generation of mainstream Jewish leaders would ever have countenanced even for a fleeting moment....Any appeal to Maimonides' criteria [see previous block quote] seemed clearly impossible.[65]

But it was not impossible. Rebbe Schneerson's followers rationalized that their dead Messiah would complete his mission later, after he resurrected from the dead. Putting aside whether or not this rationalization was coherent, Berger's reaction illustrates how big of a gap there can be between what we *think* is possible with a cognitive dissonance reduction rationalization and what actually *is* possible. Leon Festinger explains this in general terms:

> ...Where there are a number of people having the same cognitive dissonance, the phenomenon [of cognitive dissonance reduction] may be much more spectacular, even to the point where it is possible to withstand evidence which would otherwise be overwhelming....There is a tendency to seek explanations of these striking phenomena which match them in dramatic quality; that is, one looks for something unusual to explain the unusual

result. It may be, however, that there is nothing more unusual about these phenomena than the relative rarity of the specific combination of ordinary circumstances that brings about their occurrence.[66]

An Impossible To Cross Doctrinal Line?

Another barrier that some claim could never have been crossed in any rationalization by Jesus' followers is the resurrection of an individual before the general resurrection at the end of time. Like the previous objection that a dead Messiah could never be rationalized, this objection seems naïve given the human imagination's ability to overcome obstacles in cognitive dissonance situations. There is probably no new innovation that can be declared impossible for the human mind to arrive at when rationalizing.

But the Testament of Job passage mentioned earlier that has dead children being resurrected and then transported (or translated/assumed) up to heaven shows that the line of resurrection before the general resurrection could be crossed by some first-century Jews, even if it was only in a storytelling sense.

There are also two Gospel passages that suggest that resurrection before the general resurrection was not as impenetrable of a belief as some claim. The first passage comes from the Gospel of Mark. It does not matter if this passage is reporting a historical event or is a legend; it is describing purported events *before* Jesus' crucifixion, when Jesus was making a name for himself among the populace:

Jesus' name had become known. Some were saying [of Jesus], "John the baptizer has been raised from the dead; and for this reason these powers are at work in him." But others said, "It is Elijah." And others said, "It is a prophet, like one of the prophets of old." But when Herod heard of it, he said, "John, whom I beheaded, has been raised." (Mk 6:14-16)

If the idea being conveyed in this passage is that some Jews ("Herod" and some of those who "were saying") believed Jesus was John the Baptist resurrected into his final immortal body, which would seem consistent with the "powers" that Jesus is said to have in the passage, then the following comments by Robert M. Price are spot on:

> N.T. Wright comes near to resting the whole weight of his case [for Jesus' resurrection] on the mistaken contention that the notion of a single individual rising from the dead in advance of the general resurrection at the end of the age was unheard of, and that therefore it must have arisen as the result of the stubborn fact of it having occurred one day....[Wright fails] to take seriously the astonishing comment of Herod in Mark 6:14-16 to the effect that Jesus was thought to be John the Baptist *already* raised from the dead! Can Wright really be oblivious of how this one text torpedoes the hull of his argument?[67]

In other words, in Mark's story above, it did not take a discovered empty tomb or a dead person walking through locked doors to convince Herod and others that John the Baptist had resurrected from the dead before the general resurrection. All it took was Jesus performing what people thought were miracles, and all it took for Herod was hearing second hand from others that Jesus was performing miracles.

The second Gospel passage is the tradition of dead saints being raised out of their graves *before* the general resurrection (Mt 27:52-53). It is widely agreed by scholars on both sides of the aisle that this tradition is a legend that came about decades after Jesus' death. If so, then it came *after* the line of resurrection before the general resurrection had already been crossed by those who believed in Jesus' resurrection. However, it nevertheless still crosses the same line. The only nudge the rising saints tradition seems to have needed in this case was for someone else to go first. This does not seem like much of a nudge and it too suggests that the line of resurrection before the general resurrection was not as difficult to cross as some think.

N.T. Wright, one of those who advocates that a resurrection before the general resurrection could never be rationalized by first-century Jews, seems to accept that the rising saints passage *could* be a legend:

> It is impossible...to adjudicate on the question of historicity. Things that we are told by one source only, when in other respects the sources are parallel, may be suspect, especially when events like earthquakes were part of the stock in trade of apocalyptic expectation....it is better to remain puzzled than to settle for either a difficult argument for probable historicity or a cheap and cheerful rationalistic dismissal of the possibility.[68]

Wright goes on to say that the concept of bodily resurrection before the general resurrection in the rising saints passage is "without precedent in second-Temple [Jewish] expectation".[69] If so, and if this tradition is a legend, then it is an example of an *exception* to normal Jewish beliefs. The Herod passage mentioned earlier (where Jesus is thought to be John the Baptist raised from the dead) would also be an exception to normal Jewish beliefs (whether it is a legend or not). N.T. Wright agrees; he describes the Herod passage as "an exception to the general rule..."[70] Turning to pagan beliefs, Wright refers to the belief in the resurrection (and subsequent second death) of Nero as "a remarkable oddity – an exception".[71] He refers to the previously mentioned pagan traditions of heroes sometimes being bodily raised at the moment of death as "one or two isolated cases".[72] If the live bodily assumptions of Enoch, Elijah, and Moses are legends, then these beliefs too are exceptions to normal beliefs, crossing a line that had never been crossed before. I do not know if Wright thinks the live bodily assumptions of Enoch, Elijah, and Moses are history or legend, but he refers to them as "unexplained exceptions".[73] In his extensive study of ancient Jewish beliefs about the afterlife (*The Resurrection of the Son of God*, 2003) Wright does not address the Testament of Job passage mentioned earlier where dead children are bodily raised up to heaven before the general resurrection, but it seems safe to assume that he would also call this an exception.

But if all of these fictional, or potentially fictional, traditions are exceptions to normal beliefs, crossing what were previously uncrossed lines of belief without the events described actually happening, then on what basis does anyone insist that belief in Jesus' resurrection cannot also be an exception if the appropriate influences and pressures were present to create such a belief and

Jesus' burial location was not available to act as an empirical deterrent?

"In Accordance with the Scriptures"

As can be seen in the early creed, the earliest Christians were convinced that Jesus' atoning death and resurrection were "in accordance with the scriptures" (1 Cor 15:3-4). An urgent desire to anchor their rationalization in scripture would be expected not only to validate their rationalization to themselves, but also to validate it to other followers of Jesus and to defend themselves against those who might criticize their beliefs. Robert Miller describes how the Jews viewed their sacred scriptures:

> [Jews] treated the words of the prophets as coded messages beyond the prophets' own understanding....Thus the real meaning of some...prophecies could be discerned only after the predicted events had already occurred. First-century Jews...believed that God had planted throughout their writings cryptic clues about his plans for the future.[74]

While the search for scriptural confirmation of beliefs would have been enhanced by literacy and access to a copy of the Jewish scriptures, neither would have been required. As Van Buren points out:

> There is no need to imagine the disciples retiring to a Beth Midrash and pouring over texts. For all we know, they may have been unable to read. But as Jews they would have heard the Torah read again and again...[75]

Out of the thousands of verses in the Hebrew Scriptures, it is not surprising that some could be interpreted in favor of a dying and rising Messiah instead of the earthly triumphant King that had been expected by most Jews. Van Buren comments on the creativity of this interpretive process:

> To listen to...many a...Christian, is to listen to just this mistake, as though a Jew must be either blind, stupid, or perverted not to see what is so obvious to a Christian. Such Christians fail to

recognize that Jews have continued to read these texts with the closest attention over the centuries without seeing them as pointing to the gospel. They [Christians] fail as well to acknowledge their own foundations in the highly creative interpretation of Israel's scriptures.[76]

It is worth noting too that, like Christianity, the Sabbatai Sevi movement found everything they needed in the Jewish scriptures. According to Gershom Scholem:

Sabbatai's followers...believed in the holy books. Hence their first reaction – one might almost say reflex – was to search Scripture and tradition for intimations, hints, and indications of the extraordinary and bewildering events. And lo and behold – the Bible, rabbinic Haggadah, and kabbalistic literature turned out to abound in allusions to Sabbatai Sevi in general and to the mystery of his apostasy in particular....From biblical verses and fragments of verses, from rabbinic sayings whose implicit possibilities nobody had noticed before, from paradoxical expressions in kabbalistic literature, and from the oddest corners of Jewish literature, they produced material the like of which had never been seen in Jewish theology.[77]

The same thing happened in the Rebbe Schneerson movement. According to Simon Dein, "Books were published 'proving' that *Moshiach* [the Messiah] could come from the dead. These deployed passages from the Torah, Talmud, Maimonides and the Rebbe's own writings....[and were used as] proof texts to reinforce the possibility of a Messiah who suffers, dies and returns from the dead."[78]

Although it is impossible at this distance to know exactly which scriptures the earliest Christians had in mind, the most likely candidates are those which appear in the later Christian literature. For the belief that Jesus "died for our sins" some possibilities are: Isaiah 53:1, 3, 4, 11, 12; Zechariah 11:13; 12:10; 13:7; Psalm 22:1, 18; and Psalm 69:4. For the belief that Jesus was "raised" some possibilities are: Psalm 2:7; 16:10; 49:15; 68:18; 86:13; 110:1; Isaiah 25:8; Jonah 1:17; and Hosea 6:2. It would take volumes to respond to those who think that all of these passages are in fact actual predictions of the future. Although such an exercise is well beyond my scope here, a representative in-depth analysis will be done on one of the most significant of these passages later (Ps 16:10).

Conclusion

In conclusion, it is plausible that the process of cognitive dissonance reduction was the cause of the beliefs that Jesus died for our sins and was raised from the dead and that scriptural confirmation for these beliefs could be found in the Hebrew Scriptures. David Berger summarizes it well:

> In the light of what was universally understood to be the function of the Messiah, the crucifixion [of Jesus] was a terrible logical and psychological blow to Jesus' followers....There can be little doubt that many of the first-century Jews who had been attracted by Jesus' preaching sadly submitted to the conclusion forced upon them by his death. They had been mistaken....But for others this was impossible. The belief was too strong, the hurt too great, to face the terrible truth. There simply had to be an explanation, and such an explanation was found. First of all, Jesus was said to have been resurrected. Secondly, the Bible was examined with the purpose of finding what no one had ever seen there before – evidence that the Messiah would be killed without bringing peace to the world or redemption to Israel....Thirdly, there was the expectation of a second coming, at which time Jesus would carry out the task expected of the Messiah. And finally, there had to be an explanation for the first coming and its catastrophic end. The basic structure of this explanation was to shift the function of the Messiah from a visible level, where it could be tested, to an invisible one, where it could not. The Messiah's goal, at least the first time around, was not the redemption of Israel (which had clearly not taken place) but the atonement for original sin...[79]

Chapter 4

The Appearance Traditions

1 Corinthians 15:5-8: "…he appeared to Cephas, then to the twelve. Then he appeared to more than five hundred brothers and sisters at one time, most of whom are still alive, though some have died. Then he appeared to James, then to all the apostles. Last of all, as to someone untimely born, he appeared also to me [Paul]."

If cognitive dissonance reduction was the cause of the beliefs that Jesus died for our sins, was raised from the dead, and would be back very soon, the appearance traditions above can be fairly easily accounted for as phenomena expected in a highly charged religious environment.

The Appearance to Peter

It is easiest to start with the appearance to Peter (Cephas) because an *individual* seeing a dead person is not unusual or controversial at all. As resurrection defender N.T. Wright says, "Most people in the ancient world knew that visions and appearances of recently dead people occurred….That such 'seeings', even such 'meetings', occur, and that people have known about them throughout recorded history, there should be no question."[1] Still, it is worth taking a closer look at such individual experiences just to firm up what is already widely agreed on.*

---

* Although appearances of dead people will be referred to as "hallucinations" in this chapter, the result of this chapter is the same if one thinks these experiences are actual visitations of dead people from some sort of afterlife (I am agnostic on the question of the afterlife).

According to Dr. Peter Slade, professor of clinical psychology at the University of Lisbon, and Dr. Richard Bentall, Chair of Clinical Psychology at the University of Bangor, United Kingdom, "...Particular kinds of stress may elicit hallucinatory experiences. The clearest example of this concerns hallucination following bereavement."[2] Slade and Bentall point out that not counting drug use or mental illness, various studies over the last hundred years indicate that around ten percent of the population has experienced a brief auditory or visual hallucination of a dead person, with visual hallucinations being slightly more common than auditory hallucinations.[3] These studies also indicate that around one percent of the population has experienced a visual hallucination of a dead person which includes actual conversation with the hallucination.[4]

Other researchers have found similar results. For example, Dr. André Aleman, professor of cognitive neuropsychiatry at the University Medical Center in Groningen, Netherlands, and Dr. Frank Larøi, who works in the Cognitive Psychopathology Unit at the University of Liége, Belgium, report:

Research has revealed that it is common for people to see, hear, or feel the presence of the deceased person during bereavement. [For example, in one] detailed study about the hallucinations and illusions of a group of 293 widows and widowers (young, middle-aged, and older subjects), Reese (1971) found that nearly half had experiences of this kind. In total, the sense of the deceased's presence was most common (39%), followed by visual and auditory hallucinations (14% and 13%, respectively). Twelve percent of the subjects said they had talked with, and 3% said they had been touched by, the deceased.... Large population-based studies have established that people from the normal population, without psychiatric illnesses, experience hallucinations.[5]

According to another leading authority on hallucinations, Dr. Oliver Sacks, professor of neurology at New York University School of Medicine, "[Hallucinations] can mimic perception in every respect."[6]

The following four firsthand accounts from modern times serve as examples of how realistic visual hallucinations can be. They also serve as examples of the kind of visionary experience Peter could have had (the last example is a vision of Jesus).

I heard the door open and there were soft footsteps with a strange noise of knocking – I was alone at home and was rather frightened. Then the miracle happened – my beloved father came towards me, shining and lovely as gold, and transparent as mist. He looked just as he did in life. I could recognize his features quite distinctly, then he stopped beside my bed and looked at me lovingly and smiled. A great peace entered into me and I felt happier than I had felt before....Then he went away.[7]

It was on the day of the funeral, about eleven in the morning. I was just preparing the fire in the stove when suddenly I felt I was not alone – I turned round, and there this woman stood behind me. She was transparent but perfect in her glory and beauty. Her hair, gray in her lifetime, was wonderfully fair and curled halfway down her arms. Her face was clear and white, her eyes were shining, and her teeth in her smiling mouth were beautiful. Her dress, which reached up to her chin, and the sleeves which fell down over her wrists, were of an unearthly splendor.[8]

I saw Kay standing just inside the front door, looking as he always had coming home from work. He smiled and I ran into his outstretched arms as I always had and leaned against his chest. I opened my eyes, the image was gone.[9]

The thoughts tumbled over and over in my mind. Can society forgive one for such acts against humanity? Can it take this guilt off my shoulders? Can serving the rest of life in prison undo what's been done? Can anything be done? I looked at my future, my alternatives. Stay in prison. Escape. Commit suicide. As I looked, the wall in my mind was blank. But somehow I knew there was another alternative. I could choose the road many people had been pressing on me. I could follow Jesus. As plainly as daylight came the words, "You have to decide. Behold, I stand at the door and knock." Did I hear someone say that? I assume I spoke in my thoughts, but I'm not certain, "What door?" "You know what door and where it is Susan. Just turn around and open it, and I will come in." Suddenly, as though on a movie screen, there in my thoughts was a door. It had a handle. I took hold of it and pulled. It opened. The whitest, most brilliant light I had ever seen poured over me. In the center of the flood of brightness was an even brighter light. Vaguely, there was the form of a man. I knew it was Jesus. He spoke to me – literally, plainly, matter-of-factly spoke to me in my 9-by-11 prison cell: "Susan, I am really coming into your heart to stay." I was distinctly aware that I inhaled deeply, and then, just as fully, exhaled. There was no more guilt! It was gone. Completely gone! The bitterness, too, instantly gone. How could this be? For the first time in my memory I felt clean, fully clean, inside and out. In 26 years I had never been so happy.[10]

If Peter experienced the normal feelings associated with the absence of a recently deceased loved one, and he also experienced the anticipation of a raised and returning Messiah who had yet to return, it would not be surprising if he had a hallucination of Jesus similar to those described above. Such an experience would have in turn bolstered Peter's conviction that Jesus was raised from the dead.

Other Individual Appearances

As mentioned earlier, modern studies indicate that about five percent of people will experience a visual hallucination of a dead person, and about one percent will experience a visual hallucination of a dead person that involves conversation with the hallucination. However, in more superstitious cultures, such as that of first-century Palestine, the incidence of hallucination can be much higher. One informal study found that forty percent of Hawaiian natives have had auditory or visual encounters with dead people (the visual vs. auditory distinction was not separated out in the study).[11]

High emotional states mixed with superstitious beliefs can also increase the incidence of hallucination. In his 1896 Lowell Lectures, psychologist William James spoke of hallucinations which sometimes rose to epidemic proportions, thought by those in the community to be the work of the devil but which we can now interpret as the effects of suggestion.[12] A more recent example of superstition, religious beliefs, and high emotional states leading to mass hallucinations occurred a few weeks after a massive tsunami hit Asia in December of 2004. ABC news reported:

> A second surge of tsunami terror is hitting southern Thailand, but this time it is a wave of foreign ghosts terrifying locals....Tales of ghost sightings in the six worst hit southern provinces have become endemic, with many locals saying they are too terrified to venture near the beach or into the ocean...."This is a type of mass hallucination...," Thai psychologist and media commentator Wallop Piyamanotham said....Mr. Wallop said widespread trauma began to set in about four days after the waves hit. "This is when people start seeing these farangs (foreigners) walking on the sand or in the ocean," he said....Mr. Wallop said the reason almost all ghost sightings appear to involve foreign tourists stems from a belief that spirits can only be put to rest by relatives at the scene, such as was done to many Thai victims. "Thai people believe that when people die, a relative has to cremate them or bless them. If this is not done or the body is not found, people believe the person will appear over and over again to show where they are," he said.[13]

A higher rate of hallucinations in environments where there is suggestion, expectation, and/or superstitious or religious belief is backed up by more controlled studies. One 2001 study on auditory hallucinations revealed that people who place a high emphasis on spiritual experiences are more than twice as likely to experience an auditory hallucination.[14] A 2002 study revealed that people from the Caribbean are more than twice as likely to experience a hallucination as people from the United Kingdom.[15]

In the more superstitious age of two thousand years ago, and in a highly charged religious movement where the followers suffered the death and absence of their beloved leader and then came to believe he was raised from the dead and would be back very soon, it is not hard to imagine Peter's hallucination leading to a chain reaction of individual hallucinations by a moderate number of other people in the movement. The more hallucinations there were, the more plausible the hypothesis in this book becomes; however, I will try to show by the end of this chapter that there is probably not a need for any more than around ten visual hallucinations, or even less.

If some of Jesus' followers experienced a visual hallucination of Jesus, it makes sense that a much larger number would have had similar though lesser experiences, like hearing his voice, or having a strong spiritual feeling that Jesus was present, or sharing in group ecstatic experiences where Jesus' presence was felt collectively (perhaps like a spirited Pentecostal gathering today). According to Dr. Sacks, the latter two of these experiences can be almost as powerful as a visual hallucination, with the sense of conviction that someone is there being "irresistible".[16] An example of a feeling of presence, and its close association to actually seeing the person sensed, is expressed by a thirty year old member of the Rebbe Schneerson movement during one of the Lubavitch ceremonies:

> The Rebbe is here with us now. I can feel a definite presence. No, I cannot see him but I feel overwhelmed. You can definitely feel his power....A few people can see the Rebbe. People tell me, "Just open your eyes and you can see him." A few spiritually developed people have seen him – in body and in flesh looking as he did before his passing. It's not happened to me yet. Perhaps one day it will, I don't know, I hope so.[17]

Although the feeling of Jesus' presence is not explicitly stated in the Christian literature, we know that emotionally charged group gatherings where people were speaking in tongues and prophesying were occurring because Paul refers to them and in some cases tries to bring order to them (1 Cor 14:1-33; 12:1-11; 1 Thess 5:19). If these gatherings were occurring when Paul was a leader in the church, they could have been occurring in the earliest Christian community too, and they suggest that many people were feeling the presence of Jesus.

It is worth noting that the firsthand experience related by the Rebbe Schneerson follower above also indicates that visual hallucinations were occurring in the Rebbe Schneerson movement (the follower said: "A few spiritually developed people have *seen* him [the Rebbe] – in body and in flesh looking as he did before his passing"). Post-mortem visual experiences of Rebbe Schneerson are corroborated by field researchers Simon Dein and Lorne Dawson who recorded the following comment from a leading rabbi in the movement in 2005: "Some of them have seen the Rebbe in front of them."[18] David Berger reports similar findings: "Hillel Pevzner, an important messianist rabbi in France, is reported to be among the growing (though still small) number of people who claim to have seen the Rebbe since his death."[19] Some of these appearance experiences are described and discussed further at Hebrew websites and in Hebrew books, some of which have been translated into English online.[20]

All of the experiences above – visual hallucinations, auditory hallucinations, and the feeling of Jesus' presence – would have acted in a feedback loop to reinforce the belief that Jesus was raised from the dead, and this would have in turn perpetuated more of the same experiences. Although it will be assumed below that the earliest Christians knew the difference between *visually* seeing Jesus and just hearing his voice or having an ecstatic experience where his presence was just felt, this line may not have been as distinct as we think.

The Appearance to James and to Paul

1 Corinthians 15:7-8: "Then he appeared to James....Last of all, as to someone untimely born, he appeared also to me [Paul]."

Although not part of the appearance traditions in 1 Corinthians 15:3-7, it is first worth looking at Paul's own encounter with Jesus approximately three years after Jesus' death and that he refers to in 1 Corinthians 15:8 above. Although Acts says that other people witnessed this appearance with Paul (Acts 9:1-9; 22:6-11; 26:12-18) the account in Acts could be a later legendary embellishment on what was originally just a solo experience. This is how Paul's conversion appearance will be treated below.

Because the appearance to Paul marks his conversion from persecutor to leader of Christians, there have been attempts to hypothesize the exact psychological dynamics that took place within Paul's mind that led him to have such an experience. Below are a few possibilities.

According to Gerd Ludemann:

[In his letters,] Paul shows clear evidence of conflicting emotions: a radical sense of guilt and unworthiness combined with an exalted self-image that results in the need to be an authority figure....Caught up in an intellectual and emotional maelstrom that can only have been intensified by his growing familiarity with the sect he was harassing, he seems at last to have discovered the resolution of his problems for himself. The humble and self-sacrificing Jesus represents for Paul a new vision of the Almighty: no longer a stern and demanding tyrant intent on punishing even those who could not help themselves, but a loving and forgiving leader who offered rest and peace to imperfect humans who accepted his grace....Paul could become the Apostle-in-Chief of a new program of salvation with a culture-wide appeal. Something of that nature was in all likelihood the dynamic that impelled the persecutor turned proclaimer whose religious zeal stands as a measure of the inner tension that was powerfully released and transformed in a vision of Christ.[21]

Richard Carrier provides a similar explanation:

...guilt at persecuting a people he came to admire; subsequent disgust with fellow persecuting Pharisees;...beginning to see what the Christians were seeing in scripture, and to worry about his own salvation;...heat and fatigue on a long, desolate road...could have induced a convincing ecstatic event – his unconscious mind producing what he really wanted: a reason to believe the Christians were right after all and atone for his treatment of them, and a way to give his life meaning, by relocating himself from the lower, even superfluous periphery of Jewish elite society, to a place of power and purpose. We can add to this the possibility of benevolent mental disorder. We know there is a kind of "happy schizotype" who is "a relatively well-adjusted person who is functional despite, and in some cases even because of, his or her anomalous perceptual experiences"....It is entirely possible that cultural support and psychological benefits led borderline schizophrenics into comfortable situations where their visions were channeled into "appropriate" and respected religious contexts. Indeed, we would expect these "happy schizotypes" to find their most accepted place in religious avocations, and they would naturally gravitate into the entourage of miracle workers.[22]

The comments of Evan Fales, applying the work of anthropologist I.M. Lewis on mystical experiences in general, may also have some application to Paul's conversion appearance:

Central possession...typically begins with involuntary affliction interpreted as a mystical invasion; it involves gradual mastery of that affliction (and of the invading spirits); and it is a technique which, successfully deployed, is a means to social status and power....[The] invading spirit is a deity of the central cult, and is therefore a representative and guardian of the moral and institutional order....The victim must be someone whose social background places him (the gender here is usually male) in a position to aspire to social authority....However, there is a pattern. In those societies in which access to power is determined ascriptively – normally, by the passing of office from father to son or from uncle to nephew – possession does not occur. Possession is a concomitant of what are sometimes called "big-man" societies, societies in which any man (or any man from the appropriate social class) can compete for social authority. Such societies are more fluid, more meritocratic; and in them, power comes to those who have the greatest initiative or are the most charismatic. It is in that context that someone can claim [that]...he has been involuntarily chosen by the gods as their medium for communicating with humans, [and] has a means for making effective a claim to legitimate leadership. To become a "big man" requires recruiting a large enough (and influential enough) following; and the best way to recruit followers is to demonstrate that one has been oneself recruited by the gods....[The] involuntary character of the initial affliction, and its onerous character...serve to reflect and convey the crucial message that leadership has been thrust upon a resisting and unwilling individual; and therefore, that the pursuit and exercise of power does not reflect the motive of self-aggrandizement, but rather is in the service of the social whole.[23]

Although not a conversion experience, the following firsthand account of a vision experienced by Nathan of Gaza, right hand man to seventeenth-century Messiah claimant Sabbatai Sevi, serves as an example of a vision with similar motivating force to Paul's conversion appearance. This was written by Nathan himself in 1673, eight years after the experience he describes:

> He [God] sent me some of His holy angels and blessed spirits who revealed to me many of the mysteries of the Torah....[The] spirit came over me, my hair stood on end and my knees shook and I beheld the merkabah [a divine sphere], and I saw visions of God all day long and all night, and I was vouchsafed true prophecy like any other prophet, as the voice spoke to me and began with the words: "Thus speaks the Lord"....Until this day I never yet had so great a vision.[24]

Gershom Scholem remarks on the motivating effects of this vision on Nathan:

> The psychological authenticity of these autobiographical accounts is as convincing as it is decisive. Here, at last, we have the simple truth, which had escaped both historians and novelists, about the awakening of Nathan's messianic prophecy. Whatever had been lodged in the depths of his conscious or unconscious mind now came to the fore [in this vision] in a tremendous emotional upheaval...[25]

James, like Paul, was not a follower of Jesus during Jesus' lifetime. In this case, similar psychological factors, in addition to the social dynamics and expectations of being Jesus' brother, could have caused him to have a conversion experience and vision of Jesus similar to Paul's. It is also possible that James simply converted to Christianity and then later had a vision of Jesus. A third possibility for the appearance to James will be suggested later.

Paul's Qualifier "Last of all, as to someone untimely born..."

When Paul reports his experience of seeing Jesus at his conversion, he says, "*Last of all, as to someone untimely born,* he appeared also to me" (1 Cor 15:8). This qualifier suggests that when Paul had his conversion experience, which was approximately three years after Jesus' death, sightings of Jesus had long since stopped or slowed to the point that Paul did not know of any after him.

Zeroing in on Paul's qualifier "last of all", there are at least two possibilities for Paul's intent that are compatible with the hallucination hypothesis proposed above. The first explanation is that Paul simply did not have any more hallucinations of Jesus after his conversion experience, and so he considered his conversion experience to be *the* last appearance of Jesus. The second explanation takes into account the possibility that Paul experienced one or more hallucinations of Jesus *after* his conversion hallucination. In this case, Paul may have simply meant that he considered himself the last to be *chosen* to receive appearances. It is worth noting that this second explanation would also account for the possibility that other apostles saw Jesus after Paul's conversion, as long as their initial hallucination occurred before Paul's initial hallucination.

There is a third possibility for Paul's qualifier "last of all" which is proposed by some in traditional scholarship and which results in substantial difficulty for the hallucination hypothesis proposed above. This third explanation is derived from the different way that the appearances of Jesus are portrayed in Luke-Acts (same author) and in the Book of Revelation. [26] This explanation also requires the conclusion that Paul experienced one or more appearances of Jesus *after* his conversion appearance. Below is a close look at this third possibility.

Since all of the appearances relevant to this third possibility occur in Luke-Acts with the exception of one in the Book of Revelation, Luke-Acts will be covered first. In Luke-Acts, all of the appearances that occurred in the initial weeks after Jesus' resurrection (Lk 24:13-51; Acts 1:3-9; 13:31), plus the appearance to Paul at his conversion approximately three years later (Acts 9:3-7; 22:6-10; 26:12-16), are portrayed as having *extra-mental* aspects to them, that is, there are aspects of the appearance that occur in the normal space-time continuum that anyone present could see or hear. In contrast, all other appearances of Jesus in Luke-Acts, four of them (Acts 7:54-57; 9:10-12; 18:9-10; 22:17-21), the last two of which are to Paul, have *no* extra-mental aspects; they are all portrayed as occurring only in the mind of the recipient, but still sent by God. It is argued from this differentiation in Luke-Acts that Paul saw the same distinction, and that it is this distinction that Paul had in mind when he said his *conversion* encounter with Jesus was "last of all" (1 Cor 15:8). In other words, it is proposed that "last of all" meant to Paul that he thought his conversion encounter with Jesus was the last appearance of Jesus that involved real, tangible, in this world, extra-mental characteristics, like the appearances in the initial weeks after Jesus' resurrection, and all other appearances were only visions sent by God to the person's mind with no extra-mental aspects. If so, the hypothesis that Paul (and by extension others) had hallucinations of Jesus is significantly weakened because there would be no good reason for Paul to make such a precise extra-mental/non-extra-mental distinction centered on his conversion experience if all of his visions were hallucinations.

However, there is a good explanation for this distinction in Luke-Acts without Paul ever making the same distinction. To explain, it is best to start with the account of Paul's conversion experience in Acts. In the Acts account of Paul's conversion experience, there are extra-mental elements of light and voice that the others with Paul see and hear, but there is no extra-mental Jesus (Acts 9:3-7; 22:6-10; 26:12-16). Despite this, there is wide agreement among scholars that a *visual* appearance of Jesus to Paul is nevertheless intended because Acts has Jesus say to Paul during his conversion, "Get up and stand on your feet; for I have *appeared* [*ophthen*] to you for this purpose..." (Acts 26:16; see too Acts 9:17; 9:27; 22:14 for more indications that Acts intends that Paul *visually* saw Jesus at his conversion). Because of this, many have concluded that Acts intends that Paul saw Jesus in a *non-extra-mental* way, that is, in a vision sent by God to his mind while at the same time the extra-mental elements of light and voice also took place.

Given this unusual way that Paul's conversion experience is portrayed in Acts, the task for those who propose the appearance traditions originated with hallucinations is to explain two things. First, why was Paul's conversion encounter with Jesus in Acts, and the four other appearances of Jesus in Acts that also occurred years after Jesus' resurrection (Acts 7:54-57; 9:10-12; 18:9-10; 22:17-

21), legendized into appearances of Jesus that occurred only in the mind of the recipient, instead of being legendized into appearances of Jesus that were just as corporeal and extra-mental as the appearances to the disciples in Luke's Gospel and the other Gospels (e.g., Lk 24:36-51; Mt 28:8-10; Jn 20:19-29)? Second, in the legendization process, why were the extra-mental elements of light and voice added to Paul's conversion encounter with Jesus in Acts but not to the other four appearances of Jesus in Acts that occurred years after Jesus' resurrection (Acts 7:54-57; 9:10-12; 18:9-10; 22:17-21)?

Regarding the first question, by the time Luke wrote his Gospel and Acts there was the tradition that Jesus, instead of being raised to heaven and appearing from there, was raised on earth where he appeared and disappeared for some forty days and then ascended up to heaven (Acts 1:1-11; Lk 24:50-51; Jn 20:17; and in the later added ending to Mark, Mk 16:19). The Jesus Seminar considers the ascension tradition a legend:

> The earliest sequence probably regarded resurrection and ascension/exaltation as a single event: Jesus was raised and taken up into heaven at the same time. The appearances of Jesus would then have been appearances from heaven....The [resurrection and then] ascension [tradition] is an invention [or legend]...to bring the appearances to a close.[27] *

If the ascension tradition arose in order to bring the appearances to a close after a short time, or to explain why they came to a close, the reason an extra-mental Jesus does not appear at Paul's conversion in Acts (approximately three years after Jesus' death), or in the four other late appearances, is simply because in Acts, Jesus had already long ago ascended up to heaven. Although disagreeing that the ascension tradition is a legend, traditionalists

---

* The resurrection and then ascension tradition may also have arisen in order to explain to people why the very corporeal appearances of Jesus, such as we see in the Gospel stories of groups of people eating with Jesus and touching his body (presumed here to be legends that arose in the Christian community), were no longer occurring in the Christian community.

agree that the ascension tradition is the driving force behind this distinction in the appearances in Acts. As William Craig says:

> According to Luke, the appearance to Paul was in fact different from the others because Paul's was a post-ascension encounter. That is to say, after appearing to His disciples and others for some forty days, Jesus physically left this universe or dimension. He will come again at the end of history....Therefore, the appearance to Paul could not have been physical like the others; it had to be in some sense visionary. But it was not merely visionary, for it had real manifestations in the world "out there," namely, the light and the voice.[28]

If the ascension tradition is a legend, and it was the driving force behind the Acts appearances of Jesus that occur only in the mind of the recipient, then the attempt to equate a Luke-Acts extra-mental/non-extra-mental distinction in appearances with Paul's qualifier "last of all" boils down to just the second question – why in Acts does Paul's conversion encounter with Jesus have *any* extra-mental elements (light and voice) while the other four late appearances do not? One could just chalk it up to some unknown part of the legendization process, but legitimizing Jesus' appearance to Paul through the validating witness of others seems the most obvious possibility.

In sum, the extra-mental/non-extra-mental distinction in Luke-Acts is simply the result of two legendary trajectories – the ascension tradition and the legitimization of Paul's conversion – it had nothing to do with how Paul viewed his encounters with Jesus or the intent behind his qualifier "last of all".

The one appearance of Jesus after Paul's conversion that is not in Luke-Acts is in the Book of Revelation and is to John (Rev 1:9-18). However, by the time the Book of Revelation was written, the ascension tradition was well known. Therefore, for the same reasons noted above, it is not surprising if this appearance is intended to be only a vision sent by God to John's mind (John says he was "in the spirit" when he received his vision, so a vision sent by God to his mind seems to be what is intended).

There is also another difficulty with the proposal that Paul saw an extra-mental/non-extra-mental distinction between his conversion encounter with Jesus and those after. In 2 Corinthians 12:1-9, Paul refers to "visions" of the Lord:

> It is necessary to boast; nothing is to be gained by it, but I will go on to <u>visions</u> and revelations of the Lord. I know a person in Christ who fourteen years ago was caught up to the third heaven – whether in the body or out of the body I do not know; God knows. And I know that such a person – whether in the body or out of the body I do not know; God knows – was caught up into Paradise and heard things that are not to be told, that no mortal is permitted to repeat. On behalf of such a one I will boast, but on my own behalf I will not boast, except of my weaknesses. But if I wish to boast, I will not be a fool, for I will be speaking the truth. But I refrain from it, so that no one may think better of me than what is seen in me or heard from me, even considering the exceptional character of the revelations. Therefore, to keep me from being too elated, a thorn was given to me in the flesh, a messenger of Satan to torment me, to keep me from being too elated. Three times I appealed to the Lord about this, that it would leave me, but he said to me, "My grace is sufficient for you, for power is made perfect in weakness." (2 Cor 12:1-9)

Many scholars think Paul is talking about himself in this passage. Additionally, because Paul refers to this person as "in Christ", many scholars think he is talking about someone who was *already* a Christian. If both points are correct, and if Paul intends that he *saw* Jesus in this "vision" of the Lord that he is describing, then Paul is talking here about one of his *post-conversion* visions of Jesus. If so, notice that Paul accepts the possibility that this vision had *extra-mental* elements: "whether in the body or out of the body I do not know" (an "in the body" trip to the third heaven would presumably mean that a bystander would see that person's body being transported up into the sky). So in Paul's mind, an appearance of Jesus involving extra-mental elements was possible *after* his conversion. This is further indication that Paul did not make an extra-mental/non-extra-mental distinction between his conversion encounter with Jesus and those that he had after.

In conclusion, it is plausible that Paul's qualifier "last of all" in 1 Corinthians 15:8 simply meant that he considered his conversion encounter with Jesus to be *the* last appearance of Jesus or that he considered himself the last to be *chosen* to receive appearances.*

The Appearances to Groups of People

Examples of supposed simultaneous group hallucinations that are sometimes used in an attempt to explain the Christian group appearance traditions are not comparable for several reasons. For example, the well-known group sightings of the Virgin Mary appear to be associated only with the psychology of children, such as those that occurred at Medjugorje (six children/teenagers), Fatima (three children), Garabandal (four children), and La Salette (two children). The sightings at Medjugorje may also have involved drug use, and they often involved the seeing of just a faint light which has no resemblance to a person. Other group sightings of dead people have been associated with a single location where there are unique light reflections or even dust formations, such as on a window or some other surface, which was not the case with the Christian group appearance traditions. Some group sightings of dead people are the result of similar afterimages appearing in the eyes of those who have stared at the sun for prolonged periods of time (Fatima, 1917; Conyers, Georgia, 1990 and later), again, not comparable to the Christian traditions. Some group sightings are like those of Elvis, which involve groups of people seeing a person

---

* As an aside, if Paul does *not* intend that Jesus was visually *seen* in the above "vision" of the Lord (2 Cor 12:1-9), it introduces the possibility that an out of body type experience without ever seeing Jesus could qualify as an "appearance" of Jesus. That the word "visions" [*optasia*], which Paul uses in 2 Corinthians 12:1 above, and the word "appeared" [*ophthe*], which is used to refer to every appearance in 1 Corinthians 15:5-8, including Paul's *conversion* appearance, are interchangeable is evident in one Acts passage that, speaking about Paul's *conversion* appearance, has Paul say this: "I was not disobedient to the heavenly *vision* [*optasia*]" (Acts 26:19). Since this is in reference to Paul's *conversion* appearance, it means *optasia* and *ophthe* are both appropriate and interchangeable in describing Paul's conversion experience. If so, then some or many of the appearances in 1 Corinthians 15:5-8 could have been *openly accepted* as just ecstatic out of body type experiences where the person never actually *saw* Jesus.

who resembles someone who is dead, but is believed by those who see him or her to have faked their death and to be living incognito, the latter not being what Christians believed about Jesus. Lastly, some group sightings are fraudulent, such as the probable use of a light image projection device in Knock, Ireland in 1879. In summary, if the group appearance traditions in 1 Corinthians 15:5-7 are the result of people simultaneously hallucinating Jesus, there is no comparable example anywhere in history that I am aware of. In light of this, the following explanations are offered for the Christian group appearance traditions.

The Appearances to the Twelve and to All of the Apostles

1 Corinthians 15:5 & 7: "...he appeared to Cephas, then to the twelve...he appeared to James, then to all the apostles."

In the first years after Jesus' crucifixion, what the emerging Christian community must have needed badly were people who had the ability to lead, that is, the ability to teach, preach, and defend their new beliefs. Given this, it is possible that the traditions of the appearance to the Twelve and to all the apostles were born out of a desire by Christian leaders to designate with authority those who had the ability to lead, not out of a desire to accurately report appearances.* We see the importance of an appearance by Jesus to holding a position of authority in the church in Paul's argument for his own authority made to one of his Christian congregations:

> Am I not free? Am I not an apostle? Have I not *seen* Jesus our Lord? Are you not my work in the Lord? If I am not an apostle to others, at least I am to you; for you are the seal of my apostleship in the Lord. (1 Cor 9:1-2)

If authority designation was the primary motivation for these appearance traditions, it is possible that some of these people did

---

* The origin of the group known as "the Twelve" is not of interest in this discussion. It could have been a group formed by Jesus before his death or a group formed after Jesus' death.

not experience an individual appearance by Jesus but were nevertheless still very suitable for and designated as leaders. As Stephen Patterson puts it:

> Both the Twelve and the church have everything to gain by the assertion that the risen Lord had also appeared to the Twelve. Including the Twelve in the appearance formulae probably derives from a decision on the part of the early church to expand the sphere of authority that was originally confined to the "pillars" [e.g., Peter and his closest confidants] to include the Twelve as well. It is not so likely that it derives from an actual experience of the risen Jesus....[This] could also be said about the claim in 1 Cor 15:7 that Jesus also appeared to "the apostles"....[We] have in this expression a second authority-bearing designation from earliest Christianity....The inclusion of "the apostles" in this formula...derives from an ecclesial decision to expand the sphere of authority beyond James to include others who could be trusted with the task of preaching.[29]

Patterson's conclusion is echoed by the Jesus Seminar:

> The Fellows of the Jesus Seminar were doubtful that the eleven as a group ever experienced a vision of the risen Jesus at one time....The tradition probably arose as a confirmation of apostolic authority....Reports of appearances to various people in the early Christian community had political consequences. The recipient of an appearance had received the special endorsement of the source of all authority, Jesus of Nazareth, and was therefore entitled to respect and power.[30]

To some, the emergence of such traditions for the sake of conferring authority might seem implausible and amount to nothing more than calling the earliest Christians liars, which does not work because they endured hardship and death for their beliefs. However, this misses the point. I am not questioning the veracity of the earliest Christian belief that Jesus was the Messiah, their belief that he was raised from the dead, that some genuinely experienced what they thought was Jesus appearing to them, that some thought they heard Jesus speak to them, and that many honestly felt Jesus' presence after his death. These things would be enough to drive many people to endure hardship and death. But what is technically a lie can sometimes be told in order to convey what is honestly believed to be a much larger truth. This is what I think the earliest Christian leaders were doing when they claimed that Jesus appeared to the Twelve and to all the apostles. From their perspective, the inaccuracy was inconsequential given that they genuinely believed that Jesus was the Messiah, they genuinely believed that he was raised from the dead, some of the Twelve and the apostles actually did think they saw Jesus alive after his death, many or all of the Twelve and the apostles shared in group or individual ecstatic experiences where they felt Jesus' presence or heard his voice, and such an understanding added to the authority that the Twelve and the apostles deserved and needed to spread their message. Calling the earliest Christian leaders "liars" in this case does not fully represent their *intent* and that is why I do not think this term is accurate.

A more accurate description than the word "liars" would be to say that the traditions of the appearance to the Twelve and to all the apostles were, from the earliest Christian leaders' perspective, a slight stretch of the truth that supported their sincere *belief* that Jesus was raised from the dead and that message needed to be defended and spread. In other words, authority designations became more important than historical accuracy. Stretching the truth to tell what is believed to be a much larger truth would not be unusual in any human endeavor, even a well-meaning one.

A similar well-intended and from their point of view minor distortion of the truth in the early Mormon movement might serve as an example of this aspect of human nature. In the front of the Book of Mormon are two testimonies signed in 1830 by a total of eleven people asserting that they saw the physical gold plates that Joseph Smith claimed he translated the Book of Mormon from. Eight years later, when pressed, one of them changed his story slightly, but his belief in the Book of Mormon was steadfast. Mormon historian Grant Palmer explains:

> On 25 March 1838, Martin Harris testified publicly that none of the signatories to the Book of Mormon saw or handled the

physical records.... [Rather, Harris said he and the others saw the golden plates] in vision or imagination....His statement, made at the height of Ohio's banking-related apostasy, became the final straw that caused Apostles Luke S. Johnson, Lyman E. Johnson, and John F. Boynton, and high priest Stephen Burnett and seventy Warren Parish to exit the church.[31] *

Stephen Burnett, the high priest mentioned above who was present at Harris' testimony, reported on Harris' steadfast belief in the Book of Mormon despite knowing and openly saying that the nature of his witness to it had been exaggerated. After Harris' testimony Burnett talked to Harris and reported, "He [Harris] was sorry for any man who rejected the Book of Mormon for he knew it was true....[Harris lamented that] he never should have told that the testimony of the eight was false, if it had not been picked out of him but should have let it passed as it was...."[32]

Another example of this aspect of human nature comes from the Sabbatai Sevi movement. In 1665, Nathan of Gaza, one of the most ardent believers in Sevi before Sevi declared himself to be the Messiah, fabricated an ancient scroll with a prophecy on it from a twelfth-century Rabbi in order to help convince Sevi that he was the Messiah and that he should publicly proclaim so. The prophecy read as follows:

> Behold a son will be born to Mordecai Sevi in the year 5386 [1626] and he will be called Sabbatai Sevi. He will subdue the great dragon, and take away the strength of the piercing serpent and the strength of the crooked serpent, and he will be the true messiah.[33]

Although it is widely thought that when Nathan wrote this prophecy he was in a trance-like state associated with the form of Judaism he practiced (Lurianic Kabbalah), if Nathan was conscious of reality at all, including after he wrote the prophecy and looked back on it, the basic point about human nature remains

---

* Seeing things in vision or imagination was a peculiarity of that time and place, especially among those who divined for buried treasure, as Martin Harris, Joseph Smith, and others associated with the earliest Mormon movement did.

valid – people can tell what from their perspective is a minor distortion of the truth in order to convey what they believe is a much bigger and more important truth. Gershom Scholem explains:

> There is no way of telling whether he [Nathan] wrote these works in full consciousness as mystical pseudepigrapha, or in states of ecstasy wherein he felt himself to be the copyist rather than the author. There are many psychological stages of transition between downright forgery, and composition in a state of ecstasy or trance....But in the last analysis the problem of Nathan's mental states when writing is of no importance. The fact remains that the *Vision* [the prophecy above] is a literary forgery, though we may prefer to call it a "pseudepigraph" in order to avoid the moral opprobrium attached to the former term....The apocalypse [all of the writing on a scroll of which the prophecy above was only a part] is the product of Nathan's struggle with a messiah who refused the mission laid upon him by his prophet.[34]

Yet another example comes from a 1980s religious movement where a member was arrested and imprisoned for illegal weapons purchases directed by the church in preparation for the end times. One of the lead prophets of the church publicly denied, including to her own church members, any connection to the activities of the imprisoned church member. Years later, when that prophet left the movement and reflected back on her actions she said, "My truth-stretching seemed a small price to pay for saving the community."[35]

It is also worth noting that many people may never have asked the Twelve or the apostles to explain in detail their experiences of Jesus appearing to them. There is no evidence that Paul ever asked them to do so, let alone query them like a skeptic might. But there is also no reason that the Twelve and the apostles could not have responded honestly even if asked. They would have related any visions of Jesus they did have, or their hearing of Jesus talk to them, or just their feeling of Jesus' presence, along with their firm conviction that Jesus was the Messiah, was raised from the dead, and would be back very soon. Those who accepted these testimonies would have stayed in the movement, and those who did not would have left. The latter would have been people who tried to parse out the difference between seeing, hearing, and feeling the presence of Jesus, weren't bowled over by the personal authority of Christian leaders, and were not already convinced that Jesus was the Messiah and had been raised from the dead.

Being Jesus' brother, it would not be surprising if James was immediately given a leadership position in the new movement when he converted to Christianity sometime after Jesus' death. In this case, even the appearance attributed to him could have been an authority designation appearance tradition without him ever actually *seeing* Jesus.

There are two final things to say about the authority designation appearance traditions. First, the idea of authority designation appearance traditions is consistent with the fact that *all* leaders in the early church were said to have experienced an appearance by Jesus. Of course, an actual appearance by Jesus to all leaders in the early church would produce the same result, but it is worth noting that had even one early leader been left out, the authority designation hypothesis would not be possible.

Second, if you remove the appearance to the five hundred from Paul's list of appearances (1 Cor 15:6), it is interesting to note that every single appearance tradition is for a figure or group with authority, indicating a significant interest in authority by the early Christians. But is it reasonable to look at the appearance list this way, with the appearance to the five hundred removed? Highly respected evangelical New Testament scholar Richard Bauckham thinks so:

> It is possible that the summary Paul knew listed (as might be appropriate in a summary designed to assist evangelistic preaching) those appearances in which the recipients were commissioned to proclaim the Gospel, and that the appearance to the five hundred was added by Paul because of its usefulness for his purpose in 1 Corinthians 15 [1 Corinthians 15 was written approximately twenty years after Jesus' death]. The focus of verse 9 on Paul's own status as "the least of the apostles," by virtue of the anomalously late resurrection appearance to him, could lend some support to this view of a list predominantly, at least, of apostolic commissioning appearances.[36]

If the original list of appearances did not include the appearance to the five hundred, and the list was primarily intended to assist evangelistic preaching by designating those who had the authority to teach and preach (as suggested by Bauckham above), it does not follow that authority designations were the origin of the group appearance traditions, but where there is smoke there is sometimes plausibly fire.

The Appearance to Over Five Hundred People
1 Corinthians 15:6: "...he appeared to more than five hundred brothers and sisters at one time, most of whom are still alive, though some have died."

As mentioned by Bauckham above, the appearance to the five hundred may not have been part of the appearance list Paul received from early church leaders, but was an appearance tradition Paul added because it was useful for his purposes in 1 Corinthians 15 (one of which this book has argued was to prove Jesus' resurrection to the doubting Corinthians; see Chapter One). This is how this appearance tradition will be treated below; it was added by Paul because it was useful for his purposes in 1 Corinthians 15.

In trying to determine the origin of this appearance tradition, there is one glaring aspect of it that stands out. A simultaneous appearance to over five hundred people should have been one of the most, or the most, momentous appearances by Jesus, and yet it does not show up anywhere else in the historical record. As Gerd Ludemann says, "[It] is improbable that such an event witnessed by more than five hundred people should otherwise have left no trace."[37]

One possibility that would explain this peculiarity is if this appearance tradition is a fringe legend that Paul picked up from some small quarter of the Christian community and Paul believed it was true. The tradition itself may have begun as a collective spiritual experience in the early Christian community that was interpreted by some as an appearance and/or later grew into the legend of an appearance (with the number five hundred possibly growing at the same time). As Stephen Patterson says, "It is not inconceivable that an early Christian group might have interpreted an ecstatic worship experience as an appearance of the risen Jesus, however loosely this might be understood."[38] And as Bart Ehrman says, "Some of them [the appearances] were actual visions like Paul, others of them were stories of visions like the five hundred group of people who saw him."[39]

If Paul picked up this tradition from some small quarter of the Christian community well after Jesus' death, say, in the late 40s or early 50s, the additional comment that most of the five hundred "are still alive, though some have died" may have been part of the tradition when Paul received it. On the other hand, if Paul received this tradition earlier, Paul may simply be making a reasonable assumption when writing 1 Corinthians 15 (about twenty years after Jesus' death) that most of the five hundred were by that time still alive though some had died. In either case, Paul is including this information in order to convey to the Corinthians his belief that they could go check this tradition out if they wanted to.

There is also a second possibility for this appearance tradition. The stubborn absence of this tradition from the rest of the Christian origins literature leaves open the possibility that Paul the persuader, trying to prove Jesus' resurrection to a slipping congregation, is the one who, with good intentions, has turned an early collective spiritual experience into an appearance in order to bolster his case. In considering this possibility, consider these comments by Catholic scholar Raymond Brown about a different New Testament appearance tradition that he agrees may be fictitious:

> [Regarding] the raising of the holy ones and their *appearance to many* in Jerusalem (Matt 27:52-53 [the rising saints passage])....truth conveyed by drama can at times be more effectively impressed on people's minds than truth conveyed by history [emphasis added].[40]

Even evangelical scholar Michael Licona agrees with Brown that Matthew's tradition of the rising dead saints appearing to many people could be a story without any basis in history but is nevertheless intended to convey a truth:

> ...it seems to me that an understanding of the language in Matthew 27:52-53 as "special effects" with eschatological Jewish texts and thought in mind is most plausible....a poetic device added to communicate that the Son of God had died and that impending judgment awaited Israel.[41]

Paul may be doing a similar thing. His interest in leading a wayward congregation to believe what he genuinely feels is the truth about Jesus may have been more important than conveying accurate history, similar to what the early church leaders did two decades earlier with the appearance traditions to the Twelve and to all the apostles.

Paul's comment that most of the five hundred "are still alive, though some have died" is consistent with this possibility. In effect, Paul is daring the Corinthians to go check this tradition out for themselves. However, Paul's dare is at least a little disingenuous. It was over eight hundred miles from Corinth to Palestine and Paul had to know that it was unlikely that any of the Corinthians would actually pack up and travel that distance to check this tradition out. Even getting someone else already traveling in that direction to check this tradition out for them would have entailed a significant amount of effort on the part of the Corinthians and produced uncertain results, especially if the traveler was a non-Christian who would have thought their beliefs and request to interview people who supposedly saw a resurrected dead person were crazy.

A third possibility for the origin of the appearance to the five hundred is a combination of the two explanations above. Paul may have picked this appearance tradition up from the fringes of the Christian community and thought it questionable but decided to use it anyway to help bolster his case for Jesus' resurrection to the slipping Corinthian church.

It is unknown if other church leaders visited the Corinthians after Paul passed this tradition on to them. However, if they did, and if the Corinthians questioned them about it, the other church leaders may only have been able to respond that they did not know anything about it. But even if they knew this was a fringe legend, instead of telling this to a group that was notoriously skeptical of the resurrection, they may have just let it pass as a minor issue among more serious issues. It is also possible that they corrected Paul's report and the legend died right there, which would also explain why this tradition does not show up in any other records.

There is also a fourth explanation for the appearance to the five hundred if, instead of being a fringe legend, it was a well-known legend but for whatever reason does not show up in any other historical records. In this case, the appearance to the five hundred could have originated the same as suggested above – from a group ecstatic experience that was legendized into an appearance – but the pillars of the church were unable to correct it due to the legend taking on a life of its own within the early Christian community. Paul could have then picked this tradition up while he was persecuting the church and/or after his conversion, and once a Christian, assumed it was true. With Paul believing this tradition true and the pillars knowing it was false, all it would take for this tradition to show up in Paul's letter to the Corinthians twenty years later is for Paul and the pillars to have never talked about it. This does not seem so unlikely if Paul and the pillars were more interested in talking about things like theology, scriptures, the atonement, the kingdom of God, Gentiles, circumcision, collecting money, and other issues associated with running the church.

A fifth and final possibility for the appearance to the five hundred is the same as just outlined above except the legend could have grown in a location different from where the pillars were. The initial legend may have been something to the effect that Jesus appeared to many people. When word of this reached the pillars, they may have accepted it as true. When the pillars met with Paul for the first time, they may then have passed this appearance tradition on to Paul along with all of the other appearance traditions. Over the next twenty years, the number of people involved in the appearance tradition may have grown from "many" to "more than five hundred", and this is what Paul used in his letter to the Corinthians. In this case, the appearance tradition to over five hundred people could even have been part of what Paul "received" (1 Cor 15:3) from the early church leaders.

The Use of the Word "then" in the Appearance List

1 Corinthians 15:5-8: "...he appeared to Cephas [Peter], <u>then</u> to the twelve. <u>Then</u> he appeared to more than five hundred brothers and sisters at one time, most of whom are still alive, though some have died. <u>Then</u> he appeared to James, <u>then</u> to all the apostles. <u>Last of all</u>, as to someone untimely born, he appeared also to me."

The use of the word "then" in the 1 Corinthians 15:5-8 appearance list is best understood in the plain and simple chronological sense. If Peter had the first hallucination of Jesus, it makes sense that he would be listed first. If the leadership group known as "the Twelve" was designated with authority shortly after Peter's hallucination, it makes sense that they would be listed next. If the appearance to the five hundred is based on an early large group ecstatic experience that occurred shortly after the Twelve were designated as leaders (that Paul or some part of the Christian community then elevated to an "appearance"), it makes sense that it would be listed next. If James converted and was given a leadership position in the Christian movement sometime after the large group ecstatic experience (almost all scholars agree that James joined the movement late), it makes sense that he would be listed after the large group experience. If the group known as "the apostles" did not exist until after James converted and became a leader, it makes sense that they would be listed after James (even if some of their experiences were before James joined, assuming the reason for listing them was to designate them with authority, not to accurately report their appearances). And since Paul was the last of all the people above to experience a hallucination of Jesus, it makes sense that he would be listed "last of all".

It is also possible that the original list of appearances, if it did not include the appearance to the five hundred, was primarily a rank ordering list. The main point may have been that Peter was the leader of the Twelve ("he appeared to Peter, then to the twelve"), and James was the leader of all the apostles ("he appeared to James, then to all the apostles"). If rank ordering was intended in the original list of appearances, it further supports the idea that there was significant interest by early church leaders to designate with authority those who were best able to teach, preach, and defend their new beliefs, which would further support the possibility that authority designation could have been the origin of some of these appearance traditions.

Conclusion

In conclusion, it is plausible that the appearance traditions in 1 Corinthians 15:5-8 are a mix of hallucinations, collective ecstatic experiences, designations of authority, and legendary growth.

Chapter 5

Raised On the Third Day

1 Corinthians 15:4: "...he was raised *on the third day* in accordance with the scriptures..."

This is the last part of 1 Corinthians 15:3-7 that needs to be explained. According to many New Testament scholars, the Gospel accounts of Jesus predicting his resurrection on the third day after his death are not historical; they were put on his lips after his death as a form of legendary embellishment that Jesus knew all along exactly what was going to happen.[1] If true, and if there was no discovered empty tomb on the third day after Jesus' death, then what caused the third-day belief?

Some have proposed that the first vision of Jesus was on the third day after his death. However, this has the significant difficulty that the earliest tradition of Jesus' first appearance places it *later* than the third day, in Galilee (Mk 14:28; 16:7). Noting the creed's reference to "scriptures", others have proposed that instead of some *event* causing the third-day belief, the third-day belief originates from early Christian interaction with their Jewish scriptures. The most popular scriptural theories propose that the third-day belief originates from Hosea 6:2 or a Jewish sacred third-day tradition. Although both of these theories would fit well with the rest of this book, I think there is a more plausible answer. Because we are dealing with degrees of plausibility here, I will first outline for later comparison the difficulties with the Hosea 6:2 and Jewish sacred third-day theories. After that, I will present what I think is a more likely scriptural origin to the third-day belief.

The Difficulties with the
Hosea 6:2 and Sacred Third-day Theories

There are two difficulties with the idea that the third-day belief comes from Christian interaction with Hosea 6:2: "After two days he will revive us; on the third day he will raise us up, that we may live before him". First, for Hosea 6:2's phrase "on the third day" to have given birth to the third-day belief, there had to have been some other attraction to Hosea 6:2 because the phrase "on the third day" would not itself have been attractive with the third-day belief not yet born. Before the third-day belief was born, Hosea 6:2 would have in effect looked like this to Jesus' followers: "he will revive us;...he will raise us up, that we may live before him." Although Hosea 6:2 lends itself well to the idea of resurrection, it has an unavoidable group/nation focus ("revive *us*", "raise *us*") and therefore does not look like an attractive scriptural reference for those looking for scriptural confirmation of a raised *Messiah* (singular person). As William Craig points out, "[It] is very unlikely that the disciples should land upon Hosea 6.2 and apply it to Jesus' resurrection."[2] The second difficulty with Hosea 6:2 is that it is absent from the Christian literature until the beginning of the third century (Tertullian, Adversus Judaeos 13:23), and there is no claim anywhere of its earlier Christian use. The eventual Christian use of Hosea 6:2 despite its group/nation focus looks more like a product of the continuing Christian process of laying claim to as much Old Testament scripture as possible rather than because Hosea 6:2 was the origin of the third-day belief (*after* the third-day belief was born, Hosea 6:2 would have looked somewhat attractive to Christians).

The sacred third-day theory proposes that the third-day belief originates from approximately two dozen third-day related passages in the Old Testament and/or a Jewish sacred third-day tradition that was by the first century formed from those passages, such a tradition being attested to in third-century and later Jewish literature.[3] There are three difficulties with this theory.

First, if the influence of so many OT third-day scriptures or a formed sacred third-day tradition was strong enough to cause Christians to simply *assume* its application to Jesus' resurrection, it is odd that there is hardly any interest in the third day's *scriptural* significance outside of the 1 Corinthians 15:4 creed. In the entire New Testament, there is only one other general reference to the scriptural aspect of the third day (Lk 18:31-33), and only one specific OT scripture cited (Jon 1:17 in Mt 12:40). Hosea 6:2, probably the single most relevant scripture in the third-century attested Jewish sacred third-day tradition, does not appear in the Christian literature until the beginning of the third century (as already mentioned above). Another critical component of the third-century attested Jewish sacred third-day tradition, the third-day aspect of the near sacrifice of Isaac (Gen 22:4), is also not mentioned in the Christian literature, even at those points in the Christian literature that are speaking about Isaac (Rom 8:32; Heb 11:17-19; Jas 2:21-23). As William Craig correctly points out, "The appeal to the offering of Isaac as evidence that the New Testament knows of the rabbinic exegesis concerning the theological significance of the third day is counter-productive."[4] In sum, the first difficulty with the sacred third-day theory is that the New Testament's *level of interest* in the scriptural aspect of the third day does not match an origin where the third day had been elevated to a sacred or near sacred level. A scriptural solution that makes sense of the third day's inclusion in a creed of core beliefs (1 Cor 15:3-4) but the lack of scriptural interest elsewhere in the Christian literature would be more persuasive.

The second difficulty with the sacred third-day theory is similar to the first. If the influence of so many OT third-day scriptures, or a formed sacred third-day tradition, was strong enough to cause Christians to simply assume its application to Jesus' resurrection, it is odd that similar assumed applications of the third-day theme do not appear in *Jewish* literature before the third century. This gives the impression that an elevated third-day tradition did not exist in Jewish thought until the third century. As William Craig notes:

> Lehmann believes that these citations [from third-century Jewish literature] embody traditions that go back orally prior to the Christian era. But if that is the case then should not we expect to confront these motifs in Jewish literature contemporaneous with the New Testament times, namely, the Apocrypha and

Pseudepigrapha? One would especially expect to confront the third day motif in the apocalyptic works. In fact, it is conspicuously absent. The book of I Enoch, which is quoted in Jude, had more influence on the New Testament writers than any other apocryphal or pseudepigraphic work and is a valuable source of information concerning Judaism from 200 BC to AD 100. In this work the eschatological resurrection is associated with the number seven, not three (91. 15-16; 93). Similarly in 4 Ezra, a first century compilation, the eschatological resurrection takes place after seven days (7. 26-44). A related work from the second half of the first century and a good representative of Jewish thought contemporaneous with the New Testament, 2 Baruch gives no indication of the day of the resurrection at history's end (50-5 1). Neither does 2 Macc 7. 9- 42; 12. 43-45 or the Testament of the Twelve Patriarchs (Judah) 25. 1, 4; (Zebulun) 10. 2; (Benjamin) 10. 6-18. All these works, which stem from intertestamental or New Testament times, have a doctrine of eschatological resurrection, but not one of them knows of the third day motif. Evidently the number seven was thought to have greater divine import than the number three (cf. Rev 1. 20; 6. 1; 8. 2; 15. 1, 7). In 2 Macc 5. 14; 11. 18 we find 'three days' and 'third day' mentioned in another context, but their meaning is wholly non-theological, indicating only 'a short time' or 'the day after tomorrow'. Lehmann's case would be on firmer ground if he were able to find passages in Jewish literature contemporary with the New Testament which employ the third day motif or associate the resurrection with the third day. It appears that this interpretation is a peculiarity of later rabbinical exegesis of the Talmudic period.[5]

Some may point to events in the OT that happened on the third day as evidence of an elevated third day in Jewish thought well before and in the first century. However, on closer analysis, there does not seem to be any favoritism toward the third day in the OT. The results of a simple phrase search in the OT yields the following number of hits for each phrase: "First Day" (64), "Second Day" (32), "Third Day" (13), "Fourth Day" (14), "Fifth Day" (16), "Sixth Day" (10), "Seventh Day" (66), "Eighth Day" (20), "Ninth Day" (12), "Tenth Day" (20). If anything, the first day or seventh day (at five times the frequency) should have been the sacred day that the Christians adopted. For those who suggest the third day passages in the OT involved events that were more significant than those of other days, a few "first day" passages serve to show that this is not the case. God created light and dark on the first day (Gen 1:5). After Noah's flood, it was on the first day of the month that the mountain tops were seen (Gen 8:5). On the first day of Passover, hold a sacred assembly (Ex 12:16; Lev 23:7, 35; Num 28:18). On the first day of the month, Moses proclaimed to the Israelites all that the Lord had commanded him (Deut 1:3). It was on the first day that Daniel set his mind to humble himself before God that God listened to him and answered him (Dan 10:12). Why didn't the Christians assume that Jesus was raised on the first day in accordance with the scriptures instead of on the third day?

The third problem with the sacred third-day theory is that it requires the "when" of Jesus' resurrection to have been so important to the earliest Christians that they simply *assumed* a sacred-day tradition applied to it. But such an emphasis on *when* Jesus resurrected seems unwarranted; why not just leave that minor detail unanswered? A solution in which the Christians were unintentionally led to the third-day belief, instead of just assuming it, would be more persuasive.

Introduction to the Psalm 16:10 Theory

With the difficulties of the above two theories noted for later comparison, it will now be argued that the third-day belief more likely comes from early Christian interaction with the Greek or Aramaic form of Psalm 16:10: "For you will not abandon my soul to Hades, or let your Holy One experience *diaphthora*." In Aramaic, the last key word is *byt shwt*. Both the Greek and Aramaic forms of this passage will be discussed in detail later.

A Psalm 16:10 derived third-day belief has been briefly considered before but dismissed for reasons that are not very persuasive. Douglas Hill considered it a live possibility in 1967 except for its incompatibility with his view that the early resurrection belief was only "spiritual" in nature. [6] This incompatibility is not a problem in this book since it is presupposed that the earliest resurrection belief was *bodily* in nature. Hill appears to be the last to consider Psalm 16:10; he is

115

simply footnoted by Gordon Fee in 1987 and again by Anthony Thiselton in 2000.[7] Before Hill, Bruce Metzger in 1957 also briefly considered Psalm 16:10 as a possible origin to the third-day belief. He affirmed a bodily resurrection belief and an implicit three-day timeline in Psalm 16:10. However, his difficulty was with the transition from Psalm 16:10's *by* the third day timeline (to be discussed later) to the *on* the third day timeline that appears in the early creed.[8] I will attempt to show that this is not so big of a hurdle.

Before continuing, it is worth noting that this chapter is by far the most drawn out and detailed in this book. Because of this, some may wish to skip to the conclusion of this chapter where there is a very succinct summary of the Psalm 16:10 theory, and then decide whether to read through every detail.

The Nature of the Earliest
Third-Day Belief, Literal or Symbolic?

Before presenting the Psalm 16:10 theory, it is important to note that it is dependent on the conclusion that the third-day belief was understood by the earliest Christians in *literal* chronological terms, that is, Jesus' followers believed he was raised *on the third day* in the plainly understood sense. All of traditional scholarship and some of non-traditional scholarship agrees with this. However, some think this unlikely in light of the following expressions of resurrection timeline in the Gospels.

Mark, Matthew, and Luke narrate the crucifixion of Jesus to have been on Friday afternoon with a Sunday morning discovered empty tomb, a timeline of resurrection that is *on* the third day (Jews measured days from sunset to sunset and counted any part of a day as one day[9]). Also consistent with an *on* the third day timeline are Matthew's and Luke's phrases "*on* the third day", and "*the* third day" (Mt 16:21; 17:23; 20:19; 27:64; Lk 9:22; 18:33; 24:7, Acts 10:40). But a fourth-day resurrection is suggested in Mark's and Matthew's use of the phrase "after three days" (Mk 8:31; 9:31; 10:34; Mt 27:63). A fourth-day resurrection is also suggested in the "three nights" of Jonah 1:17 which Matthew cites as a scriptural sign of Jesus' resurrection: "For just as Jonah was three days and three nights in the belly of the sea monster, so for

116

three days and three nights the Son of Man will be in the heart of the earth" (Mt 12:40). A fourth day resurrection is again suggested in the Gospel of John and the non-canonical Gospel of Peter. In each, the resurrection remains on Sunday but instead of having the crucifixion *after* the Passover Seder meal as in the synoptics (Mk 14:12; Mt 26:17-19; Lk 22:7), they have Jesus crucified *before* the Passover Seder meal (Jn 18:28; 19:14; GPeter 2:5), suggesting a Thursday crucifixion. This same fourth-day timeline may also be suggested by Paul: "For our paschal lamb, Christ, has been sacrificed" (1 Cor 5:7; the paschal lamb being sacrificed in the afternoon *before* the Passover Seder meal). Further adding to the confusion, the guards in the Gospel of Peter, who witness the supposed fourth-day resurrection in that gospel, were only supposed to guard the tomb "for three days" (GPeter 8:3). To finish off, there is the ambiguous phrase "in three days" in several Gospels, which could be taken as referring to a third-day or fourth-day chronology (Mk 14:58; 15:29; Mt 26:61; 27:40; Jn 2:19, 20).

One could conclude from the different expressions of chronology above that both a literal third-day and a literal fourth-day tradition existed, with the literal third-day tradition reflected in 1 Corinthians 15:4. But one could also conclude from these expressions that their authors (or later scribes) were not concerned with precise chronology because they did not think of the third day literally. This in turn can suggest that the third-day belief was *never* intended literally.[10]

However, a consistent *on* the third day timeline in all of the literary evidence above is not as far-fetched as some might think. There are three difficulties that must be overcome in order to conclude a consistent *on* the third day timeline in all of the Christian literature – John's and GPeter's (and possibly Paul's) placement of the crucifixion before instead of after the Passover Seder, Mark's and Matthew's use of the phrase "after three days", and Matthew's use of Jonah 1:17. These will be covered in order.

Because the Gospel of John and the Gospel of Peter place Jesus' crucifixion before the Passover Seder meal instead of after the Passover Seder meal (as in the synoptics), one can easily conclude that John and Peter intend that the crucifixion occurred on Thursday with a fourth day resurrection on Sunday, and the synoptics intend that the crucifixion occurred on Friday with a third day resurrection on Sunday. However, there is another obvious possibility that is easily missed. Instead of the day of the week (e.g., Monday through Friday) that the crucifixion occurred on being moved by one day in one of these traditions, *the day of the week that the Passover meal occurred on* may have been moved by one day in one of these traditions (the day of the week that the Passover meal falls on varies year to year based on when the new moon is spotted). This is argued powerfully by John A.T. Robinson and Raymond E. Brown who conclude that John and GPeter (and Paul) preserve the historically correct tradition of a Friday night Passover meal, and the Synoptists or their tradition have simply moved the Passover meal to Thursday night.[11] If correct, every Christian narrative has a consistent Friday afternoon crucifixion with a Sunday morning discovered empty tomb, a timeline of resurrection that is *on* the third day. Note too that this now makes sense of the Gospel of Peter's guarding of the tomb "for three days" (GPeter 8:1-3).

It is worth noting here that some see a Thursday crucifixion with a fourth day resurrection on Sunday morning in Matthew's use of the plural *sabbatwn* in Matthew 28:1: "After the *sabbatwn*, as the first day of the week was dawning, Mary Magdalene and the other Mary went to see the tomb." James Tabor translates *sabbatwn* here as "After the *Sabbaths*" and concludes that Matthew is trying to convey that Jesus was crucified on Thursday and resurrected after the Passover Sabbath on Friday and the normal Sabbath on Saturday.[12] However, both Strong's and the Arndt & Gingrich (1957) Greek-English Lexicon indicate that *sabbatwn* can mean simply "week". In this case Matthew 28:1 reads "After the week" which of course is "After the Sabbath" since the Sabbath is the last day of the week, which is exactly how it is translated in the NRSV Bible. In fact, Matthew uses *sabbatwn* in exactly the same way in the next part of the same verse: "as the first day of the week [*sabbatwn*] was dawning". Translating this as "Sabbaths" instead of as "week" does not make any sense. Other uses of *sabbatwn* also suggest that "week" is the correct translation in Matthew 28:1 (see Mk 16:2; Lk 24:1; Jn 20:1, 19; Acts 20:7). If correct, then Matthew intends that the tomb was discovered empty after only one Sabbath, not two, and therefore *on* the third day.

Regarding Mark's and Matthew's phrase "after three days", this phrase could mean *on* the third day in light of Jewish inclusive time reckoning. Since *any part* of a day was counted as a day, and days were counted from sunset to sunset, a Friday afternoon death with a resurrection, say, three hours after sunset on Saturday, would still be "after" three days. Day one would be from Friday afternoon to Friday sunset. Day two would be from Friday sunset to Saturday sunset. Day three would be from Saturday sunset to three hours after Saturday sunset. We see this use of inclusive time reckoning in the OT, where being put in prison "for three days" was the same as being released *on* the third day (Gen 42:17, 18-25).[13] Although it would be circular to use an example from the Gospels to make this same point, the close proximity and apparent interest in temporal time of two phrases there may nevertheless prove to be another good example. In Matthew, the prediction that Jesus would rise "after three days" (Mt 27:63) is equated with the need to guard the tomb "*until* the third day" (Mt 27:64). But if "after three days" meant after the very end of the third day, they would need to guard the tomb until the *fourth* day.

This leads us to Matthew's use of Jonah 1:17: "For just as Jonah was three days and three nights in the belly of the sea monster, so for three days and three nights the Son of Man will be in the heart of the earth" (Mt 12:40). Although there is no way a literal "three nights" can fit into the *on* the third day chronology suggested above, it is curious that this most difficult to reconcile of the chronologies is also the only instance of the three-day chronology appearing in a scriptural reference. Because of this, there are four reasons to conclude that Matthew is here using Jonah 1:17 as an *imprecise* scriptural allusion for an *on* the third day timeline.

Significant parts of this first reason have already been discussed in Chapter One and have been alluded to in the discussion above about Mark's and Matthew's use of the phrase "after three days". They will be repeated here for clarity.

There is a trend in the Gospels that Jesus' future resurrection is never *publicly* revealed during his ministry (he only reveals it in private to his disciples). The one exception to this is Matthew's Jonah 1:17 sign, and it is aimed directly at the "scribes and Pharisees" (Mt 12:38). Note too that Matthew is also the only Gospel to post guards at the tomb, regarded by many scholars as an apologetic response to the charge of a stolen body.* Matthew posts the guards in his story by having the chief priests and Pharisees ask Pilate to guard the tomb:

> ...the chief priests and the Pharisees gathered before Pilate and said, "Sir, we remember *what that impostor said* while he was still alive, 'After three days I will rise again.' Therefore command that the tomb be made secure until the third day; otherwise his disciples may go and steal him away, and tell the people, 'He has been raised from the dead', and the last deception would be worse than the first." (Mt 27:62-64)

How did the chief priests and Pharisees in Matthew's account know that the tomb needed guarding? It appears as if they got the idea from the Jonah 1:17 announcement. As C.H. Giblin says:

> In [Matthew] 27.63, when the Pharisees recall what Jesus said while he was still living, they must be referring principally to what was told them in [Matthew] 12.40. For [Matthew] 12.40 is the only place where a burial-prediction, able to be construed as a resurrection-prediction was made to them or even stated publicly.[14]

If Matthew intends that the Jonah 1:17 announcement was where the Jewish authorities got the idea that they needed to guard the tomb, look at how long they say it should be guarded – "*until* the third day" (Mt 27:64). This gives the impression that Jonah 1:17 is being *interpreted* in Matthew's Gospel as referring to resurrection *on* the third day; otherwise they would have had to guard the tomb until the fourth day.

---

* Of course the Gospel of Peter too has the tomb guarded, but since we are missing much of that gospel, it is impossible to know if it also publicly revealed Jesus' future resurrection like Matthew's Gospel did; therefore, GPeter is left out of this comparison.

The second reason to conclude that Matthew is using Jonah 1:17 as an imprecise scriptural allusion for an *on the third day* timeline is that it is doubtful that Matthew intended his Jonah 1:17 sign to be taken in isolation from the rest of his Gospel. He may have considered it obvious to his audience that he was using Jonah 1:17 in an imprecise way to refer to the *on* the third day chronology expressed in the rest of his Gospel, especially the narrated Friday afternoon crucifixion and Sunday morning resurrection.

Third, an imprecise use of scripture would not be out of character for Matthew compared to his other inexact uses of OT scripture. For example, Matthew uses Isaiah 7:14 in Matthew 1:22-23 to refer to a virgin *conception* for someone in *his century*, as opposed to a virgin who *eight centuries earlier* married and then conceived *normally*.

Lastly, given the scriptural choices available to him, Jonah 1:17 may have been the best Matthew could do for a Messiah raised on the third day. This is not as far-fetched as some might think when one looks for alternative scriptures Matthew could have used or looks closely at what might appear to be the most obvious alternative, Hosea 6:2 ("After two days he will revive us; on the third day he will raise us up, that we may live before him"). If Hosea 6:2 was not the *cause* of the third-day belief, it would not have had any advantage over Jonah 1:17 in terms of familiarity to Matthew or his audience. With this in mind, put yourself in Mathew's shoes (or the shoes of the legendary process that created the Jonah 1:17 prediction) and consider Hosea 6:2 and Jonah 1:17 side by side. Although Hosea 6:2 has a perfect "on the third day" timeline, and it lends itself very well to resurrection, its previously mentioned group/nation focus does not lend itself very well to the singular person focus of a Messiah. In contrast, Jonah 1:17 – "Jonah was in the belly of the fish for three days and three nights" – although it has an imperfect third-day expression, it has a good *singular person* focus, and its captivity/release from the sea creature easily lends itself as an analogy to captivity/release from the earth, i.e. resurrection (which Matthew capitalizes on). One scholar has even presented a full exegetical explanation for why the sea monster in Jonah 1:17 would have been a powerful symbol of the grave to Matthew and his audience.[15] It is impossible to get into Matthew's head, and it would be inappropriate to call Jonah 1:17 a "good" scriptural sign of a Messiah raised *on* the third day, but the fact is that Hosea 6:2, due to its difficult connection to a single person, does not look any better. If Matthew had an *on* the third day timeline in mind, his choice of Jonah 1:17 over Hosea 6:2 is not so unusual. (Why Matthew would choose Jonah 1:17 over Psalm 16:10 will be addressed later.)

A final thing that counts against a symbolic third day intended in the Christian literature is that virtually all of the expressions of Jesus' resurrection chronology refer to a specific number of days. There are almost no phrases speaking of a short or vague period of time, and there does not seem to have been a shortage of such expressions nor a hesitancy to use them in other places, as the following examples show. "A *little later* someone else said..." (Lk 22:58). "For a *short time*, we were made orphans" (1 Th 2:17). "I will be with you a *little while* longer" (Jn 7:33). "The God of peace will *shortly* crush Satan" (Rom 16:20). "I will come to you *soon*, if the Lord wills" (1 Cor 4:19). Other examples can be found in Matthew 26:73; John 12:35; 13:33; 14:19; Acts 18:23; 25:4; Philippians 2:19, 24; 1 Timothy 3:14; 2 Timothy 4:9; Hebrews 10:37; 13:23; 2 Peter 1:14; 3 John 1:14; Revelation 1:1; 22:6. There is only one instance where a short period of time expression is used to refer to Jesus' resurrection (assuming it is not instead referring to Jesus' second coming): "A little while, and you will no longer see me, and again a *little while*, and you will see me" (repeated three times in John 16:16-19).

As Edward Bode concludes, "Several variant phrasings are used to express the third-day motif, but nothing demands that these expressions should not be understood as equivalent."[16] If correct, then one cannot claim inconsistency of resurrection chronology in the Christian literature as an indicator that the third-day belief was not understood literally. Furthermore, even if there were some non-literal understandings of the third-day, or even the existence of a literal fourth-day tradition, it is still entirely plausible that the earliest Christian tradition in 1 Corinthians 15:4 was that Jesus was raised on a *literal* third day.

**Plausibly Placing the Christian
Use of Psalm 16:10 in the Early 30s C.E.**

Before showing how the third-day belief was derived from
Psalm 16:10, it is first necessary to show that it is plausible that the
very earliest Christians were interacting with Psalm 16:10. Like the
third-century attested Christian use of Hosea 6:2 and the third-
century attested Jewish sacred third-day tradition, the Christian use
of Psalm 16:10 is faced with the significant difficulty of late
attestation, in this case in Acts (2:27; 13:35). It is worth noting
however that Acts is an earlier attestation by a significant margin,
dated anywhere from 60 to 125 C.E. It is worth noting too that Acts
specifically claims Psalm 16:10 was used by the earliest Christians
as a raised Messiah prophecy almost immediately after Jesus'
crucifixion (Acts 2:1-27 has Peter citing Psalm 16:10 at Pentecost).
Although an unreliable claim, it is more than can be said of Hosea
6:2 or the sacred third-day tradition, neither of which are claimed
anywhere to have been in Christian use earlier than the third
century. Suppose for the moment that Psalm 16:10 was used by the
earliest Christians. Below is an attempt to identify why Psalm
16:10 does not appear in the synoptic Gospels or the Pauline
epistles, even though those authors may have known of its
Christian use.

Tracking the use of Psalm 110:1 in the synoptic Gospels is
useful for shedding light on why Psalm 16:10 is not used in the
synoptic Gospels. Psalm 110:1 is useful for this because it is
located right next to Psalm 16:10 in Acts and it too is used in Acts
as a resurrection prophecy (and an exaltation prophecy). From Acts
(with Psalm 110:1 underlined):

> This Jesus God raised up, and of that all of us are witnesses.
> Being therefore exalted at the right hand of God, and having
> received from the Father the promise of the Holy Spirit, he has
> poured out this that you both see and hear. For David did not
> ascend into the heavens, but he himself says, "The Lord said to
> my Lord, 'Sit at my right hand, until I make your enemies your
> footstool.'" Therefore let the entire house of Israel know with
> certainty that God has made him both Lord and Messiah, this
> Jesus whom you crucified. (Acts 2:32-36)

In stark contrast to Psalm 16:10, which does not appear in any of the Gospels, Psalm 110:1 appears in Mark (12:35-37), Matthew (22:41-45), and Luke (20:41-44). And yet at that point where each Gospel uses Psalm 110:1, its resurrection aspect is *not* highlighted:

> [Jesus is publicly speaking in this scene:] How can the scribes say that the Messiah is the son of David? David himself, by the Holy Spirit, declared, "The Lord said to my Lord, 'Sit at my right hand, until I put your enemies under your feet.'" David himself calls him Lord; so how can he be his son? (Mk 12:35-37; Mark also being representative of Matthew and Luke)

Whatever the reason the synoptics do not highlight the resurrection aspect of Psalm 110:1, that could be the same reason Psalm 16:10 is not mentioned at all. The reason may be connected to the previously mentioned point that Jesus' future resurrection is never publicly revealed (with the exception of Matthew's use of Jonah 1:17 to post guards at the tomb).

The use of Psalm 110:1 can also be tracked and compared to the use of Psalm 16:10 in the Pauline epistles. There, Psalm 110:1 is used only once, in 1 Corinthians 15:23-28. But instead of using Psalm 110:1 to speak of Jesus' resurrection, Paul only uses it to speak of events that will occur when Jesus *returns* – he will put all of his enemies, including death, "under his feet" (this phrase presumably coming from Psalm 110:1), at which time the general resurrection will occur. For whatever reason Paul refers to Psalm 110:1 only once in all of his epistles, and for whatever reason Paul does not highlight Jesus' resurrection when he does refer to Psalm 110:1, that could be the same reason Paul does not mention Psalm 16:10 in any of his epistles.

Trying to get into Paul's head, note in 1 Corinthian 15, the only place in all of his epistles where Paul defends Jesus' resurrection, that he cites the primitive creed which itself asserts that Jesus was raised "in accordance with the scriptures" (1 Cor 15:4). It is hard to believe that Paul would not have included a specific scriptural citation for Jesus' resurrection in 1 Corinthian 15 if he had wanted to, given his expertise at citing scripture and that he cites specific scripture on other topics throughout 1 Corinthians (1:19, 31; 2:9, 16; 3:19, 20; 6:16; 9:9; 10:7, 26; 14:21; 15:27, 32, 54, 55). It may therefore be the case that Paul's recitation of the widely known creed (1 Cor 15:4) fulfilled any inclination he had to support Jesus' resurrection with scriptural authority. This would explain Paul's silence on the resurrection aspect of Psalm 110:1 and on Psalm 16:10 even if he had known of the Christian use of Psalm 16:10.

If the above analysis cracks the door open slightly to a possible very early Christian use of Psalm 16:10 despite its late attestation, there is one other thing that might open the door all the way. After the belief was born that Jesus was bodily raised, if there was an urge to confirm or reinforce this core belief in scriptures, then those who searched the Jewish scriptures, either by reading or remembering, would naturally have been attracted to those scriptures that most specifically and powerfully supported their raised Messiah belief. In fact, it would be incredible if there was not an immediate and powerful urge to confirm such a belief in scripture. As I hope to show in detail in the next section, Psalm 16:10 is a *very* attractive scripture to support such a belief. Modern Christians agree, Psalm 16:10 is always at or near the top of any list of resurrected Messiah prophecies. And we know of course that Luke found it attractive when he wrote Acts. As will be shown in the next section, the power of Psalm 16:10 lies in the ease with which its poetic language lends itself to a resurrection interpretation, its focus on a single person, and its (believed) King David authorship which has the obvious available connection to his descendant Messiah for those with the desire to make such a connection. If the earliest Christians were looking for a bodily raised Messiah in their scriptures, and if I can show in the next section that Psalm 16:10 lends itself very well to a bodily raised Messiah interpretation, then all the earliest Christians had to do was find Psalm 16:10 or remember it and they most certainly would have used it. In this case, Acts 2 may preserve an authentic memory of very early Christian use of Psalm 16:10, even if Peter's speech there was embellished or otherwise invented.

Psalm 16:10 as a Raised Messiah Prophecy

Below is Psalm 16:10 with the last key word in Hebrew, Greek, and Aramaic, emphasized. Following the different versions of Psalm 16:10 is the Christian interpretation of Psalm 16:10 from Acts.

Hebrew: "For you do not give me up to Sheol, or let your faithful one see the *Pit* [*tjv*]."

Greek: "For you will not abandon my soul to Hades, or let your Holy One experience *corruption* [*diaphthora*]." [17]

Aramaic: "For you do not abandon my soul to Sheol, or hand over your righteous one to see the *house of the Pit* [*byt shwt*]." [18]

Acts, written in Greek and using the Greek form of Psalm 16:10 above, interprets Psalm 16:10 this way (Psalm 16:10 and then its interpretation are underlined):

> David says…"For you will not abandon my soul to Hades, or let your Holy One experience corruption"….Fellow Israelites, I may say to you confidently of our ancestor David that he both died and was buried, and his tomb is with us to this day. Since he was a prophet, he knew that God had sworn with an oath to him that he would put one of his descendants on his throne. Foreseeing this, David spoke of the resurrection of the Messiah, saying, "He was not abandoned to Hades, nor did his flesh experience corruption." (Acts 2:25-31)

Traditionalists think Psalm 16:10 is a genuine prophecy of Jesus' resurrection. However, it will be shown below that the language of Psalm 16:10 can be totally accounted for in terms of the original psalmist's expectations for himself. After showing this, it will be shown why its language so easily lends itself to a raised

Messiah interpretation. After these things are established, then we can look at Psalm 16:10's connection to the third-day belief.

The first indication that the psalmist is referring to himself in Psalm 16:10 is that he refers to himself over twenty times in Psalm 16:1-9 and then clearly refers to himself again in the first part of verse 10 (the last sentence below):

> Protect *me*, O God, for in you *I* take refuge. *I* say to the Lord, 'You are *my* Lord; *I* have no good apart from you.' As for the holy ones in the land, they are the noble, in whom is all *my* delight. Those who choose another god multiply their sorrows; their drink-offerings of blood *I* will not pour out or take their names upon *my* lips. The Lord is *my* chosen portion and *my* cup; you hold *my* lot. The boundary lines have fallen for *me* in pleasant places; *I* have a goodly heritage. *I* bless the Lord who gives *me* counsel; in the night also *my* heart instructs *me*. *I* keep the Lord always before *me*; because he is at *my* right hand, *I* shall not be moved. Therefore *my* heart is glad, and *my* soul rejoices; *my* body also rests secure. For you do not give _me_ up to Sheol, or let your faithful one see the Pit. (Ps 16:1-10)

In the second half of Psalm 16:10 (Ps 16:10b), "faithful one" (or "Holy One" or "righteous one" in other English translations) not only would have been a normal title for a psalmist who thought highly of himself, but its linguistic parallel with the self reference in 16:10a indicates that the two are the same person. Making it impossible even on theological grounds to separate the elevated title in 16:10b from the self reference in 16:10a is that the previously presented Christian interpretation in Acts interprets *both* to refer to the same person. Therefore, there is a message in Psalm 16:10 that the psalmist is directing squarely at himself. What was that message?

There is often controversy about the meaning of the last word in Psalm 16:10, which in Hebrew is *tjv*, translated in the LXX (the Greek translation of the Hebrew Scriptures) as *diaphthora*, which in turn is usually translated into English as "corruption" (or even "decay"). The controversy centers on whether "corruption" (or "decay") is a correct English translation of *diaphthora*, and whether it is in any way representative of the original Hebrew.

Adding to the problem, yet another translation of the word *diaphthora* is offered by other scholars. According to Richard Carrier:

> Psalms 16:10 says the holy one will not enter the realm of the dead....[The] word often translated as "decay" or "corruption" is not the word that actually means those things (*phthora*) but *diaphthora*, which means thorough *destruction*....Psalms 16:10 plainly speaks of the holy one *not dying* (and not ceasing to exist).[19]

However, no matter what the originally intended meaning of the last key word in Psalm 16:10 in Hebrew or Greek (or Aramaic), the full range of meanings can be totally accounted for as applying to the psalmist himself. The psalmist is simply making a poetic expression of confidence that he will avoid death, either temporarily in some present difficult situation, or as the late Mitchell Dahood concluded (based on an analysis of Ugaritic and cognate literature), forever: "The psalmist firmly believes that he will be granted the same privilege accorded Enoch and Elijah; he is convinced that God will assume him to himself, without [ever] suffering the pains of death."[20]

Some have objected to Dahood's conclusion on the basis of Psalm 39:13: "[O Lord] turn your gaze away from me, that I may smile again, before I depart and am no more." Since this psalm expresses resignation to death, it is reasoned that the hope of bodily assumption could not possibly have been intended in Psalm 16:10.[21] However, not only does this assume the same author for both psalms, which may be incorrect, but it also assumes that a single person's fears, doubts, and ideas about death never change, an assumption in conflict with human nature.

The psalmist's expectation to avoid death, whether temporarily or permanently, is consistent with the last key word in Psalm 16:10 meaning anything from the physical "Pit" that one is buried in, to Richard Carrier's "destruction" of personhood, to the NRSV's "corruption" translation, or even a "decay" translation. The last two possibilities are especially consistent with Dahood's analysis.

Further indicating that Psalm 16:10 is simply a poetic expression of confidence by the psalmist to avoid death is the existence of virtually identical poetic language in reference to death in Psalm 30:2-3 by someone who was very sick and apparently resuscitated from the edge of death: "O Lord my God, I cried to you for help, and you have healed me. O Lord, you brought up my soul from Sheol, restored me to life from among those gone down to the Pit." What this psalmist was rescued from, the psalmist of Psalm 16:10 wants to avoid.

Even though the language of Psalm 16:10 can be totally accounted for in terms of the psalmist's expectations to avoid death, its language very easily lends itself to be reinterpreted in favor of a raised Messiah. The genealogical connection to the believed author of Psalm 16:10, King David, would have made it easy to conclude that Psalm 16:10 was speaking in code about David's descendant Messiah.

Regarding the interpretation of resurrection, consider that key word *diaphthora* in the LXX first. In light of the fact that Jesus indisputably experienced death, it would hardly have been a leap of the interpretive imagination for those looking for a bodily raised Messiah to conclude from even the most neutral translation of this word – "destruction" – that Psalm 16:10 was speaking of *flesh* that did not experience "destruction". A third-century midrash on Ps 16:10 shows the same interpretive possibility about the flesh being extracted *even from the Hebrew*: "...this verse [Ps 16:10] proves that neither corruption nor worms had the power over David's flesh....In the grave his flesh will not dissolve like the dust."[22] Given that the LXX, as in almost any translation, is "a witness to the process of transmitting tradition,"[23] and given the above Hebrew midrash on Psalm 16:10, it is reasonable to conclude that the same interpretation about decay of the flesh could be extracted from the LXX or an Aramaic form of Psalm 16:10 if that is all Jesus' earliest followers spoke.

But let's go deeper into this interpretation. Unlike the midrash above, the earliest Christians were looking for a *raised* Messiah, not a *preserved* Messiah. In this case, they would have taken Psalm 16:10b as referring to Jesus being bodily raised by God *before* his flesh *could* decay. Resurrection as an act of *rescue before decay* is implicit in the Christian use of Psalm 16:10 that shows up in Acts 13:34-37:

> As to *raising* him from the dead... [David said,] "You will not let your Holy One experience corruption." For David, after he had served the purpose of God in his own generation, died, was laid beside his ancestors, and experienced corruption; but he whom God raised up experienced no corruption.

For clarification, note here that the author of Acts is not using Psalm 16:10 to say that Jesus' body was incapable of or was protected from decay; he is using Psalm 16:10 to say that Jesus was *raised*. The *only* way to get resurrection out of Psalm 16:10 is *rescue before decay.*

Some might consider the absence of an explicit third-day reference in the above Acts passage (and in Acts 2) as an indicator that the third-day belief did not come from Psalm 16:10. However, Luke, and the earliest Christians who thought of Psalm 16:10 as a raised Messiah prophecy, *must* have had some *raised before decay time period* in mind. Luke of course believes there was a discovered empty tomb on the third day after Jesus' death (Lk 24:1-3) and that Jesus predicted he would rise on the third day (Lk 9:22; 18:33; 24:7; Acts 10:40) and so he simply views the third day as *fitting within* Psalm 16:10's before decay time period. But what Luke thinks is the origin of the third-day belief is not the question here. If the discovered empty tomb and Jesus' predictions are legends, and the third-day belief originated in scripture before that, the question is: Did that scriptural origin produce a third-day belief that just happened to fit within Psalm 16:10's before decay time window, or did Psalm 16:10's before decay time window produce the third-day belief? I hope to show it is the latter.

If the earliest Christians interpreted Psalm 16:10b as referring to a raised Messiah, how did they interpret Psalm 16:10a: "For you will not abandon my soul to Hades [or Sheol]"? The language used in this verse can be understood in one of two ways, both of which can be interpreted in favor of resurrection. According to Greg Herrick, one way to understand the intent behind this verse is that the soul was not *left in* Hades.[24] The second way to understand the intent behind this verse is that the soul did not *go to* Hades (this is the sense of the NRSV translation). It is obvious how the first can be interpreted in favor of resurrection. How the second can be interpreted in favor of resurrection will be more clearly outlined in the next section.

In summary, if the earliest Christians were looking for a raised Messiah in their scriptures, and they found or remembered Psalm 16:10, it would not be surprising if they interpreted Psalm 16:10 as Acts says they did. If Jesus' followers believed he was raised *before* his flesh could decay, then their Jewish beliefs about the *time* it normally took for flesh to decay would have interacted with that belief.

Psalm 16:10's Three-Day Time Limit

Below are second-century and later Jewish references which reflect Jewish observation that the face of a corpse distorts no later than the end of the third day after death. When reading the references below, disregard the actions of the soul that are expressed since they may not yet have been a part of Jewish belief in the first century. Also, whether the changes in the face in the references below are said to occur *only* on day three, *precisely* at the end of day three, or could occur on day one, day two, or day three, is not relevant. The only point relevant here is that the references below all reflect Jewish observation that the face of a corpse distorts *no later than the end of* the third day after death.

> Bar Kappara taught: Until three days [after death] the soul keeps on returning to the grave, thinking that it will go back [into the body]; but when it sees that the facial features have become disfigured, it departs and abandons it [the body]. Thus it says, "But his flesh grieveth for him, and his soul mourneth over him" (Job 14:22). (Mid Gen Rab 100:7. Written in the fifth century. Bar Kappara's tenure was around 200 C.E.)

> They derive testimony [concerning the identity of a corpse] only from the appearance of the whole face with the nose....They give testimony [about the identity of a corpse] only during a period of three days [after death]. R. Judah b. Baba says, "[Decay in corpses] is not alike for all men, all places, and all

131

times." (Mishnah Yebamot 16:3-4. Written in the second century. Note possible dissenting opinion from R. Judah b. Baba in addition to the three-day timeline that is clearly expressed.)

R. Abba b. R. Pappai and R. Joshua of Siknin said in the name of R. Levi: For three days [after death] the soul hovers over the body, intending to re-enter it, but as soon as it sees its appearance change, it departs, as it is written, "When his flesh that is on him is distorted, his soul will mourn over him" (Job 14:22). Bar Kappara said: The full force of mourning lasts for three days. Why? Because [for that length of time] the shape of the face is recognizable, even as we have learnt in the Mishnah: Evidence [to prove a man's death] is admissible only in respect of the full face, with the nose, and only [by one who has seen the corpse] within three days [after death]. (Mid Lev Rab 18:1. Written in the eighth century. As already noted, Bar Kappara's tenure was around 200 C.E., as was the tenure of R. Levi.)

We know today that distortion of the face is part of the process of putrefaction after death, which includes bloating of the entire corpse due to internal gasses but which *first* bloats soft tissues like the lips and eyelids of the face. Even though the time after death at which bloating begins is dependent on a variety of factors (mostly temperature), and there are inaccuracies in the Jewish measurement of time (because they counted any part of a day as one day), the upper limit of three days time for the bloating of the face described in these Jewish references is approximately confirmed by modern forensics.[25]

Given that the first outward signs of decay are distortion of the face and the accompanying foul odor from the building gasses of putrefaction, it seems reasonable to conclude that these signs would have in the first century been associated with *decay of the body in general*. We see this association – the belief that decay of the corpse in general begins no later than the end of the third day after death – in the expectation of odor from the tomb of Lazarus after three days: "Lord, already there is a stench because he has been dead for four days" (Jn 11:39).

Early Christians would have made inferences from Psalm 16:10 if such inferences were obvious and made sense to them. If, due to Psalm 16:10, the early Christians believed that Jesus was raised before decay, and they also believed that the flesh of a corpse starts to decay no later than the end of the third day after death, it would have been a natural and automatic inference for Jesus' followers to conclude that Jesus was raised no later than the end of the third day after death. If the beliefs about the soul in the midrash references above (Mid Gen Rab 100:7; Mid Lev Rab 18:1) were present in first-century Judaism, and if it was understood from Psalm 16:10a that Jesus' soul did not *go to* Hades (as noted in previous section), then this same three-day time period would have been further reinforced (i.e. the soul hovers over the body for three days, and since Jesus' soul did not *go to* Hades, Jesus must have been raised before the end of the third day). Even if the earliest Christians were not intentionally looking to answer *when* Jesus resurrected, which I do not think they were because that seems like such a minor issue, they could hardly have ignored a resurrection scripture that seemed to be telling them just that. As Bruce Metzger pointed out in 1957:

> It was believed that corruption set in on the fourth day after death....God had promised through the Psalmist (16.10) that he would not let his Holy One see corruption....[Therefore,] Jesus must rise *prior* to the fourth day.[26]

Raised *On* the Third Day

But how would a belief that Jesus was raised *by* the third day become the belief that he was raised *on* the third day? One possibility is just a slight simplification or linguistic shift in the tradition. On a common sense level, it would not be surprising for a circulated tradition about any event occurring *by* the third day to morph into the tradition that it occurred *on* the third day. Additionally, if the *on* the third day tradition was adopted into and spread through popular creed early on, which it was in this case, any previous tradition would be quickly displaced.

It is also possible that the shift from *by* the third day to *on* the third day occurred because of, or was further encouraged by, the friction between Psalm 16:10's raised before decay time period and Jewish beliefs about *resuscitation*. Jews appear to have believed that resuscitation was possible up to the point that the flesh starts to decay, and therefore like decay, up to the end of the third day after death. This belief is reflected in the same midrash references mentioned earlier with their imagery of the soul intending to *reenter* the body up until the face distorts. A first-century Jewish association of resuscitation before distortion of the flesh is still reflected in these midrash even if the expressions about the actions of the soul were not yet a part of first-century Jewish belief, i.e. regardless of the believed *cause* of resuscitation, the midrash reflects practical Jewish experience with people that sometimes "came back to life" before they started to rot, but never after they started to rot. This is entirely expected given the misdiagnosis of death that sometimes occurs in any culture, especially ancient cultures. Jan Bondeson shows that before brain waves were measured, almost all cultures used the outward signs of putrefaction as the point up to which resuscitation was thought possible.[27]

As the Christians formed their beliefs, like any human beings they would have been cognizant of how others would perceive them. The appearance of resuscitation would have been a source of tension *unavoidably inherent* in the claim of someone raised before decay (or by the third day). Anticipation of or early encounters with the accusation or misunderstanding of resuscitation would have been a hindrance to Christians who wanted people to believe that Jesus resurrected from the dead. The inclusion of the word "buried" in the creed – "and that he was buried, and that he was raised" (1 Cor 15:4) – is an indicator that the earliest Christians were sensitive to the appearance of resuscitation. As N. T. Wright says, one of the reasons for the word "buried" in the creed is "to certify that Jesus was really and truly dead."[28] Gerd Ludemann agrees: "The reference to the burial confirms the reality of Jesus' death."[29] In other words, the Christians were insisting that Jesus was really dead; he did not resuscitate after being removed from the cross. Although "burial" in the creed may close out any possibility that Jesus resuscitated, the resurrection tradition was probably not always circulated with the caveat that Jesus was buried. Therefore, sensitivity to the appearance of resuscitation may have pushed the tradition to the third day given that both day one and day two are dangerously close to and within only a couple of hours of Jesus' late afternoon death on Friday (day two began at sunset on Friday).[*]

Why Was "On the Third Day" Included in a Core Creed?

It is understandable that a core creed would include the core belief that Jesus was "raised" and the core conviction that this belief was "in accordance with the scriptures". But why would a core creed include the *day* that Jesus was raised?

As already shown above, the "before decay" aspect of Psalm 16:10 is *inseparable* from its core meaning that Jesus was raised. If Psalm 16:10 was the only raised Messiah scripture the earliest Christians had, or one of the most important ones they had (it is always near the top of any Christian list of resurrection prophesies even today), it would not be surprising if the "before decay" aspect of Psalm 16:10 was included in a creed of core beliefs that was asserting that Jesus was raised *in accordance with the scriptures*. "Raised on the third day" may be a way of expressing that in a better known and more accessible way than the more technically correct "raised before decay". As Craig Keener says:

> If "third day" is included in "according to the scriptures," Paul may think of...Jonah 1:17; but his point may simply be that Jesus was raised before he could experience decay (Ps 16:10).[30]

Michael Licona conveys the same possibility:

> If we understand these [rabbinic] texts as claiming that bodily decomposition begins on the fourth day following death, the early Christian interpretation of Ps 16:10 is that Jesus was raised prior to the fourth day. It may even be that Ps 16:10 was one of the main texts the early church had in mind in affirming that Christ's resurrection on the third day was "according to the Scriptures".[31]

---

[*] It is worth noting that if the Jewish belief that death was certain only *after* three days was the *only* determinant in when Jesus was raised (i.e. Ps 16:10 not influencing at all), it would most likely have resulted in a fourth day or later resurrection belief in order to completely avoid the appearance of resuscitation.

As an aside, and as Craig Keener suggests above, Jonah 1:17 may also have been in mind in the creed's assertion that the third day was "in accordance with the scriptures". It is worth asking on what grounds one can propose this given the following conclusion of the Jesus Seminar which would rule out such an early use of Jonah 1:17:

> Matthew [12:40] has interpreted the sign of Jonah [1:17] to mean the three days and three nights Christ is alleged to have spent in the bowels of the earth. Since Luke does not seem to know this interpretation [even though he refers to Jon 1:17 in Lk 11:29-32], we must assume it...is a Christian interpretation provided by Matthew.[32]

However, as noted earlier, Matthew's resurrection interpretation of Jonah 1:17 is done *in public* while Luke does not have *any* public proclamation of Jesus' future resurrection. If, as suggested earlier, Matthew (or the tradition he drew from) broke the public silence about Jesus' future resurrection so he could post guards at the tomb, then the application of Jonah 1:17 to Jesus' resurrection may not be a Christian interpretation original to Matthew, Matthew may just be the first to have a use for it in a narrative of events. In this case, Jonah 1:17 may have been used by Christians as a scriptural allusion to Jesus' resurrection on the third day before Matthew used it in his Gospel; hence, it could be in mind in the much earlier creed. Note however that Jonah 1:17 cannot be the scriptural *origin* of the third-day belief because its "three nights" would have led to a fourth day resurrection.

Matthew's Use of Jonah 1:17 Instead of Psalm 16:10

If Psalm 16:10 was the origin of the third-day belief, and if Matthew in his Gospel intended a scriptural illustration of a Messiah raised *on* the third day so he could post guards at the tomb (Mt 12:40), then why did Matthew refer to Jonah 1:17 instead of Psalm 16:10? This question is a splitting of hairs but is still worth looking at. If Jonah 1:17 was in Christian use before Matthew used it in his Gospel, then Psalm 16:10 would have had no advantage over Jonah 1:17 in terms of familiarity to Matthew or his audience.

As indicated earlier when this question was addressed in relation to Hosea 6:2, one can only speculate what was going on in Matthew's mind. In comparison to Hosea 6:2, it was suggested that Jonah 1:17 lent itself better to the resurrection of a *single person*. In the case of Matthew's choice of Jonah 1:17 over Psalm 16:10 the answer may lie in how well each passage lent itself as a voice for the third-day belief. Although Psalm 16:10 leads in an understandable way to the third-day belief, it does not lend itself as readily to the reverse process, that is, as a scriptural illustration (or sign) of a three-day time period. This is because Psalm 16:10 does not *state* any time period, its associated time period is instead an inferred conclusion. Therefore, Jonah 1:17's *stated* even though technically imperfect three-day time period, its singular person focus, and its captivity/release from the sea creature which lends itself well as a scriptural allusion to resurrection (burial/release from the earth), may have for Matthew made it a better scriptural sign than Psalm 16:10 of a Messiah raised on the third day.

Summarizing the relationship between Hosea 6:2, Psalm 16:10, and Jonah 1:17 from Matthew's perspective: Hosea 6:2 is lacking as a clear scriptural illustration of a resurrected Messiah, Psalm 16:10 is lacking as a clear scriptural illustration of the third day, Jonah 1:17 is a good illustration of a resurrected Messiah and a mediocre illustration of the third day. Which would you choose if you were Matthew? If Psalm 16:10 was the origin of the third-day belief, Matthew's use of Jonah 1:17 instead of Psalm 16:10 (or Hosea 6:2) is not surprising.

Conclusion

The Psalm 16:10 theory can be summarized in simplest form as follows. Compelled to find scriptural confirmation for their belief that Jesus had been bodily raised up to heaven, Jesus' earliest followers were drawn to Psalm 16:10. Believed to be written by King David, Jesus' followers interpreted Psalm 16:10 as referring to David's messianic descendant instead of to David himself. Given Jesus' indisputable death but believing him raised, Jesus' followers also interpreted Psalm 16:10 as referring to post-death rescue before decay, instead of the psalmist's originally intended poetic plea to avoid death. Since Jews believed that the flesh of a corpse starts to decay no later than the end of the third day after death, it would have been a natural and automatic inference from Psalm 16:10 that Jesus was raised no later than the end of the third day after death. A slight linguistic shift, a simplification in a growing legend, or a sensitivity to the appearance of resuscitation caused the tradition to become "on the third day". "On the third day" is included in the creed because it captures in a well-known and accessible way the inseparable "before decay" meaning in Psalm 16:10's prophetic prediction of a raised Messiah. In short, the Psalm 16:10 theory simply proposes that the third-day belief is a logical by-product of early Christian interaction with Psalm 16:10.

It might be helpful to conclude with a summary comparison of the Psalm 16:10 theory to the sacred third-day theory, where I feel there is some nuance that might not be easily noticed. First, it is easier to place the Christian use of Psalm 16:10 in the third decade of the first century than it is to place a Jewish sacred third-day tradition at that time. Four things support this conclusion. One, the Christian use of Psalm 16:10 has significantly earlier attestation in Acts than the sacred third-day tradition has in the rabbinic literature. Two, there are a lack of passages in Jewish literature contemporary with the New Testament which employ the sacred third-day motif. In contrast, the absence of Psalm 16:10 from Christian literature before Acts can be reasonably explained. Three, Acts specifically says Psalm 16:10 was used by the earliest Christians. Although an unreliable claim, it is more than can be said of the sacred third-day tradition which has no claim of Christian or Jewish use before the third century C.E. Four, Psalm 16:10 would have been a very natural passage for the earliest Christians to have been drawn to due to its potential use as a raised Messiah prophecy.

A second nuance worth noting is that the Psalm 16:10 theory explains better than the sacred third-day theory the lonely scriptural emphasis on the third day in the creed and the minimal interest in the third day's scriptural significance elsewhere in the Christian literature. The third day was included in the creed not because the third day was itself scripturally important, but because the third day was an integral and necessary part of a much more important scriptural claim – that Jesus was raised.

Lastly, it seems more realistic from a human perspective that instead of the earliest Christians simply *assuming* that Jesus was raised on a sacred day without really any compelling need to make such an assumption, that they were unintentionally led to conclude that Jesus was raised on the third day because something of much greater importance – a raised Messiah scripture – led them to that conclusion.

In conclusion, it is plausible that the Christian third-day belief originated from Psalm 16:10.

Chapter 6

A Short Summary of the Hypothesis

This book set out to explain the causes of the beliefs and traditions in 1 Corinthians 15:3-7 from the perspective of experience-based doubt in Jesus' resurrection. The answer arrived at can be summarized as follows. After his death on the cross, Jesus' body was allowed by the Romans to be removed from the cross in deference to Jewish burial sensitivities. Jesus was buried in the ground by a disinterested Jewish burial crew with none of his followers present. His grave was marked with a pile of loose rocks or chalk to warn of uncleanness. His followers returned home to Galilee never knowing where Jesus was buried in Jerusalem. During and/or after this several day trek home, some of Jesus' followers found it impossible to accept that Jesus was not the Messiah as they had hoped. To resolve this conflict between their beliefs and the harsh reality of Jesus' death, some of them rationalized as a group that Jesus died for our sins, that God raised him bodily up to heaven, and that he would be back very soon to reign as the Messiah should (a cognitive dissonance reduction rationalization). It became a highly charged religious environment of excitement and anticipation of Jesus' imminent return. Anticipating the return of Jesus and experiencing the normal feelings associated with the absence of a recently deceased loved one, Peter had a hallucination of Jesus that he interpreted as a visitation by Jesus from heaven. This led to a rash of other individuals having hallucinations of Jesus (though perhaps no more than ten or even less), while others thought they heard Jesus speak to them or thought they felt his presence. Jesus' followers immediately turned to their Jewish scriptures to find scriptural confirmation for their beliefs. Interaction with their scriptures, most likely Psalm 16:10, led Jesus' followers to conclude that it was on the third day that Jesus was raised from the dead. Within a year or so, James had second thoughts about his brother and converted to Christianity for any number of the variety of reasons that many people change their mind and convert to a particular religion or sect. Being Jesus' brother, James was immediately given a leadership position in the new movement. Somewhere along the way, the organizational need to designate leaders – those who were best able to teach, preach, and defend this new Jewish sect's beliefs – became important. This led to authority designation appearance traditions: Jesus appeared to "the Twelve", and to "all the apostles". The last person of significance to have a hallucination of Jesus was the apostle Paul about three years after Jesus' death in conjunction with his personal upheaval about the religion he was persecuting and perhaps also in conjunction with an unconscious desire to be a person of higher relative social standing, which his conversion to the Christian community would bring. As the years and decades passed, the above experiences, beliefs, and traditions gave birth to legends like Jesus' burial in a rock-hewn tomb, that tomb being discovered empty three days later, his corporeal post-mortem appearances to individuals and groups described in the Gospels, and his appearance to over five hundred people mentioned in Paul's letter to the Corinthians. Eventually Jesus was deified in a way similar to, or perhaps in challenge to, several Roman emperors of the first century who were also called or considered sons of gods (Augustus, Tiberius, Nero, Titus, and Domitian).[1] In short, Christianity started off with a bang. Immediately after Jesus' obscure burial there was a radical rationalization of Jesus' death that led to a highly charged religious environment, which in turn led to individual hallucinations, collective enthusiasm, designations of authority, scriptural interpretation, religious conversions, and legends that developed as the years and decades passed. Probably the best examples of similar extraordinary and rare events coming together in one place at the same time are the Jewish messianic movements of Sabbatai Sevi and Rebbe Schneerson.

This book does not claim that the above summary has been demonstrated to be true, but it does claim that it is *one* plausible way to read the evidence.

Chapter 7

A Comparison to the Resurrection Hypothesis

To compare the hypothesis in this book to the resurrection hypothesis I will use the widely accepted method of inference to the best explanation. This method is used by historians when there is no strong *direct* evidence for an event in history, but only *indirect* evidence.[1] It proceeds by judging competing hypotheses in five categories – explanatory scope, explanatory power, disconfirming evidence, ad hocness, and plausibility (all of which will be defined later) – to determine which hypothesis provides the best explanation for the known facts.[*]

The first step in making any comparison of hypotheses is to determine what the *known facts* are. Hypotheses cannot be compared if they are each trying to explain different facts; the two sides just end up talking past each other. To define a common set of facts that can be used in our comparison, I will draw on the work of two leading defenders of Jesus' resurrection, William Craig and Michael Licona.

William Craig's Facts

William Craig is an evangelical philosopher of religion and theologian who many regard as the world's leading defender of Jesus' resurrection on historical grounds. Craig's approach is to frame the debate this way: "Any adequate historical hypothesis about the resurrection must explain four facts: Jesus's honorable

---

[*] It is important to point out that this method of historical inquiry is only valid if the correct hypothesis is in the pool of hypotheses being considered.

burial, the discovery of his empty tomb, his post-mortem appearances, and the origin of the disciples' belief in his resurrection."[2] With the first three of his "facts" providing an explanation for his fourth, Craig spends virtually all of his efforts trying to show that his first three "facts" really are facts. Below are all of the arguments I am aware of, twenty-one of them, that Craig has put forth in an attempt to show this.

I will attempt to show that, at best, many of Craig's arguments lack precision and, at worst, none of his arguments are helpful in determining the historical or legendary nature of the three purported events that he is calling "facts". For brevity, I have paraphrased each of Craig's arguments below, but I have included in the endnote for each paraphrased argument the relevant quotes from Craig's work and the associated source.

1] The majority of scholars agree that Jesus was buried in a rock-hewn tomb and that his tomb was discovered empty.[3]

This is a good point that Craig is bringing up because scholarly consensus is probably correct more often than it is wrong. However, it is important to keep in mind the advice of one of Craig's mentors, Wolfhart Pannenberg: "A single judgment of a sober historian easily outweighs a majority vote, in my opinion. Historical judgment must remain a matter of argument. A majority vote may express the dominant mood of a group, possibly its prejudices, but is not very helpful in judging claims to historical truth or authenticity."[4]

2] There are two or more *independent* sources in the Gospels that attest to Jesus' burial in a rock-hewn tomb, that tomb being discovered empty, Jesus' appearance to the Twelve, Jesus' appearance to the women, and Jesus' appearance to the disciples in Galilee.[5]

The first thing many people might think when they hear this is that it is all but impossible that *independent* sources would come up with the same basic legend; therefore, these reports are virtually certain to be true. However, world-renowned expert on oral transmission Jan Vansina explains why the Gospels, and the oral traditions that lie behind them, are not independent sources in this sense:

> ...We cannot assume that the testimony of two different informants from the same community or even society is really independent. This is very important. In history, proof is given only when two independent sources confirm the same event or situation, but...it is not possible to do this with oral tradition wherever a corpus exists and information flows are unstemmed (i.e., in most cases). Feedback and contamination is the norm....No one will consider the three synoptic Gospels as independent sources, even though they have different authors...they stemmed from one single oral milieu, from one corpus in one community. Once this is realized, it is easy to see that it also applies to John, the fourth Gospel...[6]

The use of the term "independent sources" is widespread among scholars, but some are better than others at acknowledging the realities of the circulating oral tradition behind the Gospels noted by Vansina above. For example, Bart Ehrman defines independent sources this way:

> Technically, the term ["independent sources"] refers to sources that have not used one another for their accounts....[However,] even though these sources may be independent of one another, it is possible that the sources on which they were built – whether oral or written – may not have been independent of one another....It may be that there were independent lines of tradition that stem ultimately from a single source...[7]

In other words, the only thing "independent sources" tells us is that the story existed before the sources it appears in (i.e. it was not made up by any of the sources that we have access to). This allows the story to be dated earlier than the sources it appears in, which does increase the probability that the story is true. However, how much this increases the probability that the story is true depends on how close to the actual events the story can be dated and how fast legend was growing and displacing the historically accurate accounts of events. In the appendix of this book, I try to show that the early Christian environment was an exception to what historians normally deal with, that the environment was very conducive to legendary growth and displacement of the historical core, and that all of the stories that Craig refers to above fall easily within the timeframe available for them to be legends.

3] Jesus' burial in a rock-hewn tomb is attested in the early sermon in Acts 13:28-31.[8]

Here is what Acts 13:28-31 reports that the apostle Paul said during a sermon about fifteen years after Jesus' death:

> Even though they found no cause for a sentence of death, they asked Pilate to have him [Jesus] killed. When they had carried out everything that was written about him, they took him down from the tree and laid him in a <u>tomb</u>. But God raised him from the dead; and for many days he appeared to those who came up with him from Galilee to Jerusalem, and they are now his witnesses to the people. (Acts 13:28-31)

If this is an accurate report of an early sermon by Paul, which is a precarious assumption, the reference to a "tomb" would at first glance seem to confirm knowledge by Paul of a rock-hewn tomb burial for Jesus. The Greek word used for "tomb" in this passage is *mnēmeion*, and translating it as "tomb" is reasonable given that *mnēmeion can* mean "tomb" and given the widely accepted assumption from the Gospels that Jesus was buried in a rock-hewn tomb. It also makes sense that Luke, the author of Acts, thought *mnēmeion* meant "tomb" because he also wrote the Gospel of Luke, which has Jesus buried in a rock-hewn tomb.

However, if this is really the exact wording of an early sermon by Paul, the word *mnēmeion* is of no use in determining if Paul knew of a rock-hewn tomb burial for Jesus because *mnēmeion* is synonymous with the word "grave". In fact, this is exactly how *mnēmeion* is translated in Luke 11:44 (same author as Acts), which refers to graves in the ground: "Woe to you! For you are like unmarked *graves* (mnēmeion), and people walk over them without realizing it." The word "laid" in Acts 13:29 is also synonymous with "put" (the DBY Bible translates it this way).

145

Therefore, Acts 13:29, which we are assuming are Paul's exact words from an early sermon, could just as easily be translated into English as follows: "When they had carried out everything that was written about him, they took him down from the tree and put him in a grave."[9] There is nothing in this statement that attests to Jesus' burial in a rock-hewn tomb.

4] Jesus' discovered empty tomb is attested in the early sermons in Acts 2:29 and Acts 13:36.[10]

Here are the two Acts passages that Craig is referring to with a few verses on each side added for context and Acts 2:29 and 13:36 underlined:

> God raised him [Jesus] up, having freed him from death, because it was impossible for him to be held in its power. For [King] David says concerning him,…"you will not abandon my soul to Hades, or let your Holy One experience corruption [Ps 16:10]"….Fellow Israelites, I may say to you confidently of our ancestor David that he both died and was buried, and his tomb is with us to this day [verse 2:29]. Since he was a prophet, he knew that God had sworn with an oath to him that he would put one of his descendants on his throne. Foreseeing this, David spoke of the resurrection of the Messiah, saying, "He was not abandoned to Hades, nor did his flesh experience corruption." This Jesus God raised up, and of that all of us are witnesses. (Acts 2:24-32)

> We bring you the good news that what God promised to our ancestors he has fulfilled for us, their children, by raising Jesus; as also it is written in the second psalm, "You are my Son; today I have begotten you." As to his raising him from the dead, no more to return to corruption, he has spoken in this way, "I will give you the holy promises made to David." Therefore he has also said in another psalm, "You will not let your Holy One experience corruption [Ps 16:10]." For David, after he had served the purpose of God in his own generation, died, was laid beside his ancestors, and experienced corruption [verse 13:36]; but he whom God raised up experienced no corruption. (Acts 13:32-37)

As can be seen in both passages, the only tomb being referred to is *King David's* tomb. There is no mention of a tomb for Jesus.

The statement at the end of the first passage above that they are "witnesses" to Jesus being raised (Acts 2:32) could be referring to Jesus' discovered empty tomb, but it could just as easily be referring to the disciples' experiences of Jesus appearing to them, just like we see in another Acts passage: "But God raised him from the dead; and for many days he *appeared* to those who came up with him from Galilee to Jerusalem, and they are now his *witnesses* to the people" (Acts 13:30-31). It is also possible that the reference to them being "witnesses" is simply referring to them being witnesses to their *belief* that Jesus was raised.

But some might ask, isn't Jesus' discovered empty tomb at least *implied* in the two passages above? After all, why else would these two passages even bring up King David's tomb? The reason is obvious, and that is why I added the extra verses for context. Both passages are trying to use Psalm 16:10 to give a scriptural proof of Jesus' resurrection. To do this they have to point out that King David died and *decayed* as evidenced by the fact that David's tomb, which presumably still has or once had his bones in it, was still with them in their day. Because of this, it is argued, Psalm 16:10 cannot be referring to King David, so it must be referring to King David's messianic descendent – Jesus. In other words, the Acts passages are saying that Jesus did not experience decay; he was raised as prophesied by Psalm 16:10: "You will not let your Holy One experience corruption." The use of Psalm 16:10 in these two Acts passages clearly attests to a *belief* that Jesus' body was gone from its final resting place, but it does not attest to that final resting place ever being *discovered* empty, nor does it attest to a rock-hewn tomb burial for Jesus. (A full assessment of Psalm 16:10 as a raised Messiah prophecy was made in Chapter Five of this book, pg. 126-131.)

5] Jesus' burial in a rock-hewn tomb is implied in the phrase "he was buried" in the early creed (1 Cor 15:4).[11]

According to Craig:

...We might wonder, was the burial mentioned by the formula [1 Cor 15:4] the same event as the burial by Joseph of Arimathea [described in the Gospels]? The answer to that question is made clear by a comparison of the four-line formula [died, buried, raised, appeared in 1 Cor 15:3-5] with the gospel narratives on the one hand and the sermons in the Acts of the Apostles on the other [Craig then displays 1 Cor 15:3-5, Acts 13:28-31, and Mk 15:37-16:7 side by side with each other]. This remarkable correspondence of independent traditions is convincing proof that the four-line formula is a summary in outline form of the basic events of Jesus' passion and resurrection, *including His burial in the tomb* [emphasis added].[12]

As can be seen in Craig's comments above, one of the reasons he sees a rock-hewn tomb burial in the early creed is because the events in the early creed – died, buried, raised, appeared (1 Cor 15:3-5) – parallel the events in the Gospels: crucifixion, rock-hewn tomb burial, discovered empty tomb, corporeal post-mortem appearances. However, these events in the Gospels would still parallel the early creed if they are *legendary* expansions on earlier beliefs instead of historical expansions on earlier beliefs. Without assuming the historical reliability of the Gospels, we do not know which it is.

The second reason Craig sees a rock-hewn tomb burial in the early creed is because he sees a parallel between the four-line formula in the early creed and the events described in the early sermons in Acts. However, as already shown, the early sermons in Acts – Acts 13:28-31, Acts 2:29 and Acts 13:36 – do not mention anything about Jesus being buried in a rock-hewn tomb.

In sum, the early creed only says Jesus was "buried". Without simply assuming the historical reliability of the Gospels, we do not know whether this word is referring to a rock-hewn tomb burial or a ground burial.

6] Jesus' discovered empty tomb is implied in the phrase "he was raised" in the early creed (1 Cor 15:4).[13]

No it is not. The only thing implied in the early creed – "he was buried and he was raised" – is the *belief* that Jesus' body was gone from its burial location. There is no mention of, or any

148

implication of, a *discovered* empty tomb or *discovered* empty burial location. The same argument above with respect to the parallels between the early creed and the Gospels and the early sermons in Acts applies here.

7] Jesus' discovered empty tomb is implied in the phrase "on the third day" in the early creed (1 Cor 15:4).[14]

No it is not. The third day expression in the early creed – "he was raised on the third day in accordance with the scriptures" – could have come from Jesus' followers trying to ground their belief that Jesus was raised in their sacred Jewish scriptures. The third-day belief could be a byproduct of one of those scriptures. This would be consistent with the last part of the passage: "raised on the third day *in accordance with the scriptures*". There is no way to tell from the phrase "on the third day" what its origin is: a scripture or a discovered empty tomb. (Chapter Five of this book argues that Psalm 16:10 is the source of the third-day belief.)

8] If Jesus was not raised, the Jewish authorities would have exhumed and publicly displayed Jesus' body to debunk the resurrection claim.[15]

This is an empty argument for the reasons stated in Chapter Two of this book (pg. 42).

9] There is no attestation of a burial different from that reported in the Gospels, which adds to its likely historicity.[16]

This is an empty argument for the reasons stated in Chapter Two of this book (pg. 41).

10] The Jewish charge of a stolen body supports the historicity of the discovered empty tomb.[17]

This is an empty argument for the reasons stated in Chapter One of this book (pg. 18-21).

11] If Jesus' burial location was known to his followers, his followers could have checked for his body.[18]

True, but if Jesus' burial location was unknown except to those who buried him, which is what is suggested in this book, then his followers would not have known where he was buried and therefore could not have checked for his body.

12] Mark's discovered empty tomb account is most likely history because it is not excessively embellished.[19]

The logic does not seem correct here. Legends come in all shapes and sizes. It does not seem unusual that a legend in its initial stages might be relatively unembellished. However, if there never was a discovered empty tomb, and Mark or the tradition he drew from was the first to claim that there was a discovered empty tomb, the *claim itself* seems like a pretty extravagant embellishment to me.

13] It is unlikely that women would have been selected to find the empty tomb if it was a legend.[20]

I would agree with this if it were not for the last sentence in the Gospel of Mark: "[The women] fled from the tomb, for terror and amazement had seized them; and they said nothing to anyone, for they were afraid" (Mark 16:8). As argued in Chapter One of this book (pg. 14-18), this ending makes perfect sense if, in this first version of the discovered empty tomb legend, the women's fear-induced silence gave an answer to the question why the women's story of the empty tomb remained unknown for so long. The use of women makes perfect sense in this case – all women could do was react in fear and terror; they were so scared that they never passed the message on.

14] The appearance to Peter is independently attested by Paul and Luke.[21]

Both Paul and Luke have the exact same very short reference to Jesus' appearance to Peter: "[he] appeared to Peter" (1 Cor 15:5; Lk 24:34). Both of these reports are consistent with the hypothesis in this book that Peter simply had a hallucination of Jesus. But even if Luke had narrated an incredibly corporeal appearance of Jesus to Peter, perhaps a scene where Peter is touching Jesus and eating with him, this could simply be a legendized account of what was originally just a hallucination.

15] Paul's personal contact with the Twelve, the apostles, and some of the five hundred people he mentions in his list of appearances in 1 Corinthians 15:5-7 "guarantees" that these group appearances occurred.[22]

I do not see the "guarantee" here. The group appearance traditions to the Twelve and to the apostles could have emerged as described in Chapter Four of this book even with Paul having personal contact with them (see pg. 99-105). As also mentioned in Chapter Four, Paul's personal contact with the five hundred is unknown. He may not have had personal contact with any of them (see pg. 105-108).

16] Paul makes a distinction between appearances of Jesus and visions of Jesus that implies the resurrection appearances were physical.[23]

This is an empty argument for the reasons stated in Chapter Four of this book (pg. 92-98).

17] If all of the appearances were originally non-physical visions, the rise of the very corporeal appearances described in the Gospels cannot be explained. Christians would have avoided making corporeal appearance claims because they would have been a stumbling block to those who had difficulty accepting a physical resurrection but would have been quite happy to accept visionary appearances of Jesus.[24]

This would be a good point if someone was arguing that the earliest Christians believed Jesus was only raised spiritually. But if the earliest Christians believed Jesus was raised bodily, it makes sense that the legendary trajectory would be toward more and more corporeal appearances. Proposing that Christians would have avoided making corporeal appearance claims in order to not offend potential recruits suggests that they were tiptoeing around their real beliefs. While possible, it seems just as likely that Christians were trying as hard as they could to convince others that Jesus was raised bodily. As Craig himself says about the corporeal appearances described in Luke 24:36-51 and John 20:19-29:

Undoubtedly, the most notable feature of these appearance stories is the physical demonstrations of Jesus' showing his wounds and eating before the disciples. The purpose of the physical demonstrations is to show two things: first, that Jesus was raised physically; and second, that he was the same Jesus who had been crucified. Thus, they served to demonstrate both corporeality and continuity of the resurrection body.[25]

18] According to Edward Bode, if the discovered empty tomb story were a late legend, Mark would have used the phrase "on the third day" from the early creed (1 Cor 15:4) to indicate when the women found the tomb empty instead of using the phrase "on the first day of the week" (Mk 16:2).[26]

Craig is correct that Edward Bode makes this argument, but to understand Bode's argument it is important to look at the context in which he gives it. Here is what Bode says:

> The ancient theme of Jesus' resurrection on the third day according to the scriptures, attested by the tradition of 1 Cor 15:4, derives from the literary motif of the Old Testament which placed days of divine salvation and manifestation on the third day. This motif is absent from the empty tomb tradition except for the redactional work of Luke. Instead the tomb insists on the first day of the week. The silence of the tomb on the third-day theme is an indication that the tomb is not merely a late and legendary composition – if it had been such, it would have been careful to associate itself with the ancient, accepted and prominent notion of the resurrection on the third day.[27]

As can be seen in Bode's argument above, he thinks the third-day belief expressed in the early creed (1 Cor 15:4) came from an elevated sacred third-day tradition in Jewish thought. If this was the case, Bode is correct that one would expect the third-day motif to be used in everything from then on associated with the timing of Jesus' resurrection. However, if the third-day belief in the early creed did not originate from an elevated sacred third-day tradition in Jewish thought, but was just the day that Jesus was believed to have been raised (as was proposed in Chapter Five of this book), then Mark's use of the phrase "on the first day of the week" is not a problem – it was just the way Mark or the tradition he drew from chose to indicate which day the women went to visit the tomb.

19] Mark's phrase "the first day of the week" in his discovered empty tomb account (Mk 16:2) has linguistic indications of an Aramaic origin, so this tradition is very early.[28]

I do not know if Craig's linguistic argument is valid or not, but I grant that Mark's discovered empty tomb account may have existed in Aramaic before he wrote his Gospel. This allows this tradition to be dated earlier and increases the probability that it is true. However, determining how much more likely the story is to be true depends on *how* close to the actual events the story can be dated and how fast legend was growing and displacing the historically accurate accounts of events. As already mentioned, in the appendix of this book I try to show that the early Christian environment was very conducive to legendary growth and displacement of the historical core. Even if Mark's discovered empty tomb account circulated very early on and in Aramaic, it could still be a legend.

20] The source material for Mark's burial account can be dated to within seven years of Jesus' death, so it is unlikely that the story of Jesus' burial in a rock-hewn tomb is a legend.[29]

According to Craig:

> The account of Jesus' burial in a tomb by Joseph of Arimathea is part of Mark's source material for the passion story. This is a very early source which is probably based on eyewitness testimony and which the commentator Rudolf Pesch dates to within seven years of Jesus' crucifixion.[30]

Craig's argument has two components. The first is that, according to Rudolf Pesch, the story of Jesus' suffering and death (the passion story) can be dated to within seven years of Jesus' crucifixion. The second is that Mark's burial account was part of that passion story, so the burial account can also be dated to within seven years of Jesus' death. Let's look at both of these arguments.

Pesch's argument for dating the story of Jesus' suffering and death to within seven years of Jesus' crucifixion rests on one single idea. It is the idea that because Mark's passion narrative uses the term "high priest" to refer to Caiaphas instead of using Caiaphas' actual name during the account of Jesus' trial (Mk 14:53, 60-61, 63), Caiaphas must still have been the high priest when this story originated, for if this story had originated *after* Caiaphas' term of office, his name would have been used to distinguish him from the next high priest. Since secular records show that Caiaphas was high priest from 18 to 37 C.E., Pesch concludes that this story can be dated to no later than 37 C.E., seven years after Jesus' death (assuming Jesus died in 30 C.E.).

However, as New Testament scholar Helen Bond points out:

> Caiaphas [the high priest] and Pilate [the governor/prefect] were deposed [removed from office] within a few months of one another. Unless we are to assume that the [original] passion account [Mark's source material] was penned in the short time between Pilate's deposition (probably in January 37 [C.E.]) and Caiaphas's replacement (probably Passover 37 [C.E.; in March or April]), it is difficult to see why Pilate is named [multiple times in Mk 15:1-15] but Caiaphas is not. Surely if Pesch were correct [and if the original passion account originated before January 37 C.E.], we would expect Pilate also to be referred to as "the governor" or (more accurately) "the prefect".[31]

In other words, for Pesch's argument to hold water, the original passion story would have had to have been written within a small four month window (January to April 37 C.E.).

But there is an even bigger problem with Pesch's theory that Helen Bond points out. However, because Bond explains this difficulty while referring to a 70 C.E. dating for the Gospel of Mark, which is unnecessary and could be a distraction for those who insist that Mark's Gospel was written earlier (which I agree it may have), I will give her argument in more generic terms below.[32] ⸗

Regardless of how early the source material for Mark's Gospel can be dated, it is virtually unanimous that Mark wrote his Gospel after 37 C.E. and that Mark was a very capable narrator. If Mark had an earlier source that did not have Caiaphas' name in it for the reason that Pesch hypothesizes (Caiaphas was still the high priest when the story was recorded and so there was no reason to name him), one would have *expected* Mark to add in Caiaphas' name to his Gospel for the exact same reason that Pesch argues it would have been added into the story in the first place if the story had originated *after* 37 C.E. – to help those who heard the story distinguish Caiaphas from the current high priest. For whatever reason Mark does not add Caiaphas' name to his Gospel, that could be the same reason that whoever originated the story *after* 37 C.E. did not use Caiaphas' name.

Why Mark's Gospel uses the term "high priest" to refer to Caiaphas instead of using Caiaphas' actual name can only be guesswork and does not look to me like any kind of a sound basis upon which to date Mark's passion story to within seven years of Jesus' crucifixion. Even the highly respected Catholic scholar Raymond Brown hypothesizes that the use of the general term "high priest" in Mark's Gospel simply reflects the Gentile origin and destination of Mark's Gospel – with the name Caiaphas meaning very little to his readers, using Caiaphas' official title of "high priest" simply made more sense.[33] Again, just guesswork, but this sounds a lot more plausible to me than Pesch's hypothesis. It is also possible that Mark's passion narrative was written so late that the author simply did not know who the high priest was in the early 30s.

With regard to the second part of Craig's argument – that Mark's burial account was already part of the story of Jesus' suffering and death that Mark received before he wrote his Gospel – there is no evidence that I am aware of that Craig has put forth supporting this. It is also worth noting how wildly scholarly opinion varies on this topic. In his massive 1994 treatment of the passion, Raymond Brown gives space to an article by Marion L. Soards entitled "The Question of a PreMarcan Passion Narrative".[34] In this article, Soards tabulates the position of 35 leading scholars on the Gospel of Mark. Out of the 35 scholars, 13 see the burial account as *completely* separate from the story of Jesus' suffering and death before they were brought together in Mark's Gospel (Schenk, Schille, Czerski, Dibelius, Johnson, Donahue, Grant, Klostermann, Bultmann, Mohn, Peddinghaus, Schneider, Schreiber), and some of these 13 scholars see Mark as the *originator* of the burial account. Two of the 35 scholars also see the burial account as completely separate from the story of Jesus' suffering and death, but see the burial account as being a secondary addition to the story of Jesus' suffering and death *before* Mark wrote his Gospel (Anderson, Schweizer). Another 13 scholars out of the 35, including Pesch, agree with Craig that the burial account was an integral part of the story of Jesus' suffering and death before Mark wrote his Gospel (Schmithals, Buckley, Dormeyer, Ernst, Lane, Lightfoot, Lohse, Nineham, Luhrmann, Myllykoski, Pesch, Schenke, Taylor). Four of the scholars did not weigh in on whether or not the burial account was part of the story of Jesus' suffering and death before Mark wrote his Gospel (Kelber, Kolenkow, Kuhn, Scroggs). As for the remaining three scholars, I could not tell what their position was (Pryke, Leon-Dufour, Mohr). Soards, the author of the article, sums it up: "Scholarly opinion varies greatly on the dimensions of the preMarcan passion narrative."[35] The assertion by Craig that Mark's burial account was already a part of the story of Jesus' suffering and death that Mark received before he wrote his Gospel is only one of several possibilities.

In sum, the source material for Mark's burial account cannot be dated to within seven years of Jesus' death.

21] As a member of the Jewish Sanhedrin that condemned Jesus, Joseph of Arimathea is unlikely to be a Christian creation.[36]

The hypothesis in this book grants that Joseph of Arimathea may have been the one who actually buried Jesus (with a couple of laborers presumably helping him) and that he was not a Christian invention. However, the hypothesis in this book proposes that Joseph of Arimathea buried Jesus in the *ground*, not in a rock-hewn tomb. I know Craig objects to this and I think it might actually be a second, even if difficult to see, component of Craig's paraphrased argument above. I am surmising this based on the following statement by Craig made elsewhere:

> According to the late New Testament scholar Raymond Brown, Jesus' burial by Joseph is "very probable," since it is "almost inexplicable" why Christians would make up a story about a

Jewish Sanhedrist who *does what is right by Jesus* [emphasis added].[37]

What does Craig mean by "does what is right by Jesus"? If he is referring to Mark's account of Jesus being buried in a rock-hewn tomb by Joseph of Arimathea instead of in the ground, then his point seems to be that it is unlikely that a Christian legend would emerge that entails a member of the Jewish Sanhedrin who condemned Jesus giving him a *favorable* burial, one where he is put in a rock-hewn tomb instead of in the ground. If I am understanding Craig's argument correctly, it is worth addressing. I hope to show below that this argument not only does not have any basis, but that Craig has misunderstood what Raymond Brown was saying was "almost inexplicable".

In order for me to adequately address Craig's argument, I must give a plausible explanation for why a Christian legend would emerge that has a member of the Jewish Sanhedrin who had just condemned Jesus, put him in a rock-hewn tomb instead of in the ground. I think I have solidly done this in Chapter Two of this book (pg. 32-40). The short answer from that section of this book is that it makes sense that a hurried rock-hewn tomb burial legend would emerge (out of an actual obscure ground burial) in order to explain how some of Jesus' followers were able to see *where* he was buried, seeing where Jesus was buried being a necessary part of the discovered empty burial location legend. In the Chapter Two analysis, it was proposed that the Joseph of Arimathea in the Gospel of Mark (the first version of the burial story) did not do Jesus any favors; he had not "done what is right by Jesus" as Craig claims. He was just a pious Sanhedrist whose only desire was to carry out the Jewish law and bury a crucified criminal before sunset, and so he placed Jesus in a temporary rock-hewn tomb. In short, Christians did not make up a story about a Jewish Sanhedrist who had participated in the condemnation of Jesus and then "does what is right by Jesus"; they made up a story about a Jewish Sanhedrist who had participated in the condemnation of Jesus and then temporarily put his body in a rock-hewn tomb because of the impending sunset which marked the beginning of the Sabbath.

This leads us back to Craig's use of Raymond Brown, who he cites in order to make his point. Here again is what Craig said:

> According to the late New Testament scholar Raymond Brown, Jesus' burial by Joseph is "very probable," since it is "almost inexplicable" why Christians would make up a story about a Jewish Sanhedrist who does what is right *by Jesus* [emphasis added].[38]

Raymond Brown never says anything about Joseph of Arimathea doing what is right *by Jesus*. Here is the full quote from Raymond Brown that Craig cites in his work:

> That the burial was done by Joseph from Arimathea is very probable, since a Christian fictional creation from nothing of a Jewish Sanhedrist who does *what is right* is almost inexplicable, granted the hostility in early Christian writings toward the Jewish authorities responsible for the death of Jesus [emphasis added].[39]

According to Raymond Brown, what Mark's Joseph of Arimathea has done "right" is simply carry out the Jewish law and bury a crucified criminal before sunset; that is all: "[Mark's] Joseph was a religiously pious Sanhedrist who, despite the condemnation of Jesus by the Sanhedrin, felt an obligation under the Law to bury this crucified criminal before sunset."[40] Raymond Brown does not make an argument that the historicity of the rock-hewn tomb burial is increased because it is unlikely that a Christian legend would arise that has a Jewish Sanhedrist put Jesus in a rock-hewn tomb.

It is in a *later* Gospel that Joseph of Arimathea "does what is right by Jesus", and perhaps it is here that Craig is referring when he makes his argument. In the Gospel of Matthew, Joseph of Arimathea puts Jesus in his *own* tomb (Mt 27:60). Craig is right, it *would* be inexplicable if a Christian legend arose that had a member of the Jewish Sanhedrin who condemned Jesus put Jesus in his *own* tomb. However, by the time the Gospel of Matthew was written, Joseph of Arimathea is no longer a participant in the

Sanhedrin's condemnation of Jesus as he was in Mark; now he has been legendized into a "disciple" (Mt 27:57).

Summary of William Craig's Facts

If the above analysis has successfully shown that none of Craig's arguments are helpful in determining the historical or legendary nature of Jesus' burial in a rock-hewn tomb, that tomb being discovered empty, and Jesus' post-mortem appearances described in the Gospels, then what Craig has for a long time called "facts" should not really be called facts. Instead, Craig's arguments that these events occurred should be recognized as being *part of his hypothesis*. In order to assess Craig's hypothesis in relation to another hypothesis, like the one in this book, we have to start with real, indisputable facts, like those listed below, which would still allow Craig to remain focused on the same arguments he has always focused on:

Fact #1) Jesus' burial by Joseph of Arimathea in a rock-hewn tomb is *reported* in the Gospels of Matthew, Mark, Luke, and John.

Fact #2) The discovery of Jesus' empty tomb is *reported* in the Gospels of Matthew, Mark, Luke, and John.

Fact #3) Post-mortem appearances of Jesus are *reported* in the Gospels of Matthew, Mark, Luke, and John, and in Paul's writings.

Fact #4) Shortly after his crucifixion, Jesus' followers came to believe that Jesus was bodily raised from the dead.[*]

With the above four facts established from Craig's work, we can now look at Michael Licona's work to determine if there are additional facts that can be added to our list and used to compare our two hypotheses.

---

[*] Some will disagree that this is a fact, but I accept it as a fact and I know Craig does too. As long as those comparing hypotheses agree on what the facts are, different hypotheses can be compared, otherwise comparisons are pointless.

Michael Licona's Facts

Michael Licona is an evangelical New Testament scholar and author of the book *The Resurrection of Jesus: A New Historiographical Approach* (2010). Licona argues that Jesus' resurrection should be regarded as a historical event because, in his view, it outdistances competing hypotheses by a significant margin when using the historian's method of inference to the best explanation.[41]

One of the things interesting about Licona's book is how open he is about the uncertainty surrounding the historical reliability of the Gospels. Here are some of the things Licona says:

> The past only survives in fragments preserved in texts, artifacts and the effects of past causes....[Ancient] documents were written by biased authors, who had an agenda, who were shaped by the cultures in which they lived (and that are often foreign to us), who varied in both their personal integrity and the accuracy of their memories, who had access to a cache of incomplete information that varied in its accuracy, and who selected from that cache only information relevant to their purpose in writing. Accordingly, all sources must be viewed and employed with prudence.[42]

> Regardless of the motives involved, ancient historians, like any modern, could lie, spin and embellish. Moreover, questions pertaining to genre are not always easily answered. Thus to take texts at their face value may lead historians into all sorts of quagmires and mistakes.[43]

> There is somewhat of a consensus among contemporary scholars that the Gospels belong to the genre of Greco-Roman biography (*bios*). *Bioi* offered the ancient biographer great flexibility for rearranging material and inventing speeches in order to communicate the teachings, philosophy, and political beliefs of the subject, and they often included legend. Because *bios* was a flexible genre, it is often difficult to determine where history ends and legend begins.[44]

> Although *bioi* most often took historical matters seriously, biographers varied greatly in the amount of liberty they took,

thereby limiting the benefit of knowing the genre of the Gospels....Because the commitment to accuracy and the liberties taken could vary greatly between biographers, identifying the canonical Gospels as *bioi* will take us only so far....The conventions of *bioi* allowed for biographers to exercise literary freedom, and ancient biographers took advantage of this liberty to varying degrees. Accordingly the modern historian can only hope to create a very basic outline of what occurred.[45]

The date of composition of the canonical Gospels is disputed. Although nearly all scholars place them in the first century, more specific dating is somewhat arbitrary....The traditional authorship of Matthew, Mark, Luke and John is likewise insecure.[46]

No consensus exists pertaining to the reliability of the resurrection narratives in the canonical Gospels...[47]

It can forthrightly be admitted that the data surrounding what happened to Jesus is fragmentary and could possibly be mixed with legend...[48]

I do not believe we have enough [consensus among biblical scholars] here to warrant including the empty tomb as part of our historical bedrock.[49]

Given the above uncertainties with the Gospels, Licona sets out to make the case for Jesus' resurrection using only the most certain of historical facts saying, "Neither claims of divine inspiration nor general trustworthiness [of the Gospels] will play any part in our investigation." [50] Licona then identifies three historical facts (quoted verbatim below) that virtually everyone agrees on (including me) and that any hypothesis of Christian origins must explain.[51] Adding these three facts to the four facts derived from Craig's work, we now have seven facts:

Fact #5) "Jesus died by crucifixion."

Fact #6) "Very shortly after Jesus' death, the disciples had experiences that led them to believe and proclaim that Jesus had been resurrected and had appeared to them."

Fact #7) "Within a few years after Jesus' death, Paul converted after experiencing what he interpreted as a postresurrection appearance of Jesus to him."

The seven facts above identified from the works of Craig and Licona are what the hypothesis in this book and the resurrection hypothesis need to explain. To determine which hypothesis is the best explanation for the above seven facts, I will compare them in the five categories of the historian's method of inference to the best explanation mentioned earlier: explanatory power, explanatory scope, disconfirming evidence, ad hocness, and plausibility.

Comparing Hypotheses

Explanatory Power

In the explanatory power test, the best explanation is the one that, when temporarily *assumed* is true, is most likely to produce the evidence.

The hypothesis in this book, if true, is very likely to produce the evidence that we have and therefore has excellent explanatory power. All seven of the facts that we are interested in would be produced, and so would a host of other secondary facts: Jesus' death by crucifixion (Jesus was crucified), the origin of the disciples' belief that Jesus died for our sins, was raised from the dead, and will be back very soon (Jesus' followers experienced cognitive dissonance after his death which led to a cognitive dissonance reduction rationalization), the perception by individuals such as Peter, James, and Paul that Jesus appeared to them (individual hallucinations), the group appearance traditions to the Twelve and to all the apostles expressed in 1 Corinthians 15:5&7 (designations of authority in a growing religious movement needing leaders), the attestation in one source of an appearance by Jesus to over five hundred people (a fringe legend that Paul added to his list of appearances in 1 Corinthians 15:5-8), the belief that it was on the third day that Jesus was raised from the dead (a scriptural interpretation of Psalm 16:10), Paul's conversion (some already underway attraction to Christianity led him to a personal upheaval about the religion he was persecuting that culminated in a hallucination of Jesus and his conversion), the reports in the Gospels of a rock-hewn tomb burial, a discovered empty tomb three days later, and corporeal post-mortem appearances of Jesus (legendary growth based on earlier beliefs and traditions), the extra-mental/non-extra-mental distinction in appearances in Luke-Acts (the result of two legendary trajectories – the ascension tradition and the legitimization of Paul's conversion experience), Paul's silence on the discovered empty tomb (that legend did not yet exist or Paul knew it was an emerging legend), the abrupt fear-induced silence ending to the first version of the discovered empty tomb story found in the Gospel of Mark (the discovered empty tomb story was a late legend in which the women's fear-induced silence gave an answer to why the story had remained unknown for so long), why women were chosen in the discovered empty tomb tradition to find the tomb empty (women were more likely to be scared silent), the charge by some Jews that Jesus' body was stolen (a simplistic response by some Jews to the legend of a discovered empty tomb), and the rise of the tradition that there were guards at the tomb (a Christian apologetic legend and response to the Jewish charge of a stolen body). There are other facts that the hypothesis in this book can explain, but the above list is enough to show that it explains the seven facts of interest in our comparison and extends deeply into the secondary facts.

The resurrection hypothesis, if true, is also very likely to produce the evidence that we have and therefore also has excellent explanatory power. All seven of the facts that we are interested in would be produced, and so would the same list of secondary facts: Jesus' death by crucifixion (Jesus was crucified), the origin of the disciples' belief that Jesus died for our sins, was raised from the dead, and will be back very soon (Jesus did rise from the dead, left an empty tomb that his followers found, appeared to some of his followers, and explained these things before and after his resurrection), the perception by individuals such as Peter, James, and Paul that Jesus appeared to them (Jesus did appear to them), the group appearance traditions to the Twelve and to all the apostles expressed in 1 Corinthians 15:5&7 (Jesus did appear to these groups), the attestation in one source of an appearance by Jesus to over five hundred people (Jesus did appear to them), the belief that it was on the third day that Jesus was raised from the dead (Jesus told his followers before he died that he would rise on the third day, plus the empty tomb was discovered on the third day), Paul's conversion (Jesus appeared to Paul in a life altering way), the reports in the Gospels of a rock-hewn tomb burial, a discovered empty tomb three days later, and corporeal post-mortem appearances of Jesus (these are all historical events), the extra-mental/non-extra-mental distinction in appearances in Luke-Acts (Paul's conversion experience did have extra-mental elements of light and voice), Paul's silence on the discovered empty tomb (Paul was not trying to defend Jesus' resurrection, or the empty tomb was so well known that it was unnecessary for Paul to explicitly mention it, or some other explanation), the abrupt fear-induced silence ending to the first version of the discovered empty tomb story found in the Gospel of Mark (it was a message to beleaguered Christians encouraging them to overcome their fears and failures and spread the good news, or some other explanation), why women were chosen in the discovered empty tomb tradition to find the tomb empty (women actually did find the tomb empty), the charge by some Jews that Jesus' body was stolen (a response by some Jews to the fact of the empty tomb), and the rise of the tradition that there were guards at the tomb (there were guards at the tomb, or this may be a Christian apologetic response to the charge of a stolen body but the discovered empty tomb story is historical). Like the hypothesis in this book, there are other facts that the resurrection hypothesis can explain, but the above list is enough to show that it explains the seven facts of interest in our comparison and extends deeply into the secondary facts.

The plausibility of some of the explanations offered above will be of interest later, but looking just at explanatory power, which requires one to *assume* that an entire hypothesis is true and then assess how likely it is that the evidence would result, indicates that both of our hypotheses are equal in this test.

Explanatory Scope

In the explanatory scope test, the best explanation is the one that offers an explanation for *more* of the known facts than its rival. As pointed out above, both of our hypotheses offer an explanation for our seven facts. Additionally, I do not know of any secondary facts that either hypothesis cannot offer an explanation for. Therefore, both of our hypotheses have excellent explanatory scope and are equal in this test.

Disconfirmation

In the disconfirmation test, the best explanation is the one that has the least amount of evidence that renders the hypothesis unlikely to be true.

In a comparison of hypotheses where people are intensely passionate about their position and much of the evidence can be interpreted in different ways, I believe this test is useless for a reason stated by the prominent philosopher of history Christopher B. McCullagh: "...With sufficient ingenuity, almost any hypothesis could be rendered immune from disconfirmation...[by] creating an explanation of the evidence which is compatible with the hypothesis being defended." [52] In other words, when the evidence has multiple possible interpretations, all claims of disconfirmation by one side simply result in explanations by the other side that neutralizes the disconfirmation. However, interaction with the disconfirmation test is still beneficial. It forces each side to commit to explanations that neutralize the disconfirmations. Those explanations then become part of the hypothesis, which are subject to the other four tests, especially plausibility.

As far as I can tell, there is no disconfirming evidence for either of our hypotheses that does not already have an explanation for it built into the hypothesis. Therefore, both of our hypotheses are equal in this test.

Ad Hocness

In the ad hocness test, the best explanation is the one that requires the least number of *speculative* explanations or assumptions in order to fill in where there are gaps in the evidence.

In other words, ad hocness refers to *non-evidenced* explanations or assumptions.

Because the general trustworthiness of the Gospels and Acts is not playing a part in this investigation of Christian origins, both of our hypotheses are ad hoc. Both of our hypotheses are providing speculative explanations to make sense of *reports* in the Gospels and Acts which may or may not be true. Two examples will help to illustrate this point.

The hypothesis in this book proposes that Paul's conversion came about due to some already underway attraction to Christianity that led him to a personal upheaval about the religion he was persecuting and a hallucination of Jesus (Chapter Four, pg. 89-92). After correctly pointing out the ad hoc and speculative nature of psychological explanations like this, Licona says, "I do not mean to imply that the psychohistories proposed by Ludemann and Goulder are a priori impossible or even mistaken. Probability must be determined by weighing hypotheses."[53] Here is Licona's method for weighing hypotheses:

> For assessing hypotheses, we adopted methodical neutrality to assign the burden of proof to the one who is making a proposition, be it affirmative or negative. Accordingly no hypothesis may get the nod for being the best explanation unless its superiority to competing hypotheses can be demonstrated. Furthermore, merely stating "what-if" possibilities without supporting evidence does not challenge hypotheses with strong supporting evidence.[54]

The obvious question is, what is the "strong supporting evidence" that Paul's conversion experience was due to a resurrected Jesus appearing to him, as proposed by the resurrection hypothesis? The only thing I can find is this argument from Licona, in which he claims that Paul's statement "last of all" in 1 Cor 15:8 reflects a *belief* by Paul that his conversion encounter with Jesus was different from a vision:

> Paul believed that his experience differed from a vision that had no external reality in the material world, given his "last of all" statement in 1 Corinthians 15:8 and with Acts 9:10 [Acts 9:10 is

an example of a vision with *no* external reality in the material world] and Luke's report that his traveling companions perceived portions of the auditory and visible aspects of the experience [Acts 9:3-7; 22:6-10; 26:12-16].[55]

But this argument is confusing because Licona says only ten pages earlier:

> ...We will not take a position on the three accounts of Paul's conversion in Acts [Acts 9:3-7; 22:6-10; 26:12-16]. Instead, we will only claim that they provide a *possible* account of his conversion experience.[56]

But if one is not going to take a position on the three accounts of Paul's conversion in Acts, then the Acts accounts of Paul's companions seeing a light or hearing a voice could simply be the result of legendization over time on what was originally just a personal hallucination experience brought on by psychological factors. Paul's phrase "last of all" in 1 Corinthians 15:8 ("Last of all, as to someone untimely born, he appeared also to me") does not help either. This phrase could simply mean that Paul considered his conversion encounter with Jesus to be *the* last appearance of Jesus or that he considered himself the last to be *chosen* to receive appearances (as proposed in Chapter Four of this book, pg. 92-98). And the visionary character of Jesus' appearance in passages like Acts 9:10 could be the result of the belief that Jesus ascended into heaven long ago and so all appearances after that were sent only to the recipients mind (again, as argued in Chapter Four of this book, pg. 94-96).

If there is no "strong supporting evidence" that the resurrected Jesus appeared to Paul, it does not mean that the psychological explanation prevails, but by Licona's own method of historical inquiry, it "ties":

> Skeptical historians may accuse historians favorable to the resurrection hypothesis of speculating where the New Testament does not provide much detail – and they would be correct. However, they speculate no less when...no hard evidence exists in support of the skeptical view....The skeptical historian wins if

one embraces methodical skepticism, since he shoulders no burden of proof for his view. In methodical neutrality, he *ties* at best…[emphasis added][57]

It is a tie in this case for the simple reason that there is *insufficient evidence* to determine what really lies behind the religious conversion experience of a man two thousand years ago. Without leaning on the historical reliability of the Acts accounts of Paul's conversion experience, Licona's explanation for Paul's conversion – Jesus actually appeared to him – is just as speculative as a psychological explanation.

Without leaning on the historical reliability of the Gospels, the same dearth of evidence affects the assessment of the group appearance traditions to the Twelve and to all the apostles mentioned in 1 Corinthians 15:5&7. This book speculates that these traditions are authority designation appearance traditions (Chapter Four, pg. 99-105). Licona responds to this proposal by saying, "If this was a practice of the early Christians, then clear examples of this occurring ought to be available for support."[58] But how can Licona expect clear examples of authority designation occurring elsewhere if we do not have *anything* else from the first few years of the Christian movement? Licona focuses on the lack of authority designation examples in the Gospels, but the Gospels reflect Christian concerns and interests decades later and may or may not reflect the authority designation interests of the earliest Christians. Licona also tries to argue that the chronological order of the 1 Corinthians 15:5-8 appearance list, as indicated by the use of the word "then" in the list, counts against the authority designation explanation.[59] But as pointed out in Chapter Four of this book, the chronological order of the appearance list is consistent with an authority designation explanation (pg. 109-110).

Licona thinks he has eliminated the authority designation explanation for these appearance traditions, but he has not. Therefore, this speculative explanation stands side by side with Licona's own speculative explanation – that Jesus actually appeared to these groups.

In sum, unless one appeals to the historical reliability of the Gospels or to the Acts accounts of Paul's conversion experience, the lack of evidence makes *all* explanations for our seven facts speculative. Therefore, both of our hypotheses are ad hoc, and by an equal amount.

Ad hocness also includes background evidence. For example, the resurrection hypothesis requires the assumption, which many people feel is non-evidenced, that some supernatural entity, usually God, exists. However, since I accept that God exists (I am an agnostic), I do not see this as an ad hoc component of the resurrection hypothesis. Similarly, the hypothesis in this book assumes that psychological factors exist which can cause people to rationalize, hallucinate, and convert to another religion or sect. Since there is evidence that such psychological factors do exist, this background component of the hypothesis in this book is not ad hoc. What is ad hoc about God and the psychological factors just mentioned is each of our assumptions that they were in play at Christian origins. Other than the minimal facts that each of our hypotheses are trying to explain, there is no evidence that God acted in this case and there is no evidence that these psychological factors specifically affected the earliest Christians. In both cases, conjecture is being used to fill in where there are gaps in the evidence. Looking at background evidence, both of our hypotheses remain equally ad hoc.*

There is another piece of background evidence that is worth looking at because both Craig and Licona claim it reduces, or significantly limits, the ad hocness of the resurrection hypothesis. Licona said it best in one of his debates:

> ...To what degree is the resurrection hypothesis ad hoc? Not very much....[The three facts I lay out in my book] occur in a context charged with religious significance. At the very minimum, this context consists of three [additional] facts. Number one, Jesus claimed to have a special relationship with God. Two, Jesus taught that God had chosen him to usher in his kingdom. And three, Jesus performed deeds that awed crowds

---

* It is worth noting that one of the reasons we do not know if the psychological factors proposed in this book affected the earliest Christians (mainly Paul) is because we have nothing written by any of them before they came to believe that Jesus was raised from the dead.

and that both he and his followers regarded as divine miracles and exorcisms. All three of these facts are so strongly evidenced that they are virtually undisputed by historians of Jesus today. Thus within this context, if you had lived in the first century and seen Jesus within this context, and you saw him executed and then a few days later you saw him alive, you would normally conclude that he had been raised from the dead. And thus, the resurrection hypothesis is not contrived and the ad hoc component is minimal.[60]

But Licona points out in his book:

Perhaps one may object that this context provides an expectation for a miracle, since it is already charged with superstition. Accordingly, we are right to expect more miracle stories, and the reports of Jesus' resurrection come as no surprise....This is a thoughtful reply. It is certainly true that religiously charged contexts create an expectation for miracles, and we may presume that people in these contexts will make more out of a circumstance than may actually be there. Healing services showcasing Ernest Angley and Benny Hinn are prime examples. During worship services in which Angley and Hinn preside, people speak in tongues, receive healings and are often "slain in the Spirit." Reports of phenomena during these services can quickly become embellished and evolve into urban legends. The observation that a context charged with religious significance creates an expectation for miracle demonstrates that naturalistic explanations such as delusion, hallucination and legend can be quite reasonable in accounting for certain phenomena. It shows that a context can serve multiple purposes. And with that I am in agreement. Related to the resurrection of Jesus, we might argue that the context of Jesus as miracle-worker and eschatological agent created an expectation among his followers that resulted in their having delusions or hallucinations and in the rapid accumulation of urban legend, thus creating the resurrection narratives. I see no a priori reason for preferring a resurrection over this alternative. It is important, therefore, to weigh the hypotheses.[61]

If a context charged with religious significance can support the hypothesis in this book just as well as it can support the resurrection hypothesis, and if this background evidence reduces the ad hocness of the resurrection hypothesis, then it must reduce the ad hocness of the hypothesis in this book by the same amount. Whatever amount the ad hocness of our two hypotheses is reduced, the result in our comparison is the same – both of our hypotheses remain equally ad hoc.[*]

It is interesting to note that assessing the ad hocness of hypotheses can be subjective and result in entirely opposite conclusions, even among professionals. For example, two years after Licona published his book, McCullagh, an expert on the method of inference to the best explanation (if not one of its founders), had an exchange with Licona about his resurrection hypothesis, with one of the topics discussed being ad hocness. According to McCullagh, "The hypothesis that God raised Jesus from the dead…is weakened by the fact that it is entirely ad hoc."[62] According to Licona, "McCullagh's…assessment of [the] Resurrection Hypothesis as…ad hoc is mistaken."[63] William Craig has also noted the sometimes subjective nature of ad hocness: "Philosophers of science have found it notoriously difficult to explain what it is exactly that makes a hypothesis ad hoc."[64] And even McCullagh admits, "A fully intelligible account of arguments to the best explanation cannot yet be given, as some of the concepts involved have proved very difficult to analyse."[65]

Fortunately in our case, I do not think even large differences of opinion about ad hocness need to be settled. I think most people are willing to accept some conjecture as a part of any explanation, as long as they feel that conjecture is plausible, which is the next test. The importance of plausibility over ad hocness is also acknowledged by McCullagh:

---

[*] A context charged with religious significance is also sometimes used in the "plausibility" test to support the plausibility of Jesus' resurrection. However, for the reasons stated above, it supports the plausibility of the hypothesis in this book by the same amount. Also, as an aside, I do not think it is "virtually undisputed" among historians that Jesus thought of himself, or claimed to be, God's eschatological agent (as Licona suggests above). What I think is virtually undisputed among historians is that the "kingdom of God" was a central part of Jesus' preaching, although precisely what he meant by that is still disputed (see Licona's book, pg. 283-284).

The conditions which bear upon the acceptability of arguments to the best explanation can be divided into three groups: those about the explanatory scope and power of a hypothesis; those about the *ad hoc*ness of the hypothesis; and those about facts which render a hypothesis implausible or which disconfirm it. There is a sense in which the third group is the most important....explanatory scope and power are the next most important... [followed by] *ad hoc*...[66]

Plausibility

Since our two hypotheses have come out equal in all four tests above, everything funnels into this last test – plausibility. In the plausibility test, the best explanation is the one that is the most *probable* when measured against accepted truths *outside* of the question of interest. It is as if someone came up to you and told you a story and, before you even looked at the evidence, you made a judgment of how *likely* the story was to be true, or what the *odds* were of it being true, based on existing knowledge. As McCullagh states it, "The plausibility of a hypothesis is the same as its prior probability, prior that is to [looking at] the evidence it is designed to explain."[67] In the most simplistic terms, and incorporating the definition of plausible introduced at the beginning of this book, the most plausible hypothesis is simply the one that can be most easily *imagined* that it happened that way.

But there is already a problem. What, or who, defines what "accepted truths" and "existing knowledge" are? Many have tried to approach hypotheses of Christian origins under the pretense that the plausibility test is objective. I do not think it is. In my view, what people think are "accepted truths" and "existing knowledge" are really just the sum of their own background knowledge, biases, and personal experiences. In many cases, our background knowledge, biases, and personal experiences line up enough with others that we can assess the plausibility of something from the same basic perspective. However, sometimes our background knowledge, biases, and personal experiences do not line up very well, and I think Christian origins is one of those situations. Licona seems to agree:

[Historians] cannot look at the data devoid of biases, hopes or inclinations. No historian is exempt. Horizons [which Licona defines as "knowledge, experience, beliefs, education, cultural conditioning, preferences, presuppositions and worldview"] are of great interest to historians since they are responsible more than anything else for the embarrassing diversity among the conflicting portraits of the past....The historian who thinks that he has removed himself from his work is almost certainly mistaken....When the historical Jesus in general and the resurrection in particular are the subjects of inquiry, the horizon of the historian will be in full operation throughout the entire process.[68]

In other words, different background knowledge, biases, and personal experiences will cause people to have a different set of "accepted truths" or "existing knowledge", which in turn affects the probability that people assign to a particular hypothesis. In the most simplistic terms, the *ease* with which people are able to imagine a particular hypothesis actually happening will vary from person to person.

As an example of the strong background knowledge, biases, and personal experiences that can be present when looking at Christian origins evidence, consider this statement by Licona:

Ladies and gentleman when you see the great evidence we have out there today, he [Licona is referring to his debate opponent] says miracles don't occur? Well of course they occur. Craig Keener has just written a massive two volume set on this documenting a bunch. I've witnessed miracles. I know people who have been parts of miracles. Miracles do happen today. When you consider the existence of miracles, near-veridical apparitions, well evidenced near-death experiences of which Gary Habermas can list a hundred or more of them. And answered prayer, well gosh, the evidence for a supernatural realm is so strong today that anyone who denies a supernatural component to reality cannot be a realist.[69]

Consider too this statement by William Craig:

My knowledge of Christianity's truth, while supported by strong arguments, is not ultimately based on those arguments but on the witness of God Himself. If, therefore, I find myself confronted with a well-prepared and articulate Mormon who blows away my arguments and presents a case for Mormonism that I can't answer, I should not apostatize, since I have the witness of the Holy Spirit to Christianity's truth and so realize that although I've lost the argument, Christianity is nonetheless the truth.[70]

I would like to echo these honest statements about background knowledge, biases, and personal experiences with my own. I have read the Bible. I have even prayed to God for the ability to know the truth about it. I have done the same with the Book of Mormon. In neither case did I get anything that could even remotely be called "the witness of God Himself". In fact, I got nothing of the sort at all. I simply wondered if what these texts claimed was actually true. Add on top of this a lifetime of personal experience where I have never seen or been shown a *physically direct* intervention by God in human history, and the result on me is the same as it was on Thomas Paine two centuries ago, and I am sure on many other people:

[Jesus' disciple] Thomas did not believe the resurrection; and, as they say [in the Gospels], would not believe, without having occular and manual demonstration himself. *So neither will I*; and the reason is equally as good for me and for every other person, as for Thomas.[71]

There are probably all sorts of other background knowledge, biases, and personal experiences, many that we are not even consciously aware of, that affect the ease or difficulty with which our two hypotheses can be imagined. Because of this, the plausibility test can only be a *personal* assessment.

Based on my own background knowledge, biases, and personal experiences, I see the resurrection hypothesis explanations for Paul's silence on the discovered empty tomb and Mark's abrupt fear-induced silence ending to his empty tomb story as significantly less plausible than the explanation that this tradition is a legend, as proposed by the hypothesis in this book. But the much bigger differential in plausibility between our two hypotheses for me comes from what I stated on the first page of this book – experience-based doubt that God intervenes within human history in a *physically direct* way. Based on this specific background knowledge, bias, and personal experience, Jesus' resurrection seems *far* less plausible to me than fallible human beings rationalizing Jesus' death and the subsequent highly charged religious environment leading to individual hallucinations, collective enthusiasm, designations of authority, scriptural interpretation, religious conversions, and legendary growth.

If I try to imagine myself having the witness of God Himself, as William Craig does, and if I try to imagine a world where supernatural events are an obvious part of our reality, as Licona sees it, and if I thought those supernatural events were strongly correlated only with Christianity and not other belief systems, then I see myself accepting Jesus' resurrection as a historical fact and leaving Paul's silence on the discovered empty tomb and the strange ending to the Gospel of Mark as unexplained but insignificant details. However, I would at the same time see the hypothesis in this book as another plausible way to explain the seven facts that this historical analysis has centered on. In professing my faith, I would not claim that Jesus' resurrection from the dead is the only plausible explanation for the known facts.

Conclusion

In conclusion, when I compare the resurrection hypothesis to the hypothesis in this book using the seven facts derived from William Craig's and Michael Licona's work, our two hypotheses come out equal in every category of the historian's method of inference to the best explanation except the plausibility category. Viewing the plausibility of each hypothesis through the lens of my own background knowledge, biases, and personal experiences, the hypothesis in this book comes out on top by a large margin. Despite this, I would not confidently call the hypothesis in this book "history". The reason I would not confidently call the hypothesis in this book history is because it is too ad hoc (speculative) due to the paucity of historically reliable information. This lack of historically reliable information increases the possibility that the true explanation for Christian origins is simply not in the pool of hypotheses being considered at the present time. That is why the only thing I argue for in this book is that the hypothesis presented is *one* plausible way to read the Christian origins evidence.[*]

---

[*] Some readers may have noticed that some of the categories of inference to the best explanation have some redundancy to them. This has led some to conclude that the five categories can be collapsed into just two – explanatory power and plausibility (see for example Richard Carrier's *Proving History*, 2012). It is also worth noting (as Carrier does) that when proponents of different hypotheses are very passionate about their positions and are highly motivated to give an explanation for any piece of evidence that might not fit their hypothesis, explanatory power collapses into plausibility because those explanations given to preserve or increase explanatory power have to be evaluated for plausibility. In other words, everything funnels into plausibility, the same conclusion reached in the analysis in this chapter. It is also important to point out that many people may not think what were considered "facts" in the comparison above really are facts. Some may also think that other facts should have been included in the analysis. These views reflect how varied opinions are about the Christian origins evidence and how best to approach the issues. To those who would come at the problem with a different set of facts or from a different angle, I hope that at least some of the analysis above has been useful.

Chapter 8

Conclusion and Meaning

If Jesus did not resurrect from the dead, it is worth asking what other questions this might lead to. In addition to the beliefs and traditions that formed after Jesus' death, it seems like there had to be something else that caused Christianity to triumph over the Roman Empire's paganism and then go on to become a major world religion. What was it? Perhaps part of the answer lies with Jesus himself.

Scholars have tried to navigate the legends of the Gospels and other Christian literature to sift out a profile of the historical Jesus. One such profile comes from the Jesus Seminar. They conclude that Jesus was a sage of which there is little known except for the following basic sketch:

> [Jesus] regularly infringed the social codes in force in his society. He consorted openly with social outcasts, with "toll collectors and sinners." He did not observe kosher. He suggested that it was not what goes in to a person's body but what comes out that defiles. He did not practice fasting. He infringed the Sabbath codes on occasion. He did not observe other purity codes, such as washing his hands before eating....As a final act, Jesus went to Jerusalem, either spoke or acted against the temple and the temple authorities, and was executed by the Romans.[1]

If this profile is correct, it appears that Jesus had in view a less class-based and less ritualistic Jewish God than was prevalent among other Jews of the time. We see an expression of and probably an improvement on these same ideas in Paul's letter to the Galatians: "There is no longer Jew or Greek, there is no longer slave or free, there is no longer male and female; for all of you are one in Christ Jesus" (Galatians 3:28). The key and novel idea here (which for Paul only applies to Christians) is that all are equal in the eyes of God.

But how do we get from these ideas to a religion that triumphed over paganism and then went on to become a world religion? Perhaps the best answer comes from sociologist and Pulitzer Prize nominee Rodney Stark. Before the growth of Christianity was carried forward by the political power it obtained in the fourth century, Stark suggests there was a steady and continuous growth of Christianity among the four to six million dispersed Jews who lived outside Palestine (which was about eighty percent of all Jews at the time). Most of these Jews had been assimilated to some degree into the Greek culture there (Hellenized); almost none spoke their native Hebrew language anymore.[2] According to Stark, their remaining Jewishness put them in a socially marginalized position for which Christianity offered a solution:

> Christianity offered many of the same things to Hellenized Jews that nineteenth-century Jews found in the [Jewish] Reform Movement....A non-tribal, non-ethnic religion rooted in the Old Testament [the OT providing the familiarity and continuity], one that focused on theology and ethics rather than on custom and practice....Christianity offered to retain much of the religious content of *both* cultures and to resolve the contradictions between them...it freed them from an ethnic identity with which they had become uncomfortable.[3]

Stark argues that Christianity also grew among pagans because it offered superior answers to the misery, chaos, fear, and brutality of Greco-Roman life. Christianity taught to love and treat others as yourself. This eased the burden of the homeless, impoverished, orphaned, and widowed. It eased relations between social classes, and improved the treatment of women and slaves. Christianity offered a more compelling concept of god, one all loving and powerful God, instead of the multiple smaller gods of paganism. Pagans were able to adapt these ideas through Christianity without all of the ritual associated with Judaism.[4] Stark concludes with what he sees as the "ultimate factor" in the rise of Christianity: "Central doctrines of Christianity prompted and sustained attractive, liberating, and effective social relations and organizations."[5] Stark goes on to say, "Christianity brought a new conception of humanity to a world saturated with capricious cruelty...what Christianity gave to its converts was nothing less than their humanity."[6] Given all of this, it is no wonder that Christianity spread among many Jews and pagans in the Roman empire, went on to become a world religion, and is still a cultural success today.

That key Christian doctrine mentioned earlier – equality before God – would go on to lead in a messy and sporadic way over many centuries, and often against a Christian status quo, to some of the world's greatest cultural advancements – the abolition of slavery, better treatment for women, and the rise of democracy as a form of government. Of course non-Christians were also a part of these liberty movements, people like Elizabeth Cady Stanton in the nineteenth century women's suffrage movement, Thomas Paine's denunciation of slavery in 1775, Ernestine L. Rose's activism in the women's suffrage movement and the anti-slavery movement, John Stuart Mill's influential doctrine of liberty, and Thomas Jefferson's lead role in the birth of modern democracy. However, it is impossible to separate these people from their upbringing and their surrounding Christian culture which was based on the concept that all are equal in the eyes of God. As conservative commentator Dinesh D'Souza says about the groups that led these liberty movements:

> These groups [over a very long period of time] gave a political interpretation to the biblical notion that all are equal in the eyes of God. From this spiritual truth they derived a political proposition: because human beings are equal in God's sight, no man has the right to rule another without his consent. This doctrine is the moral root of both abolitionism and democracy....The Christian doctrine of human equality [before God] is the basis for all modern doctrines of human rights.[7]

Actually, to determine the real basis for all modern doctrines of human rights one has to determine what gave rise to the Christian doctrine of equality before God. Some might propose this concept was divinely inspired in Jesus and in the apostle Paul. But if this book is correct that Jesus did not resurrect from the dead, it is difficult to maintain that this concept was any more divinely inspired than any other idea that comes from men.

One thing indicating more human mechanisms were at work in the rise of the idea of equality before God is that similar or identical concepts of abstract human equality arose in other philosophical and religious traditions. For example, in the fourth century B.C.E. the Greek sophist Alcidamas said, "God has set everyone free. No one is made a slave by nature" (Messeniacus). Similarly, and also in the fourth century B.C.E., the Athenian poet Philemon said, "Though a man be a slave he is made of the same flesh as you. For no one was ever made a slave by nature; but chance has enslaved a man's body."[8] Although we do not know if Christianity was an influence, equality before God also appears in Judaism around 150 C.E.:

> Rabbi Judah ben Shalom said in the name of Rabbi Eleazar: It is the case by humans that if a poor man says anything, one pays little regard; but if a rich man speaks, immediately he is heard and listened to. Before G-d, however, all are equal: women, slaves, poor and rich. (Midrash Rabba, Parshat Beshalach)

Islam too, although it does not explicitly state the doctrine of equality before God, strongly implies the same idea in its pilgrimage to Mecca where people of all color, rich and poor, kings and peasants, men and women, young and old, all stand before God together at their holiest shrine. Buddhists of course could never imagine the concept of equality before God for the simple reason that they do not believe in God. But they could in the second century B.C.E. say, "Just as I am so are they, just as they are so am I" (Sutta Nipata 705, also annotated as Sutta Nipata 3.11).

I suggest that the roots of the idea of equality before God, which Jesus himself may never have articulated in the form of a "doctrine" like Paul did, was just simple human empathy. We see a codified form of empathy in Judaism as early as 1000 B.C.E.: "You shall love your neighbor as yourself" (Leviticus 19:18). We see it again in 180 B.C.E.: "What thou thyself hatest, do to no man" (Tobit 4:15). And again sometime between 30 B.C.E. and 10 C.E.: "What is hateful to you, do not do to your neighbor: that is the whole Torah; all the rest of it is commentary; go and learn" (Rabbi Hillel, Babylonian Talmud, Tractate Shabbat 31a). As the Jesus Seminar points out about the Gospel's rendition of Jesus' statement to love one's neighbor as oneself (Mark 12:31), with its application in the parable of the good Samaritan (Luke 10:25-35): "The response Jesus gives is one any Judean faithful to his or her tradition could have given, had he or she been informed by Rabbi Hillel, a contemporary of Jesus."[9] In other words, Jesus was building on the ideas of others before and around him, or perhaps more accurately, Jesus was doing what Arthur Nock describes is the role of great prophets in society:

> The receptivity of most people for that which is wholly new (if anything is) is small....The originality of a prophet lies commonly in his ability to fuse into a white heat [the] combustible material which is [already] there, to express and appear to meet the half-formed prayers of some at least of his contemporaries. The teaching of Gotama the Buddha grows out of the eager and baffled asceticism and speculation of his time, and it is not easy even now to define exactly what was new in him except his attitude. The message of John the Baptist and of Jesus gave form and substance to the dreams of a kingdom which had haunted many of their compatriots for generations.[10]

That the Christian movement was a human process that gave form and substance to empathy that was already there can be seen in the New Testament's passages about slavery. Colossians 4:1 says, "Masters, treat your slaves justly and fairly, for you know that you also have a Master in heaven" (for other passages on slavery see 1 Peter 2:18-21; Titus 2:9-10; Ephesians 6:5-9; Colossians 3:22-25; 1 Corinthians 7:17-24; and 1 Timothy 6:1-2). This admonition to treat slaves justly and fairly was revolutionary for its time, but it understandably presupposes the institution of slavery normal and acceptable. Even four hundred years later, Christian leaders were forced to theorize, "The prime cause, then, of slavery is sin" (St. Augustine, The City of God, Book XIX, Chapter 15). Not until the middle ages was there enough cultural progress that the Pope started prohibiting slavery, but even then the only prohibition was against enslaving fellow Christians: "[A] sentence of excommunication [will] be incurred by one and all who attempt to capture, sell, or subject to slavery, *baptized* residents of the Canary Islands, or those who are freely *seeking Baptism*" (Pope Eugene IV, Sicut Dudum, 1435 C.E., emphasis added). After a few more centuries, objections to enslaving non-Christians emerged and Abraham Lincoln could say, "I would not be a slave, so I would not be a master. This expresses my idea of democracy" (Definition of Democracy, 1858). After two thousand years and a civil war we can now confidently reject Paul's kinder form of slavery and say that no one should ever be, nor should anyone have ever been, a slave.

Empathy in its socialized form – compassion – appears in almost every religious and philosophical tradition, not just the Judeo-Christian tradition.[11] For example, Hindus in 150 B.C.E. said, "One should not behave towards others in a way which is disagreeable to one's self; this is the essence of morality" (Mahabharata, Anusasana Parva 113:8). Confucius in 500 B.C.E. said, "Try your best to treat others as you would wish to be treated yourself" (Mencius VII.A.4; see too Doctrine of the Mean 13). Buddhists in the second century B.C.E. said, "Hurt not others with that which pains yourself" (Udana-Varga 5:18). Zoroaster in 600 B.C.E. said, "Whatever is disagreeable to yourself do not do unto others" (Shayast-ne-Shayast 13:29). The Greek philosopher Isocrates in 375 B.C.E. said, "Do not do to others what would anger you if done to you by others." The Greek philosopher Epictetus in 135 C.E. said, "What thou avoidest suffering thyself seek not to impose on others" (Encheiridion). Mohammed in the seventh century C.E. said, "What actions are most excellent? To gladden the heart of human beings, to feed the hungry, to help the afflicted, to lighten the sorrow of the sorrowful, and to remove the sufferings of the injured" (Sahih Bukhari). The stated purpose of the world's first known legal code in 1780 B.C.E. was, "...to cause justice to prevail and to ensure that the strong do not oppress the weak" (The Law of Hammurabi).

If the idea to treat others as you would want to be treated, and the idea of an abstract equality of all people, existed in many places around the globe at and before the time of Jesus, why was it Christianity that took these ideas the furthest? This is a great question. The factors which cause some cultures to actualize certain ideas better than other cultures are complex and beyond my scope here. I have a feeling that the cultural mechanisms involved are barely understood even by those who study them.

However, an example of a different kind of cultural advancement, one in which the causes went undetected until a decade ago and not until after thirty years of research by one very curious individual, illustrates how huge cultural leaps can happen due to the most unexpected causes. In his best-selling book *Guns, Germs, and Steel*, Jared Diamond shows how those societies which first made the transition from hunter-gatherer to mass food production were catapulted thousands of years ahead of others in many other cultural aspects. The main advantages of mass food production were much larger populations, a germ resistant and carrying populace, and massive amounts of time freed up to invent things and to create societal hierarchies and organizations to efficiently direct the larger populace toward common goals. Diamond shows in excruciating detail how the transition to mass food production first occurred at those locations on the globe which simply happened to have the best selection of domesticable animal and plant species and the least geographic and ecological barriers to their spread. The Fertile Crescent was the first to make the transition to mass food production around 8500 B.C.E. Europe was next around 5000 B.C.E. The United States did not become a mass food-producing continent until the domesticated animals and plants of Europe were brought here by the Europeans (primarily cattle and a diverse suite of protein-rich cereals). Jared Diamond explains:

> It is striking that the areas of Native America without food production...are [today] some of the most productive farmlands and pasture....The former absence of food production in these

lands was due entirely to their local paucity of domesticable wild animals and plants, and to geographic and ecological barriers that prevented the crops and the few domestic animal species of other parts of the Americas from arriving.[12]

When the culturally advanced Christopher Columbus arrived in the Americas and found the Indians living in the Stone Age, it is understandable that he attributed it to their lack of Christianity. But the lack of technological and societal advancements among the Indians, like those which made Columbus' voyage and his advanced society possible, were due almost entirely, if not entirely, to just simple geography. The point I am trying to make here is that large cultural leaps can give the mistaken impression of a divine cause or lead to the mistaken conclusion that certain cultural benefits can only be obtained and sustained through a particular religious belief. This is faulty thinking.

This leads me into what I think is a main concern for many people when the foundations of a religion are questioned like this book has done. Although compassion is rooted in empathy, it is in conflict with our own self-centeredness. The prevailing wisdom is that the latter wins out without some kind of belief in God, or some kind of belief in a life after this one that is dependent on our actions here and now. As Dostoyevsky's Grand Inquisitor said, "If there is no God, all is permitted". The same implied concern is expressed by Benjamin Franklin. Franklin cautioned an acquaintance who had just written a pamphlet arguing against the existence of God to not "attempt unchaining the Tyger, but burn the Piece before it is seen by any other Person....If Men are so wicked as we now see them with Religion, what would they be if without it?"[13] Even the late atheist/agnostic Carl Sagan noted:

> There is no human culture without religion. That being the case, that immediately says that religion provides some essential meat, and if that's the case shouldn't we be a little careful about condemning something that it desperately needed?[14]

That being said, I am not advocating here that there is no God or afterlife. I personally am agnostic on those things. However, in defense of my atheist friends, I think their behavior is probably more of a mixed bag than the fears above suggest, just like the behavior of those who believe in God or an afterlife is often a mixed bag.

But if the effect of questioning religion is uncertain, why not leave well enough alone? Why write a book like this one? This is a good question, and one that I still wrestle with, but there are four main reasons. The first is simply to share with others who might have the same interest in researching Christian origins. To them, I hope my book has been useful in some way. The second springs from the claim by some Christians that Jesus' resurrection is the only plausible explanation for Christian origins. This claim bothers me because I do not think it is true, and this book is an attempt to explain why. Third, I reasoned to myself that even if this book is completely wrong, it should still help the search for what actually happened at Christian origins. Eliminating competing hypotheses is how science works and it is how we all get closer to the truth. Because of this, even Christians should welcome competing hypotheses. The fourth and final reason for publishing this book is a general belief in the benefits of truth. Christianity and other religions may bring enormous good to the world, but if this book is correct that Jesus did not resurrect from the dead, then many people have a false understanding of the world. False understandings have a way of leading to unfavorable consequences over the long term.

We occasionally see these unfavorable consequences in the interaction between the world's religions due to their mutually exclusive religious claims. As former Prime Minister Tony Blair said in 2008, "Globalization is pushing people together and there is a danger that religious faith pulls them apart."[15]

It has been said that how one orients toward religion defines one's "total-worldview", that is, it defines what one believes about the world around them at the most fundamental level. Where did I come from? Why am I here? Where am I going? Our total-worldview structures our experience and interpretation of the world around us and forms the lens through which we see everything else: politics, economics, education, relationships, science, values, etc. We tend not to question our total-worldview once it is established, and those with different total-worldviews often appear as evil, stupid, or crazy. The non-religious are not immune, for their orientation toward religion also forms a total-worldview. In short, humanity is and always has been stuck in a quagmire of conflicting total-worldviews.

The widely accepted answer to this age old problem is tolerance. However, there is a limit to the benefits of tolerance among more fundamental believers and on issues where values come into conflict. For example, in our country there is no reconciling a Christian who wants the Bible's creation story taught in public schools and the public school's decision not to. Such parents often go to a private school if they can afford it, and so too would a secular minded parent if the situation were reversed. It is not surprising that some propose we scrap our public school system and essentially segregate into schools that are consistent with our total-worldviews. Likewise, there are fundamental irreconcilable differences which cause a twelve million member church to tell their young people "not [to] take the chance of dating nonmembers...one cannot afford to take a chance on falling in love with someone who may never accept the gospel."[16] It should be no surprise if twelve million non-members of that church respectfully reach the same conclusion of incompatibility. There is an irreconcilable and radical difference between a scientist trying to raise public awareness and funds for studying the risk of a giant meteor strike, and someone who says that if God is going to let such an event happen there is nothing we can do about it.[17] These two total-worldviews have been at odds in many scientific inquiries. There is no reconciling someone who thinks God prohibits homosexuality and is therefore against any legal or social status that legitimizes gay couples, and those who agree with former vice president Dick Cheney that "people ought to be free to enter into any kind of union they wish, any kind of arrangement they wish."[18] One can hardly blame a non-Christian soldier for questioning the wisdom of going to Iraq in 2003 when he hears the president respond to a reporter asking if his father thinks the war is a good idea with, "You know, he is the wrong father to appeal to in terms of strength. There is a higher father I appeal to."[19] On the other hand, a Christian might think that such divine consultation, or at least being a Christian, is a minimum requirement for the person in the oval office.

Most of the time our differences in total-worldviews just separate us, but sometimes they are a source of tragic conflict. While tolerance goes a long way towards dealing with these problems, I think the real long-term solution may be more convergence in our total-worldviews, i.e. more convergence in that primary lens through which we see everything else. Toward that goal, this book has tried to convey to others what the founding event of a total-worldview different from my own looks like to me. That is all anyone can do. In my view, the founding event of Christianity is the basic idea of human equality, not resurrection. Additionally, and based on the evidence I am so far aware of, my experience-based doubt leads me to conclude that none of the world's religions has been founded by a divine event and none has access to the infallible will of God. If true, then one of the biggest tasks for humankind over the long term is to put their myths in proper perspective while at the same time encouraging those societal relationships that foster human empathy, its socialized form to do unto others as you would have them do unto you, and its institutionalized form, equal human rights. We would leave behind some of our divisiveness and move forward with the common understanding that whether God exists or not, we have only our own fallible hearts and minds to determine our future.

Appendix
Myth Growth Rates and the Gospels[*]

One major topic that impacts on the historical reliability of the Gospels is the rate at which myth or legend can grow over time and displace the historically accurate accounts of events. Some argue that the Gospels cannot be mostly legend, as many scholars have proposed, because that would require a myth growth rate that is implausibly high given their relatively early composition in relation to the events they claim to recount. For example, evangelical scholar William Craig says, "One of the major problems with the legend hypothesis...is that the time gap between Jesus' death and the writing of the Gospels is just too short for this to have happened."[1]

I think this topic is key for many people who try to assess the historical reliability of the Gospels. It was for me. And it was for another layman: Lee Strobel, an atheist whose investigations into the New Testament led him to become a Christian and author of the runaway best-selling book *The Case for Christ*. Strobel and I both began with the same intuitive conclusion, that the Gospels must be some kind of legendized record of Jesus. But as we each went on to look at the various factors related to Gospel reliability, we reacted differently to the myth-growth-rate argument. For me, the myth-growth-rate argument was the biggest challenge to my position as a non-Christian...until I looked at it closer. For Strobel, it was the "clincher" that led him to change his position:

> I had wanted to believe that the deification of Jesus was the result of legendary development in which well-meaning but misguided people slowly turned a wise sage into the mythical Son of God....But while I went into my investigation thinking that this legendary explanation was intuitively obvious, I emerged convinced it was totally without basis. What clinched it

[*] Parts of this essay appeared in the Feb/Mar 2013 issue of *Free Inquiry* magazine and in the May 2013 "Featured Articles" section of *The Bible and Interpretation* website (http://www.bibleinterp.com/articles/2013/kom378030.shtml).

for me was the famous study by A.N. Sherwin-White, the great classical historian from Oxford University, which William Lane Craig alluded to in our interview. Sherwin-White meticulously examined the rate at which legend accrued in the ancient world. His conclusion: not even two full generations was enough time for legend to develop and to wipe out a solid core of historical truth.[2]

Strobel and Craig are referring here to the last lecture in an eight-part lecture series presented by the late Adrian Nicholas Sherwin-White in 1961. Two years later, all eight lectures were published in a book titled *Roman Society and Roman Law in the New Testament*. The main topic of the first seven lectures was to appraise the New Testament in light of known aspects of Roman law and social background. In the last lecture, which forms the last seven pages of his book, Sherwin-White stepped out from the main topic of his lectures to, in his own words, "boldly state a case" in favor of the historical reliability of the Gospels.[3]

The focal point of Sherwin-White's case for the historical reliability of the Gospels was a two-generation rule he derived from the myth growth rates he observed in other ancient literature: "…Even two generations [about seventy years total] are too short a span to allow the mythical tendency to prevail over the hard historical core of the oral tradition."[4] Based on this two-generation rule, Sherwin-White argued that there should be enough history about Jesus in the Gospels that "the history of his mission" can be written.[5] Sherwin-White did not specify *how much* history of Jesus' mission should be able to be written, but for the sake of this essay I am going to assume it is quite a bit, based on my own subjective reading of Sherwin-White's lecture and based on Sherwin-White's 1993 obituary which refers to his "conviction of the essential historicity of the narratives in the New Testament".[6]

Before continuing any further, it might be helpful to stop at this point and clarify three things. First, virtually all scholars agree that the Gospels were written within two generations (about seventy years) after Jesus' death in the early 30s C.E. Second, Sherwin-White's two-generation rule above is not focused on how fast myth can grow; it is focused on how fast the *historical core* can be *erased.* Sherwin-White and many others acknowledge that myth can grow very fast. It is the rate at which the historical core can be *reduced* or *lost* (due to being displaced by myth) that is in dispute. Third, everything discussed in this essay is based on the Gospels *not* being written by or getting their information from firsthand eyewitnesses. Nearly all scholars acknowledge this possibility. If the Gospels did not get their information directly from eyewitnesses, then the rate at which the historical core can be pushed out of the oral tradition is of interest because the Gospels are, at best, a snapshot of the oral tradition in existence at the time each Gospel was written.

Many have rejected Sherwin-White's two-generation rule and his conclusion from it that the Gospels are essentially reliable, but few have bothered trying to explain *why* Sherwin-White's two-generation rule does not hold up. However, there is one person who has done this: Peter Brunt, another classical historian and colleague of Sherwin-White. Brunt was an expert on Alexander the Great who would later be chosen over Sherwin-White for the coveted Camden Professor of Ancient History Chair in 1970. Brunt's initial response to Sherwin-White's two-generation rule was made in private and is captured, along with Sherwin-White's response back to him, in a footnote at the very end of Sherwin-White's book. Sherwin-White wrote in this footnote:

> Mr. P.A. Brunt has suggested in private correspondence that a study of the Alexander [the Great] sources is less encouraging for my thesis. There was a remarkable growth of myth around his person and deeds within the lifetime of contemporaries [circa 300 B.C.E], and the historical embroidery was often deliberate. But the hard [historical] core still remains, and an alternative but neglected source – or pair of sources – survived for the serious inquirer Arrian to utilize in the second century A.D. This seems to me encouraging rather than the reverse.[7]

As can be seen in this footnote, despite Brunt saying that some of the Alexander sources were less encouraging for Sherwin-White's thesis, Sherwin-White stood his ground. His main point in reply to Brunt was that despite a remarkable growth of myth around Alexander the Great, the hard historical core of the oral tradition still remained, and an alternative but neglected pair of sources survived for Arrian to utilize when writing Alexander's history four hundred years later in the second century C.E. (the alternative pair of sources Sherwin-White is referring to are Ptolemy and Aristobulus).

There are only two ways I can make sense of this response by Sherwin-White. One, he was simply disagreeing with Brunt that *any* of the early Alexander sources had a shortage of historical core in them. Two, Sherwin-White was saying that *despite* the shortage of historical core in *some* of the early Alexander sources, the historical core of the oral tradition was nevertheless still captured – in this case in the alternative but neglected pair of sources (Ptolemy and Aristobulus). If this second way of understanding Sherwin-White is what he actually intended, it is useful simply to show at this point that even the author of the two-generation rule agrees with Brunt that *some* of the early Alexander sources had a shortage of historical core in them. I will come back to this possibility later, but the analysis below applies no matter which way Sherwin-White intended in his response to Brunt.

Shortly after Sherwin-White's book was published, Brunt replied to Sherwin-White's two-generation rule again, this time responding specifically to Sherwin-White's footnote above:

> Sherwin-White has done me the honour to cite a comparison I drew with our accounts of Alexander whom some of his own contemporaries treated as a god....[It is true that Alexander's history was still able to be written,] but Alexander's career was public in a sense which that of Jesus in Galilee was not....If the synoptic Gospels reflect traditions that grew and were remoulded in the changing experience of the Palestinian Church, how can we objectively distinguish between what is original and what is accretion, seeing that the Gospels themselves must be almost our only evidence for that changing experience?...Sherwin-White has not provided, as he thinks, conclusive reasons to reject the view...that the history of his [Jesus'] mission cannot be written.[8]

The key point in Brunt's response above, which is where Sherwin-White went wrong in his two-generation argument, is that

Alexander the Great, like almost everyone else classical historians normally investigate, was a figure of *significant public interest* when he was alive. Because of this, widespread knowledge of facts about him across a range of hostile, friendly, and neutral people would have limited how much the historical core could be displaced by legend in the oral and written traditions after his death. However, in the case of Jesus, this constraint would have been much less, because Jesus was very probably a figure of very little public significance except to his followers when he was alive and to his worshippers after his death.

That Sherwin-White did not fully consider the effects of public interest in a figure on the preservation of the historical core after his or her death is evident by the fact that every example he gives in his myth-growth-rate essay of people whom the historical core was preserved – Pisistratus (tyrant of Athens), Hipparchus (tyrant of Athens after Pisistratus), Gaius Gracchus (politician), Tiberius Caesar (emperor), Cleomenes (king), Themistocles (military commander), and all forty-six people in Plutarch's *Lives* (every single one a statesman, general, king, emperor, lawmaker, politician, tyrant, or consul) – *all* are figures of significant public interest.

But what about the presence and influence of firsthand eyewitnesses on the oral tradition, someone might ask. Although a few of Jesus' closest followers were probably eyewitnesses to a large part of his ministry (such as the apostles), in an enthusiastic religious movement driven by belief in Jesus' resurrection and imminent return (as outlined in this book, these were sincerely held *beliefs* that were not the result of legendary growth), these followers may by themselves have been unable to contain the growth of legend and displacement of the historical core among those in the growing church who did not know Jesus when he was alive or were not eyewitnesses of the specific events being distorted. The ability of a few of Jesus' closest followers to contain the growth of legend would have been further hampered if the legends were growing in several different locales, for in this case they would have had the nearly impossible task of being present everywhere, stamping out all of the unhistorical legends. Eyewitnesses of Jesus' ministry may also have viewed the correction of legends and policing of historical accuracy for events that occurred before Jesus' death as a relatively trivial pursuit if their focus was mainly on Jesus' future return. In this case, their priority would have been on convincing non-believers and galvanizing believers of the most important thing that they believed was true – that Jesus was the Messiah, had been raised from the dead, and would be back very soon. Any restraint a few firsthand eyewitnesses did provide would have been further diminished as they died off in the decades after Jesus' death.

The Gospel authors may also have been part of the messianic fervor and intentionally or unintentionally added some embellishments at the cost of historical core. While Sherwin-White in his myth-growth-rate essay views the Gospel writers "quite generally as primitive historians,"[9] Brunt points out that "they were not seeking to record historic incidents so much as to proclaim salvation".[10] It is human nature to embellish, and it would also be human nature if the better story became the more popular one in the growing Christian community, even if it was not the most historically accurate one. Additionally, if the Gospel accounts of Jesus' life and death were the most popular in the growing Church, and not many outside the Church knew much about Jesus because he had not been a figure of significant public interest, it makes sense that less-legendized and less-biased records, if they were ever even written, would not survive.

For those who think all of this is irrelevant because the Gospels represent *independent* strands of oral tradition, which would virtually guarantee their historicity where they agree, world-renowned expert on oral transmission Jan Vansina strongly disagrees and explains why:

> ...We cannot assume that the testimony of two different informants from the same community or even society is really independent. This is very important. In history, proof is given only when two independent sources confirm the same event or situation, but...it is not possible to do this with oral tradition wherever a corpus exists and information flows are unstemmed (i.e., in most cases). Feedback and contamination is the norm....No one will consider the three synoptic Gospels as

independent sources, even though they have different authors...they stemmed from one single oral milieu, from one corpus in one community. Once this is realized, it is easy to see that it also applies to John, the fourth Gospel...[11]

Given everything discussed above, it is plausible that the historical core surrounding Jesus' life and death is both smaller and comprises a smaller portion of the Christian origins record than historians are used to seeing in other ancient records. This would explain why a professional historian like Sherwin-White could mistakenly think the Gospels are essentially reliable. This would also explain the inability of many scholars who look critically at the Gospels to reach a consensus on a substantive history of Jesus' mission beyond the most basic facts, such as his probable start as a follower of John the Baptist, eventually attracting his own following, and getting crucified by the Romans.

In conclusion, the Gospels are an *understandable exception* to what classical historians normally deal with, because classical historians rarely if ever deal with the written records of a highly revered religious figure who had very little contemporary significance to anyone but his followers when he was alive and to his worshippers after his death and where the entire written record comes only from those who worshipped him. Because of this, using the myth growth rates observed in other ancient records as a baseline to say what should be observed in the Gospels is a mistaken approach.

In his memoir of Sherwin-White that he wrote for the British Academy in 1994, Brunt revisited Sherwin-White's myth-growth-rate essay from thirty years earlier with brutal honesty: "His remarks do not convince me that he had deeply considered this whole matter....He was himself a practising Church-man, and this may explain his unconvincing adventure into apologetics."[12]

Brunt's frank remarks above would be a good conclusion to this look into Sherwin-White's attempt to apply a two-generation rule to the Gospels; however, there are two more points to make.

First, despite Alexander the Great's huge public significance, there may actually be a written source even about him in which the historical core of the oral tradition was very significantly displaced by legend within two generations of his death. This source is known as the Alexander Romance. However, because the earliest surviving copies of the Alexander Romance date from centuries after Alexander's death, there is significant controversy about when the first version was written and what exactly was in it. This controversy will probably never be settled, but it is worth noting the opinion of Richard Stoneman, honorary fellow in the Department of Classics and Ancient History at the University of Exeter, in a widely acclaimed and highly respected book on Alexander the Great (*The Landmark Arrian*, 2010):

> Soon after his death, Alexander's life story was written up by an anonymous author....This work, known as the *Alexander Romance*, emphasized the fabulous elements of Alexander's story and added many new fables....This work seems, however, not to have been known to the Romans until it was translated by Julius Valerius in the fourth century C.E.; this has led to the mistaken view, still shared by many, that the Greek original was not written until shortly before that date. Probably it arose much earlier, perhaps in the early third century B.C.E. The *Alexander Romance* is a fictional biography that...is of interest as indicating the way that the memory of Alexander was shaped a generation or two after his death.[13]

If Stoneman is right, then the Alexander Romance shows that even for a hugely public figure, Sherwin-White's two-generation rule can fail in some quarters of the oral tradition and in the associated written sources. It also drives home the point that if one wanted to try salvaging Sherwin-White's two-generation rule, the following corollary would have to be added to it: When in some sources the mythical tendency *has* prevailed over the hard historical core of the oral tradition in the first two generations, there will *always* survive another less legendized source or sources to guide the later historian.

But this just returns us to the problem of Jesus' public insignificance. If the Gospel accounts of Jesus are similar to the Alexander Romance account of Alexander the Great, who would have written the unbiased or less legendized accounts with more of the real story? The answer is: nobody.

There is no way to know for sure, but in my opinion Sherwin-White tacitly acknowledged (in the footnote at the end of his book) that the corollary above was part of his two-generation rule. As mentioned earlier in this essay, the essence of that footnote was that Brunt thought some of the Alexander sources were less encouraging for Sherwin-White's thesis, to which Sherwin-White replied that the historical core of the oral tradition still remained and an alternative but neglected pair of sources survived for Arrian to use when writing Alexander's history four hundred years later. I think Sherwin-White may have agreed with Brunt that some of the early Alexander sources did not have the amount of historical core that he was arguing for in the Gospels, and that is why he brought up the alternative pair of Alexander sources. In doing so, Sherwin-White's point was that the historical core of the oral tradition was captured in the written record as a *whole*, even if not in *every piece* of the written record, and so his two-generation rule still held true. Sherwin-White was of course right in the case of Alexander the Great, and Sherwin-White had every right to say that this was encouraging for his thesis rather than the reverse, but in doing so he was tacitly admitting the need for the corollary above. But as already mentioned, even with this corollary, Sherwin-White's argument is stuck with a big hole in it when it comes to the Christian origins record – if Jesus was not a figure of significant public interest when he was alive or to anyone but his worshippers after his death, we very likely would not have an alternative but neglected pair of sources to fill in the record for Jesus like we did for Alexander the Great.

The second and final point to make about Sherwin-White's two-generation rule is that, as far as I can tell, it has never gathered any consensus among classical historians. If anyone were to ever try to do so, it would not surprise me if the vast majority of them either disagreed with it or gave the same response Roman historian J.J. Nicholls gave in 1964: "…the discussion, as far as it goes, is interesting, but it is too sketchy to be convincing."[14] Out of the seven reviews of Sherwin-White's book that I could find in English that specifically addressed his myth-growth-rate essay (all from the 1960s), only two were more supportive than this toward Sherwin-White's two-generation rule.[15]

That concludes my look into the effects of myth growth rates on historical core decay rates. The rest of this essay will just reinforce what is already widely agreed on – myth can grow very fast.

According to evangelical scholar Michael Licona:

> Legend emerged rapidly in antiquity. Lucian [a second century writer] reports that while sailing down a river Aristobulus handed Alexander the Great a narrative of combat between Porus and Alexander that he had just written. Alexander was so disgusted by the specific deeds of valor and achievements too great to be true that he threw the book into the river....[Another example:] When Lucian informed Cronius of Peregrinus's suicide, he added that he had conveyed the details without embellishment. However, he stated that he would dress them up for the dullards....[A third example:] Seneca [a first-century philosopher] noted that historians were often guilty of reporting incredible events in order to win approval. He adds that "some [historians] are credulous, some are negligent, on some falsehood creeps unawares....What the whole tribe has in common is this: it does not think its own work can achieve approval and popularity unless it sprinkles that work with falsehood."[16]

First-century Roman historian Tacitus echoes this sentiment:

> That everything gets exaggerated is typical for any story....[All] of the greatest events are obscure – while some people accept whatever they hear as beyond doubt, others twist the truth into its opposite, and both errors grow over subsequent generations.[17]

In 425 B.C.E., the Greek historian Herodotus reported traditions that were circulating from the Persian wars fifty five years earlier. These traditions included a temple that magically defended itself with animated armaments, lightning bolts, and collapsing cliffs, a sacred olive tree that grew an arm's length shoot in one day, a horse that gave birth to a rabbit, and a mass resurrection of cooked fish.[18] As Richard Carrier says, "[It was] an age of fable and wonder, where magic, miracles, ghosts, and gods were everywhere and almost never doubted."[19]

Another example of rapidly growing and widely believed legend is the WWI legend of the Angel of Mons, which developed over a period of just months. According to Alan Coulson:

> Under the stress of national crisis, fact and the supernatural were blended together in a myth – not a superstition, but a part-factual, part-fictional explanation of disconcerting threat and reassurance that the danger would pass. This myth was not tested scientifically; it was not analyzed; it was just accepted.[20]

Arthur Machen, the author of the fictional story that unintentionally contributed to the rise of the Angel of Mons legend would later write, "The snowball of rumor was set rolling until it was swollen to a monstrous size."[21]

In 1836, Julius Müller issued the following challenge to David Strauss after Strauss wrote a book, highly controversial in his time, proposing that the Gospels were mostly legend:

> Professor Strauss doubtless supposes that the thirty years which might perhaps be found between the death of Christ, and the composition of the oldest of our Gospels, are sufficient for it [the growth of significant legend]. But we must regard his opinion as groundless, unless he gives proof, that within thirty years, on a clear historical scene, not strange fables, – for thirty years are not requisite for that, – but a grand series of legends, the most prominent elements of which are fictitious, have anywhere gathered round an important historical individual, and been firmly fixed in the general belief.[22]

To answer Müller's challenge in the simplest way, one just needs to repeat what Sherwin-White said about Alexander the Great in his footnote quoted at the beginning of this essay: "There was a remarkable growth of myth around his person and deeds within the lifetime of contemporaries." This statement alone meets the bulk of Müller's challenge. These myths about Alexander the Great were also firmly enough "fixed in the general belief" (the other part of Müller's challenge) that, as Sherwin-White also pointed out, they were still alive four hundred years later when Arrian wrote Alexander's history in the second century.

Even if one wanted to measure Müller's challenge of "firmly fixed in the general belief" in the short term by the initial number of believers in the legends, his challenge still falls flat. Contrary to those who think there were mass conversions or huge numbers of Christians very early on, sociologist Rodney Stark suggests the same growth rate for early Christianity as has been observed for Mormonism, three to four percent per year. Like any compound-rate growth curve, it starts off very slow and gets big only much later. In order to reach the widely agreed-upon figure of six million Christians by 300 C.E., there need only have been 1000 Christians in the year 40 C.E., 1400 in 50 C.E., and only 7500 in 100 C.E., a full seven decades after Jesus' death.[23] It is not hard to imagine that as many, or more people, believed in the Alexander legends in the initial decades after Alexander's death. As James Crossley notes, "...The rapid emergence of miraculous and legendary traditions surrounding pagan figures, such as Alexander...even within their own life times...was one of the few points of agreement at the [2004] resurrection British New Testament Conference discussion."[24]

The large scale and rapid legendization of an individual is rare, but in addition to Alexander the Great, there is another person who was significantly and rapidly legendized, not only very soon after his death, but also when he was alive. Gershom Scholem, President of the Israel Academy of Sciences and Humanities, notes the rapid rise and widespread belief in legends in the very first year of the seventeenth-century messianic movement of Sabbatai Sevi: "...Legend developed and spread at an amazing speed...by the autumn of 1665...fiction far outweighed the facts...the believers moved in a dizzy whirl of legends, miracles, and revelations....The transition from mere factual reality to the transfigured reality of the heart, that is, to legend, was rapid. Collective enthusiasm quickly surrounded events with a halo."[25]

The legends that emerged in the first and second year of the Sabbatai Sevi movement included a fiery cloud encompassing the prophet with the voice of an angel coming from the cloud, the claim that the prophet had discovered the ashes of the sacred red heifer which had been hidden away until the end times, drops of oil spontaneously emerging from Sabbatai's head, Sabbatai killing a band of attacking robbers with his words, Sabbatai walking through fire unharmed, Sabbatai resurrecting some who had died years earlier, prison chains breaking and prison doors opening by themselves, lepers being healed, supernatural travel capabilities, and Sabbatai ascending into heaven when he was arrested while the archangel Gabriel assumed his form.[26] According to Scholem, "The historical truth concerning Sabbatai Sevi became obscured even in his lifetime...[and] we see Sabbatai in full-blown legendary grandeur only a few years after his death."[27]

It is more than a little interesting to note that the Sabbatai Sevi example involves another Jewish messiah movement. Perhaps the legendization that surrounds Jewish messiah movements can sometimes be especially potent because the basis for the legends is already laid in Jewish messianic expectations built up over centuries in the Old Testament. In fact, David Strauss noticed this all the way back in 1840 when he responded to Müller's challenge:

> A frequently raised objection remains...the objection, namely, that the space of about thirty years, from the death of Jesus to the destruction of Jerusalem, during which the greater part of the narratives must have been formed...is much too short to admit of the rise of so rich a collection of mythi....[But] for the period between the formation of the first Christian community and the writing of the Gospels, there remains to be effected only the transference of Messianic legends, almost all ready formed, to Jesus, with some alterations to adapt them to Christian opinions, and to the individual character and circumstances of Jesus: only a very small proportion of mythi having to be formed entirely new.[28]

In summary, this essay has tried to make five main points.

1) Although rare, legend can develop very rapidly around an individual and be believed by many people in a community, even with eyewitnesses still around.

2) An especially large amount of legend could have surrounded Jesus given the centuries of built up Jewish expectations about the Messiah.

3) If Jesus was not a figure of significant public interest when he was alive, there would have been far fewer people than normal to preserve the historical core after his death, in which case legend would have had a much easier time displacing the historical core than it would have otherwise.

4) If there was a lot of legend piled on top of a reduced historical core, a smaller portion of the Gospels would be historically reliable than historians are used to seeing in other ancient records.

5) If Jesus was a figure of little significance to anyone but his worshippers when the record about him was being written, less legendized sources which might have added more balance to the historical record would have been less likely to have been written or to have survived.

In short, the Gospels are an understandable exception to what classical historians normally deal with, because classical historians rarely if ever deal with the written records of a highly revered religious figure who had very little contemporary significance to anyone but his followers when he was alive and to his worshippers after his death and where the entire written record comes only from those who worshipped him. Because of this, even traditions which can be dated very shortly after Jesus' death could still plausibly be legends.

Afterword

The first edition of this book published in 2009 brought to a close a personal inquiry into Christian origins that I sincerely enjoyed. Writing this second edition was different. My personal interest in the puzzle of Christian origins had passed, but I felt the need to answer some critiques made of the first edition, polish some of the ideas in it, and add some additional ideas that appeared in various works since the first edition was published. Although writing this book was more tedious and not as enjoyable the second time around, I feel confident that I have improved it to the best of my ability. But this second edition will probably also receive criticism, and there will always be new ideas and perspectives that could be used to update the hypothesis in this book, or render it obsolete. Since keeping track of and updating for such changes is a significant amount of work, it is doubtful that there will be another edition of this book. I wish the reader all the best in their personal inquiry into Christian origins and I hope that my book has contributed something to that inquiry. – Kris Komarnitsky

Endnotes

Introduction

[1] Thomas Paine, *The Age of Reason*, Part One. See Jn 20:24-29 for the doubting Thomas scene.

[2] Gary Habermas and Michael Licona, *The Case for the Resurrection of Jesus* (Grand Rapids, Michigan: Kregal, 2004), 128.

[3] Lee Strobel, *The Case for Christ* (Grand Rapids, Michigan: Zondervan, August 18, 1998), 356 (pg. 264 in the September 1, 1998 publishing).

[4] ZDenny's Blog at http://zdenny.com/?p=2618 [cited Nov 30, 2009].

[5] *The Five Gospels* (New York, NY: Polebridge, 1993); *The Acts of Jesus* (New York, NY: Polebridge, 1998); Robert J. Miller, *The Jesus Seminar and Its Critics* (New York, NY; Polebridge, 1999), 76. The Jesus Seminar's home page along with a list of Fellows can be found at: http://www.westarinstitute.org

[6] For a good summary of the reasons for this conclusion, as well as a list of a broad range of scholars who agree, see Michael R. Licona, *The Resurrection of Jesus: A New Historiographical Approach* (Downers Grove, IL: InterVarsity, 2010), 223-235.

[7] Jim Collins, *Good to Great* (New York, NY; HarperCollins, 2001), 9, 11.

[8] N.T. Wright, *The Resurrection of the Son of God* (Minneapolis, MN: Fortress, 2003), 706.

[9] Licona, *Resurrection of Jesus*, 123 (Copyright (c) 2010 by Michael R. Licona. Used by permission of InterVarsity Press, PO Box 1400, Downers Grove, IL 60515. www.ivpress.com).

[10] Craig L. Blomberg, *The Historical Reliability of the Gospels* (Downers Grove, IL: InterVarsity, 2007), 284, 291, 295.

[11] Wright, *Resurrection of the Son of God*, 696.

[12] Dinesh D'Souza, *What's So Great About Christianity* (Washington D.C.: Regnery, 2007), 78-79.

Chapter One

[1] John Dominic Crossan and Jonathan L. Reed, *In Search of Paul* (New York, NY: HarperCollins, 2004), 379.

[2] *The Expositor's Bible Commentary*, Vol. 11 (ed. Tremper Longman III and David E. Garland; Grand Rapids, Michigan; Zondervan, 2008), 247. See too another strongly traditional scholar, Wolfhart Pannenberg, who, speaking of Paul's list of appearances in 1 Cor 15:5-8 says, "The intention of this enumeration is clearly to give proof by means of witnesses for the facticity of Jesus' resurrection" (Wolfhart Pannenberg, *Jesus: God and Man*, Second Edition (Philadelphia: Westminster John Knox Press, 1977), 89.

[3] Craig S. Keener, *1-2 Corinthians* (New York, NY; Cambridge University Press, 2005), 124.

[4] G.W.H. Lampe, "Easter: A Statement" in *The Resurrection* (ed. William Purcell, Philadelphia: Westminster, 1966), 43. See too Roy W. Hoover, "Was Jesus' Resurrection an Historical Event? A Debate Statement with Commentary," *The Fourth R* 23.5 (Sep/Oct 2010): 8; Uta Ranke-Heinemann, *Putting Away Childish Things* (San Francisco: Harper, 1994), 131; R. Bultmann, *The History of the Synoptic Tradition* (New York: Harper, 1968), 290.

[5] Full analysis by Metzger in *A Textual Commentary on the Greek New Testament* (Stuttgart, Germany: Biblia-Druck, 1971), 122-126 and online at: http://www.bible-researcher.com/endmark.html

[6] Craig L. Blomberg, *The Historical Reliability of the Gospels* (Downers Grove, IL: InterVarsity, 2007), 140.

[7] Wilhelm Bousset (1913) as quoted by Rudolf Bultmann (1976) and then Gerd Ludemann (1994) in Gerd Ludemann's book, *The Resurrection of Jesus* (Minneapolis, MN: Fortress, 1994), 116-117. See too Michael J. Cook, "Jews and Gospel Dynamics," *The Fourth R* 22.2 (Mar/Apr 2009): 13.

[8] Ludemann, *Resurrection of Jesus*, 117.

[9] Earl Doherty, "Challenging the Verdict, A Cross-Examination of Lee Strobel's *The Case For Christ*" n.p. [cited 10 Oct 2007] Online: http://pages.ca.inter.net/~oblio/CTVExcerptsThree.htm#Twelve

[10] Michael Goulder, "Jesus' Resurrection and Christian Origins: A Response to N.T. Wright," *Journal for the Study of the Historical Jesus*, Vol. 3.2 (2005), 192.

[11] R.E. Brown, "The Burial of Jesus," *Catholic Biblical Quarterly* Vol. 50.1 (Jan 1988): 233-234.

[12] C.H. Giblin, "Structural and Thematic Correlations in the Matthean Burial-Resurrection Narrative (Matt. xxvii.57-xxviii.20)," *New Testament Studies* 21 (1974-75): 419. Cambridge University Press.

[13] R.E. Brown, *Death of the Messiah*, II (ABRL, 7; New York: Doubleday, 1994), 1312.

[14] William Lane Craig, "The Guard at the Tomb," *New Testament Studies* 30 (1984): 281. Cambridge University Press.

[15] William Craig during interview on the John Ankerberg show, "William Lane Craig on the Historical Jesus - Interview 2001," Time stamp 1:45:20-1:47:30 [cited Apr 15, 2013] Online: http://www.youtube.com/watch?v=xUKW2Bm5P2k. Also available as a short clip taken from the interview: "Were there guards at the tomb of Jesus?" [cited Apr 15, 2013] Online: http://www.youtube.com/watch?feature=player_embedded&v=b8UMb7NlxkU

[16] The Jesus Seminar, *The Acts of Jesus* (New York, NY: Polebridge, 1998), 265-266.

Chapter Two

[1] The Jesus Seminar, *The Acts of Jesus* (New York, NY: Polebridge, 1998), 121-122, 133, 145-146, 152.

[2] More detailed arguments in favor of removal from the cross for burial can be found at: Craig A. Evans, "Jewish Burial Traditions and the Resurrection of Jesus," *Journal for the Study of the Historical Jesus*, Vol. 3.2 (2005), 233-248, also online at: http://craigaevans.com/Burial_Traditions.pdf; Richard C. Carrier, "The Burial of Jesus in Light of Jewish Law," in *The Empty Tomb* (ed. Robert M. Price and Jeffery Jay Lowder; Amherst, NY: Prometheus, 2005), 373-379, some of the information from this reference is online at: http://www.secweb.org/index.aspx?action=viewAsset&id=125#11; Byron R. McCane, *Roll Back the Stone* (Harrisburg, PA: Trinity, 2003), 92-95, also online at: http://enoch2112.tripod.com/ByronBurial.htm.

[3] John J. Rousseau and Rami Arav, *Jesus and His World: An Archaeological and Cultural Dictionary* (Minneapolis, MN; Augsburg Fortress, 1995), 167; Amos Kloner, *The Necropolis of Jerusalem in the Second Temple Period*, Ph.D. diss., Hebrew University, 1980 (Hebrew, English summary).

[4] Jodi Magness, "What did Jesus' Tomb Look Like?," *Biblical Archaeology Review*, Jan/Feb 2006: 41, 47, 48. Biblical Archaeology Society, Washington, D.C. (www.biblicalarchaeology.org).

[5] William Lane Craig, "Was Jesus Buried in Shame? Reflections on B. McCane's Proposal," *The Expository Times* 115 (2004): 405; see too Num 11:31-34; Ezek 39:9-16.

[6] Boaz Zissu, "Odd Tomb Out: Has Jerusalem's Essene Cemetery Been Found?," *Biblical Archaeology Review*, Mar/Apr 1999: 52. Biblical Archaeology Society, Washington, D.C. (www.biblicalarchaeology.org).

[7] Hershel Shanks, "Who Lies Here? Jordan Tombs Match Those at Qumran," *Biblical Archaeology Review*, Sep/Oct 1999: 51. Biblical Archaeology Society, Washington, D.C. (www.biblicalarchaeology.org).

[8] See Zissu, "Odd Tomb," 55.

[9] Magness, "Jesus' Tomb," 48.

[10] Ibid., 48.

[11] Zissu, "Odd Tomb," 52.

[12] The Mishnah: Maaser Sheni, 5.1; English translation from Herbert Danby, *The Mishnah, Translated from the Hebrew with Introduction and Brief Explanatory Notes* (London: Oxford, 1958), 80; Jon Davies, *Death, Burial and Rebirth in the Religions of Antiquity* (New York, NY: Routledge, 1999), 102.

[13] William Lane Craig, "Was Jesus Buried in Shame? Reflections on B. McCane's Proposal," *The Expository Times* 115 (2004): 406.

[14] R.E. Brown, *Death of the Messiah*, II (ABRL, 7; New York: Doubleday, 1994), 1017 and "The Burial of Jesus," *Catholic Biblical Quarterly* Vol. 50.1 (Jan 1988): 236 n. 7.

[15] Brown, "Burial," 233-234.

[16] William John Lyons, "On the Life and Death of Joseph of Arimathea," *Journal for the Study of the Historical Jesus*, Vol. 2.1 (2004), 32-33.

[17] Brown, *Death of the Messiah*, 1214.

[18] Donald Senior, *The Passion of Jesus in the Gospel of Mark* (Wilmington, Del: Glazier, 1984), 133.

[19] Brown, "Burial," 240, 243; *Death of the Messiah*, 1216, 1239.

[20] Brown, *Death of the Messiah*, 1212, n. 28.

[21] Ibid., 1244 n. 4, 1245-1246.

[22] Amos Kloner, "Did a Rolling Stone Close Jesus' Tomb?," *Biblical Archaeology Review*, Sep/Oct 1999: 23, 25, 28-29. Biblical Archaeology Society, Washington, D.C. (www.biblicalarchaeology.org).

[23] Brown, *Death of the Messiah*, 1248, 1254, n. 34.

[24] Richard Carrier, "The Burial of Jesus in Light of Jewish Law," in *The Empty Tomb* (ed. Robert M. Price and Jeffery Jay Lowder; Amherst, NY: Prometheus, 2005), 383 and his "Reply to Glenn Miller on the Burial of Jesus (2002)," Infidels.org Library, n.p. [cited Oct 3, 2007] Online: http://www.infidels.org/library/modern/richard_carrier/replytomiller.html

[25] Brown, *Death of the Messiah*, 1218.

[26] Kloner, "Rolling Stone," 29.

[27] *The Complete Gospels* (ed. Robert J. Miller; Santa Rosa, CA; Polebridge Press, 1994), 337. Some translations use the word "shamefully" instead of "in the sand", but the latter is the correct literal translation; see *The Complete Gospels* reference just given and Peter Kirby, "The Case Against the Empty Tomb," *Journal of Higher Criticism*, 9/2 (Fall 2002), 190, online at: http://depts.drew.edu/jhc/.

[28] Gerald Bostock, "Do We Need an Empty Tomb?," *The Expository Times* (1994): 204.

[29] Peter Carnley, *The Structure of Resurrection Belief* (Oxford: Clarendon Press, 1987), 58.

Chapter Three

[1] N.T. Wright, *The Resurrection of the Son of God* (Minneapolis, MN: Fortress, 2003), 690.

[2] R. L. Timpe, *Baker Encyclopedia of Psychology and Counseling* (ed. David G. Benner and Peter C. Hill; Grand Rapids, MI: Baker Books, 1999), 220.

[3] Wright, *Resurrection of the Son of God*, 697-701; William Craig, "Doubting the Resurrection," Reasonable Faith podcast 21 Feb 2011, n.p. [cited 1 Apr 2011]. Online: http://www.reasonablefaith.org/doubting-the-resurrection. The critique by Craig was in response to the first edition of this book.

[4] Wright, *Resurrection of the Son of God*, 698.

[5] Robert M. Price, *Book Reviews*, n.p. [cited July 7, 2007]. Online: http://www.robertmprice.mindvendor.com/rev_ntwrong.htm

[6] Henri Zukier in *Extending Psychological Frontiers, Selected Works of Leon Festinger* (ed. Stanley Schachter and Michael S. Gazzaniga; New York, NY: Russell Sage Foundation, 1989), xi, xxii.

[7] *Cognitive Dissonance, Progress on a Pivotal Theory in Social Psychology* (ed. Eddie Harmon-Jones and Judson Mills; Washington, DC: American Psychological Association, 1999), 3.

[8] Ibid., 6-7, 86-91.

[9] Leon Festinger, Henry W. Riecken, and Stanley Schachter (New York, NY: Harper & Row, 1956).

[10] Examples from: Leon Festinger, Henry W. Riecken, and Stanley Schachter, *When Prophecy Fails* (New York, NY: Harper & Row, 1956), 166-167.

[11] Ibid., 168.

[12] Ibid., 169-171.

[13] Leon Festinger in *Extending Psychological Frontiers*, 255-256.

[14] Festinger, *Prophecy Fails*, 232.

[15] Ibid., 3, 27-28. See too Leon Festinger, *A Theory of Cognitive Dissonance* (Stanford, California: Stanford University Press, 1957, renewed by the author in 1985), 18, 200-202, 233-234, 243-259 and Joel Cooper, *Cognitive Dissonance: Fifty Years of a Classic Theory* (Thousand Oaks, California: Sage, 2007), 60-61.

[16] *Advent Herald*, October 30, 1844, pg. 93, quoted in *Prophecy Fails*, 19-20.

[17] Luther Boutelle, *Sketch of the Life and Religious Experience of Elder Luther Boutelle* (Boston, MA: Advent Christian Publication Society, 1891), 65, quoted in *Prophecy Fails*, 20.

[18] Wikipedia, *Seventh-day Adventist Church* [Cited 26 Dec 2006] Online: http://en.wikipedia.org/wiki/Seventh-day_Adventist_Church

[19] Gershom Scholem, *Sabbatai Sevi, the Mystical Messiah* (Princeton, NJ: Princeton, 1973), 792-795.

[20] Ibid., 800-801.

[21] Ibid., 795.

[22] Simon Dein, "A Messiah from the Dead: Cultural Performance in Lubavitcher Messianism," *Social Compass*, Vol 57:4 (2010), 542 and "What Really Happens When Prophecy Fails: The Case of Lubavitch," *Sociology of Religion*, Vol 62:3 (2001), 394.

[23] Dein, "What Really Happens When Prophecy Fails," 395.

[24] Simon Dein, *Lubavitcher Messianism* (New York, NY: Bloomsbury Academic, 2012), 58 and Dein, "A Messiah from the Dead," 543.

[25] Dein, "What Really Happens When Prophecy Fails," 397.

[26] Ibid., 397.

[27] Marcus J. "The Once and Future Messiah in Early Christianity and Chabad," *New Testament Studies* 47.3 (July 2001), 394, Cambridge University Press; reference thanks to Simon Dein, *Lubavitcher Messianism*, 61.

[28] Dein, "What Really Happens When Prophecy Fails," 397-398. See too Dein's *Lubavitcher Messianism*, 63.

[29] David Berger, *The Rebbe, the Messiah, and the Scandal of Orthodox Indifference* (Portland, OR: Littman Library of Jewish Civilization, 2008), 11, 41.

[30] Dein, *Lubavitcher Messianism*, 63.

[31] David Berger, *The Rebbe*, xxxi, xxxvi, 26. Berger gives numerous examples throughout his book indicting that the belief in Rebbe Schneerson's resurrection has a significant following (see for example pgs. xxxi, xxxii, xxxv, xli, 24, 31, 33, 36, and 55-57). See too an excellent lengthy article by New York Times Magazine reporter Jonathan Mahler, who describes a visit to a Lubavitch community in 2003, reporting the beliefs and schisms he observed at that time ("Waiting for the Messiah of Eastern Parkway," *New York Times Magazine*, September 21, 2003, 45. Also online: http://www.nytimes.com/2003/09/21/magazine/waiting-for-the-messiah-of-eastern-parkway.html?pagewanted=all&src=pm). See too Simon Dein and Lorne Dawson, "The 'Scandal' of the Lubavitch Rebbe: Messianism as a Response to Failed Prophecy," *Journal of Contemporary Religion* 23.2 (May 2008): 168 and endnote #4: "There are no reliable estimates of the number of Lubavitchers in each group. In the UK, messianists [those who believe Rebbe Schneerson will resurrect from the dead as the Messiah] constitute a small portion of Lubavitchers; in the US their numbers are much larger.... Many still speak of the possibility of the Rebbe's resurrection as *Mosiach*." (Taylor & Francis Ltd, www.tandfonline.com, reprinted by permission of the publisher.)

[32] Berger, *The Rebbe*, 28.

[33] Dein, "What Really Happens When Prophecy Fails," 399, "A Messiah from the Dead," 550, and *Lubavitcher Messianism*, 139. It is also worth noting that Dein and others have moved beyond cognitive dissonance theory, which provides an explanation for temporary belief formation and maintenance, to look at the role of ritual and performance in sustaining beliefs: "The authoritative provision of a plausible rationalisation, communicated promptly and persuasively, can offset the cognitive dissonance initially experienced by individuals. If further actions are taken at this juncture to reaffirm the group's cohesion, such as special rituals, ceremonies, and educational events, the dissonance can be significantly dissipated" (Simon Dein and Lorne Dawson, "The 'Scandal' of the Lubavitch Rebbe: Messianism as a Response to Failed Prophecy," *Journal of Contemporary Religion* 23.2 (May 2008), 175 (Taylor & Francis Ltd, www.tandfonline.com, reprinted by permission of the publisher)). See too Dawson, "When Prophecy Fails and Faith Persists: A Theoretical Overview," *Nova Religio: The Journal of Alternative and Emergent Religions*, Vol. 3, No. 1 (Oct 1999), 65, 70, 71, 72 and Dein, "A Messiah From the Dead," 545-550.

[34] Dein, "A Messiah from the Dead," 551 n. 5.

[35] Berger, *The Rebbe*, 3, 25 n. 9.

[36] Dein, *Lubavitcher Messianism*, 133.

[37] Festinger, *Prophecy Fails*, 24-25.

[38] "...the majority of scholars do not regard the predictions as historical" (Michael Licona, *The Resurrection of Jesus: A New Historiographical Approach* (Downers Grove, IL: InterVarsity, 2010), 300-301 (Copyright (c) 2010 by Michael R. Licona. Used by permission of InterVarsity Press, PO Box 1400, Downers Grove, IL 60515. www.ivpress.com)).

[39] The Jesus Seminar, *The Five Gospels* (New York, NY: Polebridge, 1993), 36, 75, 83, 94, 212, 225, 312, 371, 397, 406.

[40] Paul M. van Buren, *According to the Scriptures* (Grand Rapids, MI: Eerdmans, 1998), 21-22.

[41] David Berger, private email on Dec 4, 2013 (used with permission): "A Lubavitch hasid attracted by the idea that Rabbi Schneerson was raised to heaven bodily might well be deterred by the movement's doctrine that there must be a physical prince (*nasi*) of any given generation residing in a specific location. In the absence of a prince of the generation in the physical world who mediates the divine force that sustains the world, it [the world] would cease to exist. Some hasidim who accept the Rebbe's physical death have struggled to deal with this problem by maintaining that in the exceptional moments before the final redemption, the critical divine energy can be mediated through the Rebbe's gravesite." Berger conveys some of these same ideas in his book *The Rebbe*, pg. xxxii.

[42] William Lane Craig, *Reasonable Faith: Christian Truth and Apologetics* (Wheaton, IL: Crossway, 2008), 394.

[43] John Dominic Crossan and Jonathan L. Reed, *In Search of Paul* (New York, NY: HarperCollins, 2004), 383.

[44] I owe my entire understanding of this to Paul M. van Buren, *According to the Scriptures* (Grand Rapids, MI: Eerdmans, 1998).

[45] Scholem, *Sabbatai Sevi*, 30.

[46] Van Buren, *Scriptures*, 47-48.

[47] Ibid., 48.

[48] Scholem, *Sabbatai Sevi*, 795.

[49] Bruce Chilton and Jacob Neusner, *Judaism in the New Testament* (New York, NY: Routledge, 1995), 2.

[50] Mitchell Dahood, *Psalms I, 1-50* (AB 16; Garden City, NY: Doubleday, 1965), 91.

[51] Reference from Robert M. Price, "Brand X Easters," *The Fourth R* 20.6 (Nov/Dec 2007): 13.

[52] Ibid., 13.

[53] Ibid., 14.

[54] Reference from Daniel A. Smith, "Appearance or Disappearance?: Early Beliefs About Jesus' Vindication," *The Fourth R* 21.1 (Jan/Feb 2008): 5.

[55] Stephen J. Patterson, *The God of Jesus* (Harrisburg, PA: Trinity, 1998), 222.

[56] Ibid., 232-233, 237. See too Francis Watson, "'Historical Evidence' and the Resurrection of Jesus," *Theology* 90 (1987): 367-368, Roy W. Hoover, "Was

Jesus' Resurrection an Historical Event? A Debate Statement with Commentary," *The Fourth R* 23.5 (Sep/Oct 2010): 6, and David Berger, *The Rebbe, the Messiah, and the Scandal of Orthodox Indifference* (Portland, OR: Littman Library of Jewish Civilization, 2008), 156-157.

[57] Wright, *Resurrection of the Son of God*, 203.

[58] Ibid., 193, 160, 142 respectively.

[59] Ibid., 142.

[60] Ibid., 95.

[61] Ibid., 95.

[62] James G. Crossley, "Against the Historical Plausibility of the Empty Tomb Story and the Bodily Resurrection of Jesus: A Response to N.T. Wright," *Journal for the Study of the Historical Jesus*, Vol. 3.2 (2005), 171.

[63] Dein, *Lubavitcher Messianism*, 50, 44-45.

[64] Berger, *The Rebbe*, 18, 41, xli.

[65] Ibid., 13, 24.

[66] Leon Festinger, *A Theory of Cognitive Dissonance* (Stanford, California: Stanford University Press, 1957, renewed by the author in 1985), 233, 247.

[67] Robert M. Price, *Book Reviews*, n.p. [cited 27 Apr 2011]. Online: www.robertmprice.mindvendor.com/rev_ntwrong.htm

[68] Wright, *Resurrection of the Son of God*, 636.

[69] Ibid., 636. See too pg. 595 n. 17.

[70] Ibid., 413.

[71] Ibid., 68. Wright also calls the pagan belief in the resurrection (and subsequent second death) of Alcestis an "exception" (Ibid., 28 n. 67).

[72] Ibid., 57.

[73] Ibid., 94, 95.

[74] Robert Miller, *Born Divine* (Santa Rosa, California; Polebridge, 2003), 97.

[75] Van Buren, *Scriptures*, 26.

[76] Ibid., 72.

[77] Scholem, *Sabbatai Sevi*, 802-803.

[78] Dein, *Lubavitcher Messianism*, 63, 135. See too Berger, *The Rebbe*, 24.

[79] David Berger and Michael Wyschogrod, *Jews and 'Jewish Christianity'*, (New York: Ktav Pub Inc, 1978), 20-21; repeated in 2008 in Berger, *The Rebbe*, 156-157.

Chapter Four

[1] N.T. Wright, *The Resurrection of the Son of God* (Minneapolis, MN: Fortress, 2003), 689-690.

[2] Peter Slade and Richard Bentall, *Sensory Deception: a Scientific Analysis of Hallucination* (Baltimore: John Hopkins University Press, 1988), 88; reference thanks to Keith Parsons, "Peter Kreeft and Ronald Tacelli on the Hallucination Theory," in *The Empty Tomb* (ed. Robert M. Price and Jeffery Jay Lowder; Amherst, NY: Prometheus, 2005), 442.

[3] Ibid., 68-70; reference thanks to Richard Carrier, "The Spiritual Body of Christ," in *The Empty Tomb* (ed. Robert M. Price and Jeffery Jay Lowder; Amherst, NY: Prometheus, 2005), 185-186. See too Oliver Sacks (M.D. and professor of neurology at NYU School of Medicine), *Hallucinations* (New York: Alfred A. Knopf, 2012), 57.

[4] Slade and Bentall, *Sensory Deception*, 70-71. 8.4% of 14.3% is 1.2% of the total sample, or about 1%.

[5] André Aleman and Frank Larøi, *Hallucinations: The Science of Idiosyncratic Perception* (Washington D.C.: American Psychological Association, 2008), 14, 67; for a summary of several other studies, with citations for each, see pgs. 31, 37, 40-41, 61-64, 70, and 76.

[6] Oliver Sacks, *Hallucinations* (New York: Alfred A. Knopf, 2012), ix.

[7] Firsthand account from a subject in Aniela Jaffe's book *Apparitions: An Archetypal Approach to Death Dreams and Ghosts*, with foreword by psychiatrist C.G. Jung (Irving, TX: Spring Publications, 1979), 57; reference thanks to Gerd Ludemann, *The Resurrection of Christ* (Amherst, NY: Prometheus, 2004), 164-165.

[8] Ibid., 57.

[9] Firsthand account from Y. Spiegel, *The Grief Process: Analysis and Counseling* (Nashville, TN: Abingdon Press, 1978), 182.

[10] Susan Atkins, who was involved with Charles Manson in a series of murders in the 1970s, in M.J. Meadow and R.D. Kahoe, *Psychology of Religion* (New York: Harper and Row, 1984), 90; reference thanks to Michael Goulder, "The Baseless Fabric of a Vision," in *Resurrection Reconsidered*, ed. G. D'Costa (Oxford: One World, 1996), 49. For several more firsthand accounts of hallucinations see Sacks, *Hallucinations*, 214, 232, 234, 235, 248-249.

[11] Slade and Bentall, *Sensory Deception*, 77-78.

[12] Sacks, *Hallucinations*, 244. Sacks notes similar phenomena in the French village of Loudun in 1634 and during the Salem witch trials in 1692.

[13] ABC News Online, "Thai Tsunami Trauma Sparks Foreign Ghost Sightings," reported on Jan 14, 2005. [cited Nov 15, 2007] Online: http://www.abc.net.au/news/newsitems/200501/s1282281.htm, or http://www.abc.net.au/cgi-bin/common/printfriendly.pl?http://www.abc.net.au/news/newsitems/200501/s1282281.htm

[14] Aleman and Larøi, *Hallucinations*, 79.

[15] Ibid., 29.

[16] Sacks, *Hallucinations*, 212.

[17] From the fieldwork of Simon Dein, "A Messiah from the Dead: Cultural Performance in Lubavitcher Messianism," *Social Compass*, Vol 57:4 (2010), 547.

[18] Simon Dein and Lorne Dawson, "The 'Scandal' of the Lubavitch Rebbe: Messianism as a Response to Failed Prophecy," *Journal of Contemporary*

Religion 23.2 (May 2008): 174 (Taylor & Francis Ltd, www.tandfonline.com, reprinted by permission of the publisher).

[19] David Berger, *The Rebbe, the Messiah, and the Scandal of Orthodox Indifference* (Portland, OR: Littman Library of Jewish Civilization, 2008), xxxiv.

[20] Some apparently firsthand accounts of seeing the dead Rebbe Schneerson alive can be found in English at http://seeingtherebbe.wordpress.com/ [cited Sep 3, 2013]. Note especially the accounts of R' Adam Rozhnik, Mrs. Heidi Amit, Rabbi Mordechai Rottenstein, Mrs. Rochel Hendel, and Yigal Mord, which seem a lot like what one would expect from a hallucination. The website says these accounts come from a Hebrew book titled *Lifkoach et Ha'einayim* ("Open Your Eyes") which was published in 2006, but I could not find any more information about this book. Berger, *The Rebbe*, xxxiv refers readers fluent in Hebrew to the following website for information about sightings of Rebbe Schneerson: http://forum.chabad.fm/141/12924.html [cited Sep 16, 2013].

[21] Gerd Ludemann, *The Resurrection of Christ* (Amherst, NY: Prometheus, 2004), 170-171.

[22] Carrier, "Spiritual Body," 187; Carrier's quoted label "happy schizotype" and the quoted description of that label is from professional psychiatrist Dr. Claridge McCreery, "A Study of Hallucination in Normal Subjects," *Personality and Individual Differences* 2:5 (November 1996): 739-747.

[23] Evan Fales, "The Case of St. Teresa (Scientific Explanations of Mystical Experiences, Part 1)," *Religious Studies* 32.n2 (June 1996): 148. Cambridge University Press.

[24] Gershom Scholem, *Sabbatai Sevi, the Mystical Messiah* (Princeton, NJ: Princeton, 1973), 203-205.

[25] Ibid., 206-207.

[26] This argument can be found at William Craig, "Visions of Jesus: A Critical Assessment of Gerd Lüdemann's Hallucination Hypothesis," *Leadership U*, n.p. [cited 15 Nov 2008]. Online: http://www.leaderu.com/offices/billcraig/docs/visions.html

[27] The Jesus Seminar, *The Acts of Jesus* (New York, NY: Polebridge, 1998), 493-494.

[28] William Lane Craig, *The Son Rises: Historical Evidence for the Resurrection of Jesus* (Chicago: Moody, 1981), 110.

[29] Stephen J. Patterson, *The God of Jesus* (Harrisburg, PA: Trinity, 1998), 234-236.

[30] Jesus Seminar, *Acts of*, 484, 485, 492.

[31] Grant H. Palmer, *An Insider's View of Mormon Origins* (Salt Lake City, UT: Signature Books, 2002), 204.

[32] Ibid., 204

[33] Scholem, *Sabbatai Sevi*, 224- 225. Some people think Abraham Yakhini fabricated the scroll, but Scholem explains why he thinks this is wrong on

pages 166-167, 229. However, this is unimportant for the point being made because all indications are that Yakhini believed in Sevi just as sincerely as Nathan did (see Scholem pages 135, 381, 427).

[34] Ibid., 231-233.

[35] Erin Prophet, *Prophet's Daughter: My Life with Elizabeth Clare Prophet Inside the Church Universal and Triumphant* (Guilford, CT: The Globe Pequot Press, 2009), 192-193.

[36] Richard Bauckham, *Gospel Women: Studies of the Named Women in the Gospels* (Grand Rapids: Eerdmans, 2002), 308. Reference thanks to Michael Licona, *The Resurrection of Jesus: A New Historiographical Approach* (Downers Grove, IL: InterVarsity, 2010), 342 n. 249. Licona reports in the same footnote that Bauckham clarifies elsewhere that this possibility is very unlikely. However, I think Licona has misread Bauckham. On page 309 Bauckham says, "Explanations (1), (2) and (5) seem to me to have some plausibility", and it is clear on page 308 that Bauckham's explanation #2 is that Paul could have added the appearance to the 500 to his list of appearances. On pages 279-280 (the pages Licona refers to in Bauckham's book purportedly indicating Bauckham thinks explanation #2 is very unlikely), it is actually explanation #3 that Bauckham is clarifying is very unlikely (that there was competition for the first appearance of Jesus).

[37] Ludemann, *Resurrection of Christ*, 73-74.

[38] Stephen J. Patterson, *The God of Jesus* (Harrisburg, PA: Trinity, 1998), 236.

[39] Bart Ehrman in his March 28, 2006 debate with William Lane Craig "Is There Historical Evidence for the Resurrection of Jesus?" at the College of the Holy Cross, Worcester, Massachusetts. Pg. 29 of transcript that can be found at: http://academics.holycross.edu/files/crec/resurrection-debate-transcript.pdf

[40] R.E Brown, *Death of the Messiah*, II (ABRL, 7; New York: Doubleday, 1994), 1311-1312.

[41] Michael Licona, *The Resurrection of Jesus: A New Historiographical Approach* (Downers Grove, IL: InterVarsity, 2010), 552-553 (Copyright (c) 2010 by Michael R. Licona. Used by permission of InterVarsity Press, PO Box 1400, Downers Grove, IL 60515. www.ivpress.com).

Chapter Five

[1] Michael Licona, *The Resurrection of Jesus: A New Historiographical Approach* (Downers Grove, IL: InterVarsity, 2010), 300-301: "...the majority of scholars do not regard the predictions as historical" (Copyright (c) 2010 by Michael R. Licona. Used by permission of InterVarsity Press, PO Box 1400, Downers Grove, IL 60515. www.ivpress.com). The Jesus Seminar, *The Five Gospels* (New York, NY: Polebridge, 1993), 75, 83, 94, 212, 225, 312, 371, 397, 406.

[2] William Lane Craig, "The Historicity of the Empty Tomb of Jesus," *New Testament Studies* 31 (1985): 45. Cambridge University Press.

3 This theory was initiated by Karl Lehmann, *Auferweckt am dritten Tag nach der Schrift* (QD 38; Freiburg: Herder, 1968) 262-290. It was further built up by Edward Bode, *The First Easter Morning* (AB 45; Rome: Biblical Institute Press, 1970), 119-126 and Harvey K. McArthur, "'On the Third Day'", *New Testament Studies* 18 (1971) 81-6, Cambridge University Press. As an aside, this theory usually proposes that the phrase "in accordance with the scriptures" (1 Cor 15:4) is referring to the scriptures in general instead of to specific scripture(s).

4 William Craig, "Historicity," 48. This insightful point, including the references (Rom 8:32; Heb 11:17-19; Jas 2:21-23) are also from Craig.

5 Ibid., 47.

6 Douglas Hill, "On the Third Day", *The Expository Times* 78 (1967): 266-67.

7 Gordon D. Fee, *The First Epistle to the Corinthians* (Grand Rapids, Michigan: Eerdmans, 1987), 727; Anthony C. Thiselton, *The First Epistle to the Corinthians* (Grand Rapids, Michigan: Eerdmans, 2000), 1196.

8 Bruce M. Metzger, "A Suggestion Concerning the Meaning of I Cor. XV. 4b," *Journal of Theological Studies* 8 (1957): 122.

9 See Jerusalem Mishnah Shabbat 12a, 15, 17.

10 "Even more telling [that the third-day is not meant literally] is the way this three-day symbol dances around in the gospel story" (John Shelby Spong, *Jesus for the Non-Religious* (New York, NY: HarperCollins, 2007), 124). "'In the course of three days' will mean 'in a day or two', 'soon'" (Bernard P. Robinson, "Peter and His Successors: Tradition and Redaction in Matthew 16.17-19," *Journal for the Study of the New Testament* 6 (1984): 93).

11 John A.T. Robinson, *The Priority of John* (London: SCM Press, 1985), 147-156. Raymond E. Brown, *The Gospel According to John* (AB 29; Garden City, NY: Doubleday, 1970), 555-556.

12 *The Jesus Dynasty* (New York, NY: Simon & Schuster, 2006), 199.

13 Reference thanks to Bode, *First Easter*, 110.

14 C.H. Giblin, "Structural and Thematic Correlations in the Matthean Burial-Resurrection Narrative (Matt. xxvii.57-xxviii.20)," *New Testament Studies* 21 (1974-75): 419. Cambridge University Press.

15 Evan Fales, "Taming the Tehom: The Sign of Jonah in Matthew," in *The Empty Tomb* (ed. Robert M. Price and Jeffery Jay Lowder; Amherst, NY: Prometheus, 2005), 322-324.

16 Bode, *First Easter*, 124.

17 This English translation of the Greek form of Ps 16:10 (designated LXX 15:10 in the Septuagint, the Greek translation of the Hebrew Scriptures) is taken from the standard NRSV Bible because the original author of Acts, writing in Greek, quoted LXX 15:10 verbatim in Acts 2:27.

18 Aramaic translation by David M. Stec, *The Targum of Psalms, Translated, with a Critical Introduction, Apparatus, and Notes* (Aramaic Bible 16; Collegeville, Minn: Liturgical, 2004), 47.

[19] Richard Carrier, "The Spiritual Body of Christ and the Legend of the Empty Tomb," in *The Empty Tomb* (ed. Robert M. Price and Jeffery Jay Lowder; Amherst, NY: Prometheus, 2005), 210.

[20] Mitchell Dahood, *Psalms I, 1-50* (AB 16; Garden City, NY: Doubleday, 1965), 91.

[21] "David clearly believed that he would die someday (cf. Psalm 39:13)" (Greg Herrick, "The Use of Psalm 16:8-11 in Acts 2:25-28," *Bible.org Trustworthy Bible Study Resources*, n.p. [cited 15 Jan. 2006]. Online: http://www.bible.org/page.php?page_id=1784).

[22] Midr. Ps 16:9, 10; actual versification is 11, 12 in the midrash itself (reference thanks to Herrick, "Use of," footnote #58, which refers the reader to Leon Nemoy, Saul Lieberman and Henry A. Wolfson, eds., *The Midrash on the Psalms*, trans. William G. Braude (Yale: New Haven, 1987), 201-202).

[23] Mogens Müller, *The First Bible of the Church: A Plea for the Septuagint* (JSOT-SS 206; Sheffield, England: Sheffield, 1996), 99, see too pg. 110.

[24] "Since eij can mean 'in,' the phrase can be translated as: 'you will not leave my soul *in* Hades.'" (Herrick, "Use of," n.p.).

[25] See for example: "Postmortem Changes and Time of Death", Department of Forensic Medicine, University of Dundee, pg. 15 [cited 17 Jan 2007] Online: http://www.dundee.ac.uk/forensicmedicine/notes/timedeath.pdf. Also see: "Time of Death and Changes after Death", pg. 21 [cited 17 Jan 2007] Online: http://home.comcast.net/~drdeathmd/doc/spitz_chapt02-1.pdf. Also: "Stages of Decomposition" [cited 17 Jan 2007] Online: http://everything2.com/index.pl?node_id=1478719

[26] Metzger, "A Suggestion," 122.

[27] *Buried Alive*; Darby, PA: Diane, 2004.

[28] N.T. Wright, *The Resurrection of the Son of God* (Minneapolis, MN: Fortress, 2003), 321.

[29] Gerd Ludemann, *The Resurrection of Christ* (Amherst, NY: Prometheus, 2004), 42.

[30] Craig S. Keener, *1-2 Corinthians* (New York, NY; Cambridge University Press, 2005), 123.

[31] Licona, *The Resurrection of Jesus*, 329 n. 208 (Copyright (c) 2010 by Michael R. Licona. Used by permission of InterVarsity Press, PO Box 1400, Downers Grove, IL 60515. www.ivpress.com).

[32] Jesus Seminar, *Five Gospels*, 189.

Chapter Six

[1] All five examples from Robert Miller, *Born Divine* (Santa Rosa, California; Polebridge, 2003), 140, 238-239. For the title "Son of God" not being used to convey Jesus' divinity until the late first century and as a possible challenge to Roman emperors see Larry Hurtado, *Lord Jesus Christ: Devotion to Jesus in Earliest Christianity* (Grand Rapids, MI: Eerdmans, 2005), 75-76, 104.

Chapter Seven

[1] C. B. McCullagh, *The Logic of History: Putting Postmodernism in Perspective* (New York, NY: Routledge, 2004), 49-52.

[2] William Craig, "Visions of Jesus: A Critical Assessment of Gerd Lüdemann's Hallucination Hypothesis," *Leadership U*, n.p. [cited Mar 29, 2008] Online: http://www.leaderu.com/offices/billcraig/docs/visions.html.

[3] William Craig in his March 28, 2006 debate with Bart Ehrman "Is There Historical Evidence for the Resurrection of Jesus?" at the College of the Holy Cross, Worcester, Massachusetts, pg. 3, 4, 5, and 7 of transcript that can be found at: http://academics.holycross.edu/files/crec/resurrection-debate-transcript.pdf. Craig says that Jesus' burial in a rock-hewn tomb and the discovered empty tomb are "agreed to by most scholars", "widely accepted by historians", "agreed upon by the majority of scholars", "most New Testament critics concur that Jesus was buried by Joseph of Arimathea in a tomb", "by far most exegets hold firmly to the reliability of the biblical statements concerning the empty tomb."

[4] Wolfhart Pannenberg, "The Historical Jesus as a Challenge to Christology," *Dialog* 37 (1998): 22-23. Reference thanks to Michael R. Licona, *The Resurrection of Jesus: A New Historiographical Approach* (Downers Grove, IL: InterVarsity, 2010), 279.

[5] William Lane Craig, *On Guard: Defending Your Faith with Reason and Precision* (Colorado Springs, CO: David C. Cook, 2010), 223, 226, 236 (Publisher required credit line: Copyright 2010 William Craig. *On Guard: Defending Your Faith with Reason and Precision* published by David C Cook. Publisher permission required to reproduce. All rights reserved). Craig says that in addition to the Gospel of Mark "...independent testimony to Jesus' burial by Joseph is also found in the sources behind Matthew and Luke and the Gospel of John....[In addition to the Gospel of Mark] there are good reasons to discern independent sources for the empty tomb in the other gospels...Matthew is clearly working with an independent source...Luke also has an independent source...given John's independence of the other three gospels, we have yet another independent report of the empty tomb.... The gospel accounts provide multiple, independent reports of postmortem appearances of Jesus... The appearance to the Twelve is independently reported by...Luke, and John (Luke 24:36-53; John 20:19-31) ....the appearance to the women disciples is independently reported by Matthew and John (Matt. 28:9-10; John 20:11-17)....that Jesus appeared to the disciples in Galilee is independently reported by Mark, Matthew, and John (Mark 16; Matt. 28:16-20; John 21)." Craig defines independent sources as sources "which don't rely on each other or on a common source" (pg. 195), and says, "Historians think they've hit historical pay dirt when they have two independent accounts of the same event" (pg. 226).

[6] Jan Vansina, *Oral Tradition as History* (Madison, WI: University of Wisconsin, 1985), 159.

[7] Bart Ehrman, "More on the Criterion of Independent Attestation," at Christianity in Antiquity (CIA): The Bart Ehrman Blog, post dated Oct 1, 2012, n.p. [cited Oct 10, 2013] Online: http://ehrmanblog.org/more-on-the-criterion-of-independent-attestation-for-members/#post-comments

[8] William Lane Craig, with Joseph E. Gorra, *A Reasonable Response: Answers to Tough Questions on God, Christianity, and the Bible* (Chicago, IL: Moody, 2013), 118-119. Referring to Acts 13:28-31 Craig says, "...the early apostolic sermons in the book of Acts, which are probably not wholly Luke's creation but preserve the early preaching of the apostles... make mention of Jesus' interment in a tomb." Craig may also be referring to Acts 2:29 and 13:36. These two Acts passages will be covered next in reference to Craig's claim that these two passages mention Jesus' discovered empty tomb, which of course would also entail a burial in a rock-hewn tomb.

[9] Thanks to Richard Carrier (Ph.D. Greco-Roman intellectual history) for confirmation of the Greek in this passage. The reader can also confirm this for themselves at http://www.blueletterbible.org/ (the original Greek and English translation for each word is displayed side by side; compare Acts 13:29 and Luke 11:44). See too John 5:28-29: "...the hour is coming when all who are in their graves [mnēmeion] will hear his voice and will come out – those who have done good, to the resurrection of life, and those who have done evil, to the resurrection of condemnation." This passage is referring to all dead people, so that must include dead people buried in the ground as well those buried in rock-hewn tombs, and it must include graves with objects designed to preserve or recall the memory of the deceased as well as those graves marked only with chalk or a pile of loose rocks to preserve the memory that a dead person was buried there to indicate uncleanness.

[10] Craig in Craig-Ehrman debate, pg. 5 of transcript. "On the Sunday after the crucifixion, Jesus' tomb was found empty by a group of his women followers....The story of the empty tomb...[is] mentioned in the sermons in the Acts of the Apostles (2.29; 13.36)." See too William Craig, "Independent Sources for Jesus' Burial and Empty Tomb," Q&A #103 at Reasonable Faith website, n.p. [cited May 1, 2013] Online: http://www.reasonablefaith.org/independent-sources-for-jesus-burial-and-empty-tomb. "Jesus' empty tomb is also mentioned in the early sermons independently preserved in the Acts of the Apostles (2.29; 13.36)."

[11] Craig in Craig-Ehrman debate, pg. 23 of transcript. "...When you look at that four line formula in I Corinthians 15 [verses 3-5]...[it] is like an outline of the events of the death of Jesus, the burial by Joseph of Arimathea, the empty tomb, and then the appearance narratives. Compared to the Acts of the Apostles on the one hand and the Gospels on the other hand, this summary in I Corinthians 15 is like an outline, which includes as the second line [1 Cor 15:4] *Joseph's burial of Jesus in the tomb* [emphasis added]."

[12] Craig, *A Reasonable Response*, 118.

[13] Craig, *On Guard*, 222-225 (Copyright 2010 William Craig. *On Guard: Defending Your Faith with Reason and Precision* published by David C Cook. Publisher permission required to reproduce. All rights reserved). "…A comparison of the four-line formula [1 Cor 15:3-5] with the gospel narratives on the one hand and the sermons in Acts on the other reveals that the third line ['he was raised'] is, in fact, a summary of the empty tomb story."

[14] Ibid., 225-226. "…The expression 'on the third day' [in 1 Cor 15:4] implies the empty tomb…"

[15] Ibid., 221. "…The Jewish authorities would have exposed the whole affair simply by pointing to Jesus' tomb or perhaps even exhuming the body as decisive proof that Jesus had not been raised."

[16] This is the one argument that I could not find a citation for, but I had it written down as one of Craig's arguments after listening to several of his debates. It is possible that Craig is not making this argument anymore.

[17] Craig, *On Guard*, 229-230 (Copyright 2010 William Craig. *On Guard: Defending Your Faith with Reason and Precision* published by David C Cook. Publisher permission required to reproduce. All rights reserved). "…The Jewish claim that the disciples had stolen the body [recorded in Mt 28:11-15] presupposes that the body was missing.…[This is] evidence…that Jesus' tomb was, indeed, found empty…"

[18] Ibid., 221. "[If] the location of Jesus' tomb was known in Jerusalem to both Jew and Christian alike…the disciples could not have believed in Jesus' resurrection if His corpse still lay in the tomb."

[19] Ibid., 227. "Mark's account of the empty tomb is remarkably simple and unembellished by theological motifs likely to characterize a later legendary account."

[20] Ibid., 228. "If the empty tomb story were a legend, then the male disciples would have been made to be the ones who discover the empty tomb. The fact that women, whose testimony was deemed worthless, were the chief witnesses to the fact of the empty tomb can only be plausibly explained if, like it or not, they actually *were* the discoverers of the empty tomb…"

[21] Ibid., 236. "The appearance to Peter is independently mentioned by Paul and Luke (1 Cor. 15:5; Luke 24:34)."

[22] Craig in Craig-Ehrman debate, pg. 5 of transcript. "…Groups of people experienced appearances of Jesus alive from the dead.…Paul's list of eyewitnesses to Jesus' resurrection appearances guarantees that such appearances occurred." See too Craig, *On Guard*, 232, 234 (Copyright 2010 William Craig. *On Guard: Defending Your Faith with Reason and Precision* published by David C Cook. Publisher permission required to reproduce. All rights reserved). "…Paul himself had contact with the members of the Twelve…[The] appearance [to all the apostles] is guaranteed by Paul's personal contact with the apostles themselves… [Regarding the appearance to the 500,] Paul himself apparently had personal contact with these people, since he knew that some had died…There can hardly be any purpose in

mentioning the fact that most of the 500 are still alive, unless Paul is saying, in effect, 'The witnesses are there to be questioned.'...Paul could never have said this if the event had not occurred."

[23] Craig, *On Guard*, 238-239 (Copyright 2010 William Craig. *On Guard: Defending Your Faith with Reason and Precision* published by David C Cook. Publisher permission required to reproduce. All rights reserved). "Paul, and indeed all the New Testament, makes a distinction between an *appearance* of Jesus and a *vision* of Jesus....[that] implies that the resurrection appearances were physical."

[24] William Lane Craig, *Reasonable Faith: Christian Truth and Apologetics* (Wheaton, IL: Crossway, 2008), 383. "If all the appearances were originally non-physical visions, then one is at a complete loss to explain the rise of the Gospel accounts. For physical, bodily appearances would be foolishness to Gentiles and a stumbling block to Jews, since neither, for different reasons, could countenance physical resurrection from the dead but would be quite happy to accept visionary appearances of the deceased."

[25] Ibid., 378.

[26] Ibid., 366. "According to the Markan account, the empty tomb was discovered by the women 'on the first day of the week.' We've already seen from the Christian tradition quoted by Paul that the earliest Christians proclaimed the resurrection of Jesus 'on the third day.' As E.L. Bode explains, if the empty tomb story were a late legend, it would almost certainly have been formulated in terms of the accepted and widespread third-day motif."

[27] Edward Bode, *The First Easter Morning* (AB 45; Rome: Biblical Institute Press, 1970), 161.

[28] Craig, *Reasonable Faith*, 366. "...although 'the first day of the week' is very awkward in the Greek (*te mia ton sabbaton*), employing a cardinal instead of an ordinal number and 'Sabbath' for 'week,' the phrase when translated back into Aramaic is perfectly natural. This suggests that the empty tomb tradition is not a late-developing legend."

[29] Ibid., 362. "The account of Jesus' burial in a tomb by Joseph of Arimathea is part of Mark's source material for the passion story. This is a very early source which is probably based on eyewitness testimony and which the commentator Rudolf Pesch dates to within seven years of Jesus' crucifixion."

[30] Ibid., 362.

[31] Helen K. Bond, *Caiaphas: Friend of Rome and Judge of Jesus?* (Louisville, Kentucky: Westminster John Knox Press, 2004), 100.

[32] Ibid., 100-101.

[33] R.E. Brown, *The Gospel According to John XIII-XXI* (New Haven, CT: Yale University Press, 1970), 821. Reference thanks to Bond, *Caiaphas*, 101.

[34] R.E. Brown, *Death of the Messiah*, II (ABRL, 7; New York: Doubleday, 1994), 1492-1524.

[35] Ibid., 1492.

[36] Craig, *A Reasonable Response*, 119. "As a member of the Jewish Sanhedrin that condemned Jesus, Joseph of Arimathea is unlikely to be a Christian creation."

[37] Craig, *Reasonable Faith*, 364.

[38] Ibid, with citation for Raymond Brown's work that reads as follows "Raymond E. Brown, *The Death of the Messiah*, 2 vols. (Garden City, N.Y.: Doubleday, 1994), 2:1240-41."

[39] R.E. Brown, *Death of the Messiah*, II (ABRL, 7; New York: Doubleday, 1994), 1240-1241.

[40] Ibid., 1239.

[41] Michael Licona, *The Resurrection of Jesus: A New Historiographical Approach* (Downers Grove, IL: InterVarsity, 2010), 610.

[42] Ibid., 38 (Copyright (c) 2010 by Michael R. Licona. Used by permission of InterVarsity Press, PO Box 1400, Downers Grove, IL 60515. www.ivpress.com).

[43] Ibid., 95.

[44] Ibid., 34.

[45] Ibid., 127, 204, 338-339.

[46] Ibid., 205-206.

[47] Ibid., 485 n. 64.

[48] Ibid., 185.

[49] Ibid., 463.

[50] Ibid., 208.

[51] Ibid., 617.

[52] C.B. McCullagh, *Justifying Historical Descriptions* (New York, NY: Cambridge University Press, 1984), 30.

[53] Licona, *The Resurrection of Jesus*, 508. See too 586. (Copyright (c) 2010 by Michael R. Licona. Used by permission of InterVarsity Press, PO Box 1400, Downers Grove, IL 60515. www.ivpress.com.)

[54] Ibid., 467.

[55] Ibid., 394.

[56] Ibid., 382.

[57] Ibid., 99.

[58] Ibid., 343. Entire argument on pgs. 339-343.

[59] Ibid., 341-343.

[60] Michael Licona in his July 2012 debate with Greg Cavin at Antioch Church, "Did Jesus Rise from the Dead?" Timestamp 21:10-22:10 [cited May 24, 2013]. Online: http://www.youtube.com/watch?v=0rJqfsEN_Fo. See too Craig, *On Guard*, 261.

[61] Licona, *The Resurrection of Jesus*, 301-302 (see too 281, 283). (Copyright (c) 2010 by Michael R. Licona. Used by permission of InterVarsity Press, PO Box 1400, Downers Grove, IL 60515. www.ivpress.com.)

[62] C.B. McCullagh, "The Resurrection of Jesus: Explanation or Interpretation?" *Southeastern Theological Review* 3.1 (Summer 2012): 49.

[63] Michael Licona, "In Reply to Habermas, McGrew, and McCullagh," *Southeastern Theological Review* 3.1 (Summer 2012): 67.

[64] Craig, *Reasonable Faith*, 398.

[65] McCullagh, *Justifying Historical Descriptions*, 19.

[66] Ibid., 28.

[67] Jun 13, 2013 email correspondence with McCullagh (used with permission).

[68] Licona, *The Resurrection of Jesus*, 38, 39, 41 (Copyright (c) 2010 by Michael R. Licona. Used by permission of InterVarsity Press, PO Box 1400, Downers Grove, IL 60515. www.ivpress.com).

[69] Licona-Cavin debate. Timestamp 1:12:20-1:13:00.

[70] William Craig, "Counterfeit Claims to the Witness of the Spirit," Q&A #167 at Reasonable Faith website, n.p. [cited May 1, 2013] Online: http://www.reasonablefaith.org/counterfeit-claims-to-the-witness-of-the-spirit

[71] Thomas Paine, *The Age of Reason*, Part One. See Jn 20:24-29 for the doubting Thomas scene.

Chapter Eight

[1] The Jesus Seminar, *The Acts of Jesus* (New York, NY: Polebridge, 1998), 530-531.

[2] Rodney Stark, *The Rise of Christianity: A Sociologist Reconsiders History* (Princeton, NJ: Princeton, 1996), 58.

[3] Ibid., 53, 54, 214; see too pgs. 57-59, 69.

[4] I owe this excellent succinct summary of Stark's ideas to someone but could not find the reference. In any case, the ideas themselves are found on the following pages of Stark's *The Rise of Christianity*: 88, 161-162, 188, 211-215.

[5] Ibid., 211.

[6] Ibid., 214, 215.

[7] Dinesh D'Souza, *What's So Great About Christianity* (Washington D.C.: Regnery, 2007), 71-73.

[8] Frg. 95 in Kock, Theodore, *Comicorum Atticorrum fragmenta* 2: 508, Leipzig, Teubner, 1984; Glotz, Gustave, *The Greek City and its Institutions*, 260-261, New York Knopf, 1929; reference thanks to William Linn Westermann, *The Slave Systems of Greek and Roman Antiquity* (Darby, Pa: Diane, 1955), 24.

[9] Jesus Seminar, *Acts of*, 128.

[10] Arthur Darby Nock, *Conversion: The Old and the New in Religion from Alexander the Great to Augustine of Hippo* (Oxford: Clarendon, 1933), 9-10; reference thanks to Stark, *Rise of Christianity*, 55.

[11] Many of the references in this paragraph are from Michael Shermer, *The Science of Good and Evil* (New York, NY: Henry Holt, 2004), 25-26.

[12] *Guns, Germs, and Steel* (New York, NY; Norton, 1999), 356.

[13] Benjamin Franklin, *Representative Selections* (ed. Chester E. Jorgensen and Frank Luther Mott; New York, 1936), 485.

[14] From Carl Sagan's keynote address "Wonder and Skepticism" at the CSICOP Conference, Seattle, WA, June 23-26, 1994. Transcript in the *Skeptical Inquirer*, Volume 29, No. 4, July/August 2005, 36.

[15] Tony Blair, *The Daily Show with Jon Stewart*, Sept 18, 2008. First two minutes of interview.

[16] Mormon President Spencer W. Kimball from, "The Miracle of Forgiveness," 1969.

[17] Person who called in to National Public Radio, Jan 7, 2005, "Science Friday" segment.

[18] National Press Club Speech, Washington D.C., June 1, 2009.

[19] George W. Bush quoted in Bob Woodward, *Plan of Attack* (London: Simon & Schuster, 2004), 421.

Appendix

[1] William Lane Craig, *On Guard: Defending Your Faith with Reason and Precision* (Colorado Springs, Colorado: David C. Cook, 2010), 190 (Publisher required credit line: Copyright 2010 William Craig. *On Guard: Defending Your Faith with Reason and Precision* published by David C Cook. Publisher permission required to reproduce. All rights reserved). See too William Craig, "The Evidence for Jesus," n.p. [cited Sep 30, 2008] Online: http://www.leaderu.com/offices/billcraig/docs/rediscover2.html.

[2] Lee Strobel, *The Case for Christ* (Grand Rapids, Michigan: Zondervan, August 18, 1998), 357 (pg. 264 in the September 1, 1998 publishing).

[3] A. N. Sherwin-White, *Roman Society and Roman Law in the New Testament* (Oxford, NY: Oxford University, 1963), 186, entire discussion pg. 186-193.

[4] Ibid., 190.

[5] Ibid., 187.

[6] Obituary, *The Times* (UK); 15 November 1993, pg. 17; available for a fee online at http://www.newstext.com.au/

[7] Sherwin-White, *Roman Society*, 192.

[8] Peter Brunt, "A Historian of Rome on the New Testament," *The Oxford Magazine*, New Series Vol. 4 No. 13 (20 February 1964), 209-210.

[9] Sherwin-White, *Roman Society*, 192.

[10] Brunt, *Historian of Rome*, 210.

[11] Jan Vansina, *Oral Tradition as History* (Madison, WI: University of Wisconsin, 1985), 159.

[12] Peter Brunt, "1994 Lectures and Memoirs," *Proceedings of the British Academy*, Vol. 87 (1995), 462, 467.

[13] Richard Stoneman in *The Landmark Arrian* (ed. James Romm; New York, NY: Anchor, 2010), 388-389.

[14] J.J. Nicholls, *Journal of Religious History*, Vol. 3, Issue 1 (June, 1964), 95.

[15] Three reviews that were critical of Sherwin-White's myth-growth-rate essay are: Peter Brunt (already cited above); Frederick Grant, *The Journal of*

Theological Studies, New Series, Vol. 15, Part 2 (October 1964), 352-358; and Rudolph C. Gelsey, *The American Journal of Legal History*, Vol. 8, No. 4 (October, 1964), 348-351. Two reviews that were supportive of Sherwin-White's myth-growth-rate essay are: Robert M. Grant, *Classical Philology*, Vol. 59, No. 4, (October, 1964), 304 and A.E. Raubitschek, *The Classical World*, Vol. 56, No. 9 (June, 1963), 294. Two reviews that were ambiguous toward Sherwin-White's myth-growth-rate essay are: John Crook, *The Classical Review*, New Series, Vol. 14, No. 2 (June, 1964), 198-200 and J.J. Nicholls, *Journal of Religious History*, Vol. 3, Issue 1 (June, 1964), 92-95.

[16] Michael R. Licona, *The Resurrection of Jesus: A New Historiographical Approach* (Downers Grove, IL: InterVarsity, 2010), 584-585 (Copyright (c) 2010 by Michael R. Licona. Used by permission of InterVarsity Press, PO Box 1400, Downers Grove, IL 60515. www.ivpress.com).

[17] Tacitus, *Annals* 3.44, 3.19; reference thanks to Richard Carrier, "The Spiritual Body of Christ," in *The Empty Tomb* (ed. Robert M. Price and Jeffery Jay Lowder; Amherst, NY: Prometheus, 2005), 170.

[18] Examples from Carrier, "Spiritual Body," 173. Exact citations for each legend are provided in Carrier's work.

[19] Ibid., 171.

[20] Alan Coulson, "Legends & Traditions of the Great War: The Case of the Elusive Angel of Mons," [cited Jan 16, 2008] Online: http://www.worldwar1.com/heritage/angel.htm; see too http://en.wikipedia.org/wiki/Angels_of_Mons.

[21] Arthur Machen, *The Angel of Mons: The Bowmen and Other Legends of the War* (London, 1915), 5, 7; reference from Coulson, "Legends".

[22] Julius Müller, *The Theory of Myths in Its Application to the Gospel History Examined and Confuted* (London: John Chapman, 1844), 29. (Originally published in German in 1836.)

[23] Rodney Stark, *The Rise of Christianity: A Sociologist Reconsiders History* (Princeton, NJ: Princeton, 1996), 7.

[24] James G. Crossley, "Against the Historical Plausibility of the Empty Tomb Story and the Bodily Resurrection of Jesus: A Response to N.T. Wright," *Journal for the Study of the Historical Jesus*, Vol. 3.2 (2005), 181, including footnote#39.

[25] Gershom Scholem, *Sabbatai Sevi, the Mystical Messiah* (Princeton, NJ: Princeton, 1973), 265, 417.

[26] Ibid., 265, 266, 375, 391, 535, 605.

[27] Ibid., 928-929.

[28] David Friedrich Strauss, *The Life of Jesus Critically Examined, 4th German edition* (1840), Translated by George Eliot (London: G. Allen & Co., 1913), 86. Online at: http://quod.lib.umich.edu/g/genpub/ajh1242.0001.001/86?page=root;rgn=full+text;size=100;view=image (see introduction, section 14).

Selected Bibliography

Aleman, André and Frank Larøi. *Hallucinations: The Science of Idiosyncratic Perception.* Washington D.C.: American Psychological Association, 2008.

Bauckham, Richard. *Gospel Women: Studies of the Named Women in the Gospels.* Grand Rapids, MI: Eerdmans, 2002.

Berger, David. *The Rebbe, the Messiah, and the Scandal of Orthodox Indifference.* Portland, OR: Littman Library of Jewish Civilization, 2008.

Blomberg, Craig L. *The Historical Reliability of the Gospels.* Downers Grove, IL: InterVarsity, 2007.

Bode, Edward. *The First Easter Morning.* AB 45; Rome: Biblical Institute Press, 1970.

Bond, Helen K. *Caiaphas: Friend of Rome and Judge of Jesus?* Louisville, Kentucky: Westminster John Knox Press, 2004.

Bondeson, Jan. *Buried Alive.* Darby, PA: Diane, 2004.

Bostock, Gerald. "Do We Need an Empty Tomb?" *The Expository Times* 105.7 (1994): 201-205.

Brown, Raymond E. *The Gospel According to John.* AB 29; Garden City, NY: Doubleday, 1970.

———. "The Burial of Jesus," *Catholic Biblical Quarterly Vol. 50.1* (Jan 1988).

———. *Death of the Messiah, II.* ABRL, 7; New York: Doubleday, 1994.

Brunt, Peter. "A Historian of Rome on the New Testament," *The Oxford Magazine,* New Series Vol. 4 No. 13 (20 February 1964): 209-210.

———. "1994 Lectures and Memoirs," *Proceedings of the British Academy,* Vol. 87 (1995): 455-470.

Bultmann, Rudolph. *The History of the Synoptic Tradition.* New York: Harper, 1968.

Carrier, Richard C. "Reply to Glenn Miller on the Burial of Jesus (2002)," Infidels.org Library, n.p. [cited Oct 3, 2007] Online: http://www.infidels.org/library/modern/richard_carrier/replytomiller.html

———. "The Spiritual Body of Christ and the Legend of the Empty Tomb," in *The Empty Tomb.* Edited by Robert M. Price and Jeffery Jay Lowder. Amherst, NY: Prometheus, 2005. FAQ at: http://www.richardcarrier.info/SpiritualFAQ.html

———. "The Burial of Jesus in Light of Jewish Law," in *The Empty Tomb.* Edited by Robert M. Price and Jeffery Jay Lowder. Amherst, NY: Prometheus, 2005. FAQ at: http://www.richardcarrier.info/BurialFAQ.html

———. *"Stephen Davis Gets It Wrong."* n.p. (2006) Online: http://www.richardcarrier.info/Carrier--ReplyToDavis.html

———. *Not the Impossible Faith: Why Christianity Didn't Need a Miracle to Succeed.* Lulu, 2009.

————. "Why the Resurrection is Unbelievable," in *The Christian Delusion: Why Faith Fails*. Edited by John Loftus. Amherst, NY: Prometheus, 2010.

————. "Christianity's Success Was Not Incredible," in *The End of Christianity*. Edited by John Loftus. Amherst, NY: Prometheus, 2011.

Chilton, Bruce and Jacob Neusner. *Judaism in the New Testament*. New York, NY: Routledge, 1995.

Collins, Jim, *Good to Great*. New York, NY; HarperCollins, 2001.

Cooper, Joel. *Cognitive Dissonance: Fifty Years of a Classic Theory*. Thousand Oaks, California: Sage, 2007.

Craig, William. *The Son Rises: Historical Evidence for the Resurrection of Jesus*. Chicago: Moody, 1981.

————. "The Guard at the Tomb," *New Testament Studies* 30 (1984). Cambridge University Press.

————. "The Historicity of the Empty Tomb of Jesus," *New Testament Studies* 31 (1985). Cambridge University Press.

————. "Was Jesus Buried in Shame? Reflections on B. McCane's Proposal," *The Expository Times* 115.12 (2004): 404-409.

————. *Reasonable Faith: Christian Truth and Apologetics*. Wheaton, IL: Crossway, 2008.

————. *On Guard: Defending Your Faith with Reason and Precision*. Colorado Springs, CO: David C. Cook, 2010.

————. And Joseph E. Gorra. *A Reasonable Response: Answers to Tough Questions on God, Christianity, and the Bible*. Chicago, IL: Moody, 2013.

Crossan, John Dominic and Jonathan L. Reed. *In Search of Paul*. New York, NY: HarperCollins, 2004.

Crossley, James G. "Against the Historical Plausibility of the Empty Tomb Story and the Bodily Resurrection of Jesus: A Response to N.T. Wright," *Journal for the Study of the Historical Jesus* Vol. 3.2 (2005): 171-186.

Dahood, Mitchell. *Psalms I, 1-50*. AB 16; Garden City, NY: Doubleday, 1965.

Danby, Herbert. *The Mishnah, Translated from the Hebrew with Introduction and Brief Explanatory Notes*. London: Oxford, 1958.

Davies, Jon. *Death, Burial and Rebirth in the Religions of Antiquity*. New York, NY: Routledge, 1999.

Dawson, Lorne L. "When Prophecy Fails and Faith Persists: A Theoretical Overview," *Nova Religio: The Journal of Alternative and Emergent Religions*, Vol. 3, No. 1 (Oct 1999): 60-82.

Dein, Simon. "What Really Happens When Prophecy Fails: The Case of Lubavitch," *Sociology of Religion* Vol 62:3 (2001): 383-401. Used by permission of Oxford University Press.

————. And Lorne Dawson. "The 'Scandal' of the Lubavitch Rebbe: Messianism as a Response to Failed Prophecy," *Journal of Contemporary Religion* 23.2 (May 2008): 163–180.

————. "A Messiah from the Dead: Cultural Performance in Lubavitcher Messianism," *Social Compass*, Vol 57:4 (2010), 537-554.

————. *Lubavitcher Messianism*. New York, NY: Bloomsbury Academic, 2012.

Diamond, Jared. *Guns, Germs, and Steel*. New York, NY; Norton, 1999.

D'Souza, Dinesh. *What's So Great About Christianity*. Washington D.C.: Regnery, 2007.

Ehrman, Bart. *Jesus, Interrupted: Revealing the Hidden Contradictions in the Bible (And Why We Don't Know About Them)*. New York, NY: HarperOne, 2009.

Evans, Craig A. "Jewish Burial Traditions and the Resurrection of Jesus," *Journal for the Study of the Historical Jesus* Vol. 3.2 (2005): 233-248.

Fales, Evan. "The Case of St. Teresa (Scientific Explanations of Mystical Experiences, Part 1)." *Religious Studies* 32.n2 (June 1996): 143-163. Cambridge University Press.

————. "Taming the Tehom: The Sign of Jonah in Matthew," in *The Empty Tomb*. Edited by Robert M. Price and Jeffery Jay Lowder. Amherst, NY: Prometheus, 2005.

Fee, Gordon D. *The First Epistle to the Corinthians*. Grand Rapids, Michigan: Eerdmans, 1987.

Festinger, Leon & Henry Riecken & Stanley Schachter. *When Prophecy Fails*. New York, NY: Harper & Row, 1956.

————. *A Theory of Cognitive Dissonance*. Stanford, California: Stanford University Press, 1957.

Giblin, C.H. "Structural and Thematic Correlations in the Matthean Burial-Resurrection Narrative (Matt. xxvii.57-xxviii.20)." *New Testament Studies* 21 (1974-75). Cambridge University Press.

Goulder, Michael. "The Baseless Fabric of a Vision," in *Resurrection Reconsidered*. Edited by G. D'Costa. Oxford: One World, 1996.

————. "Jesus' Resurrection and Christian Origins: A Response to N.T. Wright." *Journal for the Study of the Historical Jesus* Vol. 3.2 (2005): 187-195.

Habermas, Gary and Michael Licona. *The Case for the Resurrection of Jesus*. Grand Rapids, Michigan: Kregal, 2004.

Harmon-Jones, Eddie and Judson Mills. *Cognitive Dissonance, Progress on a Pivotal Theory in Social Psychology*. Edited by Eddie Harmon-Jones and Judson Mills. Washington, DC: American Psychological Association, 1999.

Herrick, Greg. "The Use of Psalm 16:8-11 in Acts 2:25-28." *Bible.org Trustworthy Bible Study Resources*, n.p. [cited 15 Jan. 2006]. Online: http://www.bible.org/page.php?page_id=1784.

Hill, Douglas. "On the Third Day." *The Expository Times* 78 (1967).

Jacoby, Susan. *Free Thinkers*. New York, NY: Henry Holt, 2004.

Jaffe, Aniela. *Apparitions: An Archetypal Approach to Death Dreams and Ghosts*. Irving, TX: Spring Publications, 1979.

Keener, Craig S. *1-2 Corinthians*. New York, NY; Cambridge University Press, 2005.

Kirby, Peter. "The Case Against the Empty Tomb." *Journal of Higher Criticism* 9/2 (Fall 2002): 175-202.

Kloner, Amos. *The Necropolis of Jerusalem in the Second Temple Period.* Ph.D. dissertation. Hebrew University, 1980.

———. "Did a Rolling Stone Close Jesus' Tomb?" *Biblical Archaeology Review* Sep/Oct 1999. Biblical Archaeology Society, Washington, D.C. (www.biblicalarchaeology.org).

Lampe, G.W.H. "Easter: A Statement" in *The Resurrection.* Edited by William Purcell, Philadelphia: Westminster, 1966.

Licona, Michael R. *The Resurrection of Jesus: A New Historiographical Approach.* Downers Grove, IL: IVP Academic, 2010.

———. "In Reply to Habermas, McGrew, and McCullagh," *Southeastern Theological Review* 3.1 (Summer 2012): 55-69.

Longman, Tremper III and David E. Garland. *Expositor's Bible Commentary,* Vol 11. Grand Rapids, Michigan; Zondervan, 2008.

Ludemann, Gerd. *The Resurrection of Jesus.* Minneapolis, MN: Fortress, 1994.

———. *The Resurrection of Christ.* Amherst, NY: Prometheus, 2004.

Lyons, William John. "On the Life and Death of Joseph of Arimathea." *Journal for the Study of the Historical Jesus* Vol. 2.1 (2004): 29-53.

Magness, Jodi. "What did Jesus' Tomb Look Like?" *Biblical Archaeology Review* Vol. 32 No. 1 (Jan/Feb 2006): 38-49. Biblical Archaeology Society, Washington, D.C. (www.biblicalarchaeology.org).

McArthur, Harvey K. "'On the Third Day'" *New Testament Studies* 18 (1971). Cambridge University Press.

McCane, Byron R. *Roll Back the Stone.* Harrisburg, PA: Trinity, 2003.

McCullagh, Christopher B. *Justifying Historical Descriptions.* New York, NY: Cambridge University Press, 1984.

———. *The Logic of History: Putting Postmodernism in Perspective.* New York, NY: Routledge, 2004.

———. "The Resurrection of Jesus: Explanation or Interpretation?" *Southeastern Theological Review* 3.1 (Summer 2012): 41-53.

Meadow, M.J. and R.D. Kahoe. *Psychology of Religion.* New York: Harper and Row, 1984.

Metzger, Bruce M. "A Suggestion Concerning the Meaning of I Cor. XV. 4b." *Journal of Theological Studies* 8 (1957): 118-123.

———. *A Textual Commentary on the Greek New Testament.* Stuttgart, Germany: Biblia-Druck, 1971.

Miller, Robert J. *The Complete Gospels.* Editor. Santa Rosa, California: Polebridge, 1994.

———. *Born Divine.* Santa Rosa, California; Polebridge, 2003.

Müller, Julius. *The Theory of Myths in Its Application to the Gospel History Examined and Confuted.* London: John Chapman, 1844.

Müller, Mogens. *The First Bible of the Church: A Plea for the Septuagint.* JSOT-SS 206; Sheffield, England: Sheffield, 1996.

Nock, Arthur Darby. *Conversion: The Old and the New in Religion from Alexander the Great to Augustine of Hippo.* Oxford: Clarendon, 1933.

Pannenberg, Wolfhart. "The Historical Jesus as a Challenge to Christology." *Dialog* 37 (1998): 22-27.

Parsons, Keith. "Peter Kreeft and Ronald Tacelli on the Hallucination Theory" in *The Empty Tomb.* Edited by Robert M. Price and Jeffery Jay Lowder. Amherst, NY: Prometheus, 2005.

Patterson, Stephen J. *The God of Jesus.* Harrisburg, PA: Trinity, 1998.

Perper, Joshua A. "Time of Death and Changes After Death: Part 1, Anatomical Considerations." [cited 17 Jan 2007] Online: http://home.comcast.net/~drdeathmd/doc/spitz_chapt02-1.pdf.

Pounder, Derrick J. "Postmortem Changes and Time of Death." Department of Forensic Medicine, University of Dundee, 1995. [cited 17 Jan 2007] Online: http://www.dundee.ac.uk/forensicmedicine/notes/timedeath.pdf.

Price, Robert M. "Brand X Easters." *The Fourth R* 20.6 (Nov/Dec 2007).

Prophet, Erin. *Prophet's Daughter: My Life with Elizabeth Clare Prophet Inside the Church Universal and Triumphant.* Guilford, CT: The Globe Pequot Press, 2009.

Ranke-Heinemann, Uta. *Putting Away Childish Things.* San Francisco: Harper, 1994.

Robinson, Bernard P. "Peter and His Successors: Tradition and Redaction in Matthew 16.17-19." *Journal for the Study of the New Testament* 6 (1984): 85-104.

Robinson, John A.T. *The Priority of John.* London: SCM Press, 1985.

Rousseau, John J. and Rami Arav. *Jesus and His World: An Archaeological and Cultural Dictionary.* Minneapolis, MN; Augsburg Fortress, 1995.

Sacks, Oliver. *Hallucinations.* New York: Alfred A. Knopf, 2012.

Sagan, Carl. "Wonder and Skepticism" at the CSICOP conference in Seattle, WA, June 23-26, 1994. Transcript printed in the *Skeptical Inquirer*, Vol. 29.4, July/August 2005.

Schachter, Stanley and Michael S. Gazzaniga. *Extending Psychological Frontiers, Selected Works of Leon Festinger.* Edited by Stanley Schachter and Michael S. Gazzaniga. New York, NY: Russell Sage Foundation, 1989.

Scholem, Gershom. *Sabbatai Sevi, the Mystical Messiah.* Princeton, NJ: Princeton, 1973.

Senior, Donald. *The Passion of Jesus in the Gospel of Mark.* Wilmington, Del: Glazier, 1984.

Shanks, Hershel. "Who Lies Here? Jordan Tombs Match Those at Qumran." *Biblical Archaeology Review* Sep/Oct 1999. Biblical Archaeology Society, Washington D.C. (www.biblicalarchaeology.org).

Shermer, Michael. *The Science of Good and Evil.* New York, NY: Henry Holt, 2004.

Sherwin-White, A.N. *Roman Society and Roman Law in the New Testament.* Oxford, NY: Oxford University, 1963.

Slade, Peter and Richard Bentall. *Sensory Deception: a Scientific Analysis of Hallucination.* Baltimore: John Hopkins University Press, 1988.

Smith, Daniel A. "Appearance or Disappearance?: Early Beliefs About Jesus' Vindication." *The Fourth R* 21.1 (Jan/Feb 2008).

Spong, John Shelby. *Jesus for the Non-Religious.* New York, NY: HarperCollins, 2007.

Stark, Rodney. *The Rise of Christianity: A Sociologist Reconsiders History.* Princeton, NJ: Princeton, 1996.

Stec, David M. *The Targum of Psalms, Translated, with a Critical Introduction, Apparatus, and Notes.* Aramaic Bible 16; Collegeville, Minn: Liturgical, 2004.

Stoneman, Richard. *The Landmark Arrian.* Edited by James Romm. New York, NY: Anchor, 2010.

Strauss, David Friedrich. *The Life of Jesus Critically Examined,* 4th German edition (1840). Translated by George Eliot. London: G. Allen & Co., 1913. Also online at: http://quod.lib.umich.edu/cgi/t/text/text-idx?c=genpub;idno=AJH1242.0001.001.

Strobel, Lee. *The Case for Christ.* Grand Rapids, Michigan: Zondervan, 1998.

Tabor, James. *The Jesus Dynasty.* New York, NY: Simon & Schuster, 2006.

The Jesus Seminar. *The Five Gospels.* New York, NY: Polebridge, 1993.

———. *The Acts of Jesus.* New York, NY: Polebridge, 1998.

Thiselton, Anthony C. *The First Epistle to the Corinthians.* Grand Rapids, Michigan: Eerdmans, 2000.

Van Buren, Paul M. *According to the Scriptures.* Grand Rapids, MI: Eerdmans, 1998.

Vansina, Jan. *Oral Tradition as History.* Madison, WI: University of Wisconsin, 1985.

Watson, Francis. "'Historical Evidence' and the Resurrection of Jesus," *Theology* 90 (1987): 365-372.

Westermann, William Linn. *The Slave Systems of Greek and Roman Antiquity.* Darby, Pa: Diane, 1955.

Wright, N.T. *The Resurrection of the Son of God.* Minneapolis, MN: Fortress, 2003.

Zissu, Boaz. "Odd Tomb Out: Has Jerusalem's Essene Cemetery Been Found?" *Biblical Archaeology Review* Mar/Apr 1999. Biblical Archaeology Society, Washington, D.C. (www.biblicalarchaeology.org).

Index of Subjects, Authors, and Scriptures

N

O

P

R

Expanded Table of Contents

Lightning Source UK Ltd.
Milton Keynes UK
UKOW04f1809220615

253939UK00001B/77/P